AF477840

A LEGAL HISTORY
OF MISSISSIPPI

A LEGAL HISTORY

of

MISSISSIPPI

Race, Class, and the Struggle for Opportunity

JOSEPH A. RANNEY

University Press of Mississippi / Jackson

www.upress.state.ms.us

The University Press of Mississippi is a member
of the Association of University Presses.

First printing 2019

∞

Library of Congress Cataloging-in-Publication Data

Names: Ranney, Joseph A., 1952– author.
Title: A legal history of Mississippi: race, class, and the struggle for
opportunity / Joseph A. Ranney.
Description: Jackson: University Press of Mississippi, [2019] | "First
printing 2019." | "This book is part of a project, now more than
twenty-five years old, to examine the history of American states' legal
systems. The project has long had a Southern tinge."—Provided by
publisher. | "Through close research, qualitative analysis, published
court decisions, statutes, and law review articles, along with unusual
secondary sources including nineteenth-century political and legal
journals and journals of state constitutional conventions, Ranney
indicates how Mississippi law has both shaped and reflected the state's
character and, to a certain extent, how Mississippi's legal evolution
compares with that of other states. Ranney examines the interaction of
Mississippi law and society during key periods of change including the
colonial and territorial eras and the early years of statehood when the
legal foundations were laid; the evolution of slavery and slave law in
Mississippi; the state's antebellum role as a leader of Jacksonian legal
reform; the unfolding of the response to emancipation and wartime
devastation during Reconstruction and the early Jim Crow era;
Mississippi's legal evolution during the Progressive Era and its legal
response to the crisis of the Great Depression; and the legal response to
the civil rights revolution of the mid-twentieth century and the cultural
revolutions of the late twentieth century. Histories of the law in other
states are starting to appear, but there is none for Mississippi. Ranney
fills that gap to help us better understand the state as it enters its
third century."—Provided by publisher. | Includes bibliographical
references and index. |
Identifiers: LCCN 2018054031 (print) | LCCN 2018056148 (ebook) | ISBN
9781496822598 (epub single) | ISBN 9781496822581 (epub institutional) |
ISBN 9781496822611 (pdf single) | ISBN 9781496822604 (pdf institutional)
| ISBN 9781496822574 (cloth)
Subjects: LCSH: Law—Mississippi—History.
Classification: LCC KFM6678 (ebook) | LCC KFM6678 .R36 2019 (print) | DDC
349.76209—dc23
LC record available at https://lccn.loc.gov/2018054031

British Library Cataloging-in-Publication Data available

To Carol, again—and to Emily, who has roots in both
North and South and loves both, critically but truly.

CONTENTS

PREFACE

This book is part of a project, now more than twenty-five years old, to examine the history of American states' legal systems. The project has long had a Southern tinge.

As a child in central Illinois in the 1950s, the homeland of Abraham Lincoln, but also a borderland where Northern and Southern influences met and the ghost of Jim Crow was still visible, I became fascinated with the history of slavery and the Civil War. As I grew up, I was also drawn to the grittier but equally important history of the civil rights struggle that has continued from the Reconstruction era to the present. When I began the project by writing a legal history of my home state, Wisconsin, another theme soon emerged: the legal history of Southern states and what part that history might play in explaining the South's distinctiveness. In 2006, I published *In the Wake of Slavery*, a history of how Southern states shaped their legal systems during and after Reconstruction, often in very different ways, to respond to the demise of slavery and the ruin of war. After completing another book on Wisconsin's legal history, this time with a focus on how that history compared to other states, I decided to write the legal history of a Southern state. Mississippi seemed to be an ideal candidate because of its rich political and cultural history—and indeed it was.

A passage from President Lincoln's First Inaugural Address (1861) addressing the differences between North and South has provided continuing inspiration for this book. "Physically speaking," said Lincoln, "we cannot separate. We cannot remove our respective sections from each other nor build an impassable wall between them. . . . Suppose you go to war, you cannot fight always; and when, after much loss on both sides and no gain on either, you cease fighting, the identical old questions, as to terms of intercourse, are again upon you." Today, as Americans experience a level of polarization not seen in many years, and as we come to realize that the wake of slavery is longer than many of us had hoped, it is more important than ever for Americans of all regions and backgrounds to understand each other's perspectives. I hope that this book will assist readers in that endeavor.

Many people have encouraged and helped me during the course of this project. For many years, Marquette Law School has given me an academic perch from which to conduct the project. I am particularly grateful to Dean Joseph Kearney and to professors David Ray Papke, the late Gordon Hylton (of the Marquette and the University of Virginia law schools), and Dan Blinka for their advice and support, and I also appreciate the support of other Marquette faculty members and my legal history students at Marquette who have patiently provided a forum for my ideas. Thanks also to the management of my law firm, DeWitt Ross & Stevens S.C., for its support of my quest to lead a dual life of law practice and scholarship. Last but not least, I am very grateful to Craig Gill, Vijay Shah, Emily Bandy, and others at the University Press of Mississippi for their editorial encouragement and assistance, and to the anonymous readers whose constructive comments and criticisms have made this a better book.

A LEGAL HISTORY
OF MISSISSIPPI

INTRODUCTION

To understand the world, you have to understand a place like Mississippi.
—Willie Morris, attributed to William Faulkner[1]

For most of its two hundred years of existence, the state of Mississippi has maintained a hold on the American imagination out of all proportion to its modest size and its location far from the main centers of American power. Writers and other artists of great talent have addressed Mississippi's culture, its landscape, its economy, its racial sins, and its racial promise. But no one has comprehensively examined the evolution of Mississippi's legal system or examined the role that law has played in the state's larger culture. This book, written as Mississippi marks its bicentennial, aims to create a broader understanding of the state from this heretofore little-explored perspective.

State legal systems are a central but under-examined part of American life. The American federal system reserves vast amounts of power to the states and gives them freedom within the limits of the US Constitution to shape their worlds as they see fit, and it is state law that governs most aspects of our daily lives. Yet scholars, commentators, and the media pay more attention to federal laws and court decisions than to state legislatures and courts. Only a handful of state legal histories have been written, and regional legal histories are virtually nonexistent. With this book, Mississippi becomes the first Southern state to possess a comprehensive history of its legal system.

As a state's legal system evolves, it both shapes and is shaped by cultural and economic forces, and its evolutionary pattern illuminates the state's general character and points of distinctiveness. Mississippi's legal history features two overarching but conflicting themes: a steadfast quest for a purified democracy, coupled with an equally steadfast quest to create a diametrically opposite legal system for its black half. These themes have been present from the beginning.

Mississippi was a key part of the federal government's experiment in creating a democratic empire through the Northwest and Southwest Ordinances (1785–90), the first system in the world's history that allowed colonized territories to join their colonizers on fully equal terms as new states. In 1798, Mississippi became the first portion of the southern trans-Appalachian lands to be granted territorial status. It remained to be seen whether the remote territory, governed under French and Spanish civil law for more than a century and now dominated by a small elite of planters and merchants based in the Natchez district, would throw off civil law and aristocracy and adopt American democratic ideals. Mississippi more than fulfilled those hopes. It quickly adopted an Americanized common-law system, and as it filled up with white yeoman farmers after 1820, it amended its laws and constitution to give the new settlers a full place in the state's political and economic world. Territorial-era limits on suffrage were eliminated, and, in the 1830s, Mississippi reached a high point of direct democracy; it became the first state to choose all of its judges by popular election (1832) and the first state to enact a law giving women the right to control property they brought to their marriages (1839), a major advance in an era when the law denied most married women any legal existence separate from their husbands.

Mississippians supported other democratizing reforms of the Jacksonian era, but they did so on their own terms. Jacksonians fought a long battle against a Federalist-dominated American judiciary that viewed with suspicion their efforts to decentralize political and economic power. It was not until 1837 that US Chief Justice Roger Taney, recently appointed by Jackson, affirmed that state legislatures had broad power to enact laws for the common welfare even where those laws incidentally affected property rights. Mississippi did not participate actively in that fight because it did not need to: from the state's earliest days, its Supreme Court adopted a policy of deference to the will of the legislature. Mississippians, whose cotton economy depended on Eastern and international financial networks for credit and customers, initially disavowed the Jacksonian view that banks' economic power made them a threat to democracy. But when the depression of 1837–40 put an end to the cotton boom they turned against banks with a vengeance, even though that did long-term damage to the state's credit.

Most Mississippians tacitly acknowledged the paradox of a society that prized freedom and equality for its white members but relied on the forced labor of its black members. Mississippi's law of slavery reflected the ambivalence that accompanied that acknowledgment. The state shifted from colonial French and Spanish codes that allowed slaves a measure of personal independence to a British-influenced code that strictly limited their freedoms, but it also gave slaves a limited right to be heard in court and to receive due process of law—an admission that even in the heart of the slave belt, slaves were something more than property. In a series of cases enforcing planter Isaac Ross's wish to free his slaves by sending them to Africa at his death, Mississippi's Supreme Court left open a small passageway to freedom notwithstanding state laws placing strict limits on emancipation. The court's liberalism ended as intersectional tensions increased and war approached; in 1858, a new generation of justices overturned the rule of the *Ross* cases and held that thenceforth, Mississippi would not permit the freeing of slaves under any circumstances. According to Justice William Harris, Mississippi's "climate, soil and productions . . . her people, their habits, manners and opinions . . . *require slave labor.*"

War then turned Mississippi's world upside down, and in the summer of 1865, delegates assembled in Jackson to rebuild the state's legal system. Some delegates argued for resistance and a return to the old racial order, but delegate Edmund Goode cut them short: "There was a wager of law, as well as of battle," said Goode, and "the question was decided against us." Rebuilding was needed not only to define the rights and roles of newly emancipated black Mississippians but also to accommodate the new balance of power between the state and an ascendant federal government and define Mississippi's postwar economic course. The challenges were fundamental and difficult but they had to be met in a hurry, and the process was a messy one. During the immediate postwar Restoration period (1865–67), white Mississippians enacted a harsh black code that recreated slavery in all but name. National opinion demanded more: in 1867 Congress placed Mississippi under military rule and required that its black citizens be given basic civil rights and voting rights as a condition of readmission to representation in Washington. A coalition of blacks and white Unionists produced a constitution that met these conditions. During the short period of domestic Reconstruction that followed (1869–75), that coalition followed a comparatively cautious course. Its signature achievement was an 1873 law that prohibited racial discrimination in places of public accommodation, a law that the Reconstruction supreme court, dominated by white Unionists, somewhat surprisingly upheld.

When white conservatives returned to power in 1875, they recognized that there could be no return to the antebellum racial order. The federal Fourteenth and Fifteenth Amendments gave black citizens a permanent guarantee of basic civil rights and voting rights and put an end to any notion that they could be classified as less than fully human under the law. White Mississippians worked around the amendments and maintained racial supremacy through custom and violence, but the amendments acted as a check. There was an odd parallel between the amendments and Mississippi's old slave code in that each was laxly enforced but nonetheless hovered over daily life in Mississippi, always available for use against those who flouted them too obviously. But accommodation of the federal amendments took a toll; the need for white solidarity to counteract blacks' voting power made it difficult to discuss, let alone resolve, the growing economic and social divide between black-belt merchants and planters in west Mississippi and white-belt farmers in east and south Mississippi. In 1890, a new constitutional convention devised innovative suffrage requirements that were racially neutral on their face but effectively excluded most blacks (and many poor whites) from voting, thus allowing white Mississippians to return to their intramural disputes. The new measures became a model for other Southern states, and a series of Jim Crow laws mandating segregation in places of public accommodation completed the new order. Mississippi's supreme court readily upheld the new racial laws, and the US Supreme Court somewhat reluctantly followed suit.

Mississippi's dual themes of democratic innovation for whites and strict subordination of blacks continued during the state's Progressive era. Between 1895 and 1915, Mississippi adopted several Progressive reforms including one of the nation's first direct-primary laws, measures allowing voters to enact legislation directly, hours laws designed to protect women and children industrial workers, and public-health laws combatting disease, malnutrition, and impure food and drugs. Reform laws met resistance from judges in other parts of the United States who worried that the laws would interfere with businessmen's liberty and property interests and freedom of contract, but surprisingly, such laws met with little resistance from Mississippi's Supreme Court and other Southern courts. That pattern repeated itself twenty years later during the Great Depression when Mississippi joined other states in enacting relief measures such as mortgage moratoria and bank reorganization laws, enthusiastically supported federal relief programs such as the Social Security Act, and, in 1936, enacted a pioneering Balance Agriculture with Industry (BAWI) law, providing state subsidies and tax incentives for businesses that would relocate to Mississippi and guarantee new jobs. The BAWI law faced a serious constitutional challenge, but in 1938 Mississippi's supreme court upheld it, proclaiming that if law "ceases to grow and keep pace with social and economic needs it becomes a hindrance." BAWI was widely copied in other states and became an enduring model for state economic development.

Jim Crow continued his journey alongside economic progressivism, but in the early 1930s, the first signs of change appeared when the US Supreme Court served notice that it would now look closely at whether black Mississippians truly received due process in criminal cases and segregated facilities equal to those provided to whites. Mississippi judges were torn between their desire to support the existing social order, and their distaste for the compromises they often had to make between legal ideals and the imperatives of racial supremacy. They complied grudgingly with Supreme Court directives and occasionally overturned criminal convictions that involved egregious miscarriages of justice, but they resisted the idea slowly growing in other parts of the nation that law should be used to effect meaningful racial change.

Mississippi experienced a double transformation after World War II. Between 1954 and 1970, a second civil rights revolution, as violent and as far-reaching as Reconstruction, again overturned the state's racial order, and since 1970, the state has edged into the national legal mainstream in its response to the many legal changes that modern individualistic concepts of liberty have generated. Mississippi lawmakers responded to the Supreme Court's outlawing of school segregation in *Brown v. Board of Education* (1954) with expressions of defiance and resistance laws. Moderate "practical segregationists" such as Governor James Coleman (1956–60), insisted on channeling resistance through forms of law rather than violence, but in 1961, when direct legal challenges to segregation finally began in Mississippi, the state's judges joined in the resistance. Change came only after repeated application of blunt legal force from outside. The federal Fifth Circuit Court of Appeals repeatedly reversed Mississippi judges' decisions and gradually forced integration of schools, bus stations, and other public places. In 1964–65, Congress enacted landmark civil rights and voting rights laws that finally broke the resistance movement in Mississippi. During the late 1960s and early 1970s, a new generation of Mississippi judges, led by Coleman after his appointment to the Fifth Circuit, signaled its commitment to enforce the new laws but argued that laws alone could not change the racial order and that gradual change might be the best path. In the mid-1970s, as opposition to integration through busing and breakup of neighborhood schools grew, their arguments received wide attention.

Mississippi's recent legal history has also been defined by the state's response to expressive individualism, a shift from the traditional American concept of liberty as freedom to dissent only within a universe of positions deemed tolerable by the community at large, to a broader concept of liberty as freedom to express one's personality virtually without limit. Expressive individualism has manifested itself in many ways, for example, the gay rights movement that began in the late 1960s; the abortion rights movement that has been a subject of continuous controversy since *Roe v. Wade* (1973); the erosion of traditional belief in public schools as a vehicle for assimilation of all students into a shared value system and the accompanying rise of private schools and school voucher programs; and increasing dissent and division among judges in courts across the nation. Expressive individualism has elicited a powerful reactive movement; the legal contest between the two forces is still in progress. Mississippians have generally sided with the reactive movement, but expressive individualism has influenced their lives and their law more than is commonly realized.

No account of Mississippi's legal history would be complete without mention of some of the individuals, white and black, who have helped shape it. The book tells the stories of Winthrop Sargent, a stern New Englander who tried to impose an equally stern code on an unruly new territory as its first governor (1798–1801); of Isaac Ross, whose efforts to free his slaves led to a family feud, a slave revolt against his grandson, eventual freedom for the slaves, and a transformation of Mississippi slave law; and of Piety Smith Hadley, a women's rights pioneer whose life provides a vivid glimpse into politics and business in antebellum Mississippi. The book also resurrects two largely forgotten figures from the Reconstruction and post-Reconstruction eras. Horatio Simrall, a conservative Unionist, resisted extension of rights to Mississippi blacks as a Restoration-era legislator, enforced those rights as a Reconstruction-era Supreme Court justice, and ended his career by helping shape the 1890 constitution's suffrage restrictions. Isaiah Montgomery, who rose from slavery to become one of the most prominent postwar figures in the Delta, also ended his political career as a delegate to the 1890 convention, torn between the need to accommodate the forces that led to the convention and a desire to preserve some shred of black rights and self-respect in the process.

The stories continue into the twentieth century. The book introduces the reader to Justices William Anderson and Virgil Griffith, who alone among their colleagues sometimes spoke up against egregious denials of due process to black criminal defendants and denounced the corrosive effect of lynchings on Mississippi justice, and to Sidney D. Redmond, the leading black lawyer of the Jim Crow era who regularly directed the justices' attention to such wrongs at great personal risk. The book's portrait of James Coleman, whose service as attorney general, governor, and federal judge put him at the heart of Mississippi's modern civil rights revolution, tries to give the reader a sense of how Coleman and other practical segregationists viewed the world and adapted to the revolution.

The book's value lies not only in its description of the historical arc of Mississippi law, but in its comparison of Mississippi's arc to the arcs of other states. Mississippi's long legal history of slavery and freedom, and the pursuit of political equality among whites (and now among all Mississippians), have been central forces in shaping its arc. The book's account of the arc provides a template for examination of other Southern state arcs and provides clues as to what those arcs might look like. Mississippi law has also shaped, and has been shaped by, states outside the South. The book examines the interweaving of those influences and again provides a template for investigating legal interweaving in other states. For example, the book looks at New York's influence on law in Mississippi and other states, particularly through the decisions and writings of its chancellor, James Kent; at the places that Mississippi and other states occupied in the Jacksonian legal reform movement and the Progressive movement; and at Mississippi's place in the modern legal struggle between expressive individualism and its opponents.

Two generations of lawmakers have now followed Judge Coleman's generation, and Mississippi increasingly has focused on legal issues of nationwide concern rather than uniquely Southern issues. What journeys of heart and mind have modern Mississippi lawmakers taken during their lives? Do Mississippi's modern legal trends reflect a complete acceptance of new ways, or will old racial and social traditions inform new lawmakers' responses to the problems they meet as the twenty-first century progresses? It may be too soon to tell: the Jim Crow era and the civil rights revolution are fading into history, but there are still many Mississippians who remember and were directly touched by those events. The questions are important ones. The author hopes that this book will be of help to Mississippians, as well as to all who seek to understand the world by understanding Mississippi, in their search for answers.

CHAPTER ONE

"A Refractory and Turbulent Spirit": Origins of Mississippi Law

There prevails in the country of our destination, a refractory and turbulent spirit, with parties headed by men of perverseness and cunning.
They have run wild in the recess of Government, and every moment's
delay in the adoption of rules and regulations . . . must be productive of
growing evils and discontent.

—Winthrop Sargent (1798)[1]

In April 1798, President John Adams needed to find a governor for the newly
created Mississippi Territory, and when Winthrop Sargent came to his attention
he believed he had found an excellent candidate. Sargent, like Adams, came
from New England and was a loyal Federalist. He had made a good military
record in the American Revolution; perhaps more important, he had served
as secretary and acting governor of the Northwest Territory on whose system
Mississippi's new government was modeled. But Sargent proved an awkward
fit for Mississippi: he had trouble impressing American law on a territory
whose settlers had functioned under Spanish law for several decades and were
familiar with a social order based more on personality and power than on laws.
Mississippians did not take kindly to Sargent's often puritanical ways and his
status as the representative of a distant, only recently established government.[2]

Sargent was not able to promulgate laws until a majority of the territory's
new judges arrived in Natchez, the capital, nearly a year after the territory
was established. The new laws he and his colleagues created, labeled "Sargent's

Code," were criticized for imposing unduly harsh criminal penalties and for concentrating power in Sargent and his allies. "Law is the crie," exclaimed a frustrated Sargent, but "all are unfitted for it."[3] Residents petitioned for the right to elect their own legislators, a request granted by Congress in 1800, and they petitioned Congress to replace Sargent with a more responsive governor. In 1801, after Thomas Jefferson defeated Adams for the presidency he replaced Sargent with the more democratically minded William C. C. Claiborne. Sargent remained in Mississippi but never again held office.[4]

Three years later, Jefferson appointed Harry Toulmin the judge of an additional court that Congress had created for the territory's Tombigbee district comprising most of present-day Alabama, a district that was both geographically and culturally distant from Natchez. Toulmin shared Sargent's combative streak and his taste for culture and writing, but their similarities ended there. Toulmin had spent his life as a dissident; originally a minister, he had left his native England over doctrinal differences with the Anglican church. After settling in Kentucky, he served as its secretary of state but he was forced out when his political opponents gained power.[5] Toulmin's experience with Southern culture and politics gave him advantages in the new territory not possessed by Sargent, and over the course of the next decade, Toulmin set his stamp on Mississippi's culture and politics as well as its legal system.

Toulmin annually rode a circuit of more than three hundred miles through the wilderness, arranging sessions of court, encouraging local sheriffs and justices of the peace in their duties, and attempting to cultivate respect for law as he went. Like other prominent American territorial judges, Toulmin became deeply involved in the social and political life as well as the legal life of his adopted homeland. He frequently carried out local assignments for territorial governors, served as an intermediary between American settlers and Spanish authorities in nearby West Florida, and reported regularly on territorial affairs to Presidents Jefferson and Madison.[6] In his spare time, he compiled a code of territorial laws to replace Sargent's old code and authored a guide for Mississippi magistrates. Toulmin's efforts earned him enemies who petitioned federal authorities for his removal. Unlike Sargent, however, Toulmin withstood all opposition, retaining his judgeship until Mississippi gained statehood in 1817 and later becoming a prominent figure in his new state of Alabama.[7]

The contrasts between Sargent's and Toulmin's careers illuminate central themes of Mississippi's early law, themes that would also inform later eras of the state's legal history. Early Mississippi was a unique mix of aristocracy and democracy, of provincialism and globalism. During the late eighteenth and early nineteenth centuries, it moved from an autocratic, centralized civil-law system under Spanish rule to an American system that venerated popular democracy, federalism, and the common law. But Spanish influences remained in place after the Spanish ceded political control. The planter and merchant aristocracy that arose in Natchez under Spanish rule remained in power throughout Mississippi's territorial period and first years of statehood, and the civil-law penchant for codification lived on in Sargent's and Toulmin's work. Frontier Mississippi was as removed from the center of American power as it was possible to be, but from the beginning its economy depended heavily on world trade, on access to the ports at New Orleans and Mobile through which trade flowed, and on the good will of Spanish officials who controlled that access.[8]

Early lawmakers shaped Mississippi's legal system with three goals in mind: establishing a basic system of legal order and in the process preserving the planter-merchant aristocracy's power as much as possible against newer settlers' democratic sensibilities; clearing the obstacles to sovereignty posed by neighboring Spanish authorities and Indian nations; and, as Mississippi grew and moved to statehood, integrating the new state into the larger American system while responding to Mississippians' strong need for a separate identity. This chapter describes the ways in which lawmakers tried to achieve those goals.

The Transition from Civil to Common Law

Mississippi spent the first century of its political existence under French and Spanish civil law. When British and American settlers began entering the territory in the late 1700s, bringing common-law sensibilities with them, the question of how the two legal systems would interact became an urgent one.

France began serious efforts to colonize the lower Mississippi River Valley at the end of the seventeenth century. When Pierre d'Iberville founded New Orleans in 1718, he also established small settlements at Natchez, on Mississippi's Gulf coast, and on the Yazoo River, all of which were incorporated into the province of Louisiana.[9] New Orleans flourished as the Mississippi Valley's great port and as the colonial capital, and Natchez likewise flourished due to its proximity to New Orleans and its status as the center of a fertile agricultural area. Civil law played an important role in Natchez and New Orleans, but other Mississippi Valley settlements remained small and remote, with little need of formal law. Most legal disputes were simple matters involving debts, family quarrels, land disputes, and petty crime, and most were settled by local military commanders and justices of the peace. Spanish civil law encouraged settlement of disputes through arbitration rather than resort to courts and commandants; arbitration proved popular among early Mississippi settlers, and remained so well into the nineteenth century. But it was not a panacea because settlers also petitioned Spanish authorities at different times for a local court to assist with collection of debts, debtor relief laws, and laws requiring cattle owners to keep their animals fenced in.[10]

In 1762, facing defeat by Great Britain in the Seven Years War (1756–63), France ceded the lower Mississippi Valley to Spain. Mississippi quickly became a legal borderland. The line between Spanish territory and the adjacent British territory ceded to the United States at the end of the American Revolution was hazy, and Georgia claimed the Mississippi territory based on equally hazy terms in its colonial charter. British and American settlers soon made up a large majority of the local population, and in 1795, Spain formally ceded the Mississippi territory to the United States. Spanish authorities were slow to evacuate and planters and merchants in Natchez, who had forged a good relationship with the generally easygoing officials, were not eager to see them replaced by American officials.[11]

Even though civil law had only shallow roots in much of the Mississippi Valley, it would play a role in the region's legal development under American rule. The public was always an interested party in civil-law disputes, and civil law permitted flexible application of rules where necessary to achieve a result deemed socially beneficial. By contrast, common law gave individual rights priority over the common good, and laws creating such rights were strictly followed regardless of whether the outcome benefited society.[12] Three points of difference between the systems would prove particularly important in Mississippi's early legal history: first, the concept of a constitution guaranteeing basic rights to citizens and limiting the scope of government's power, a concept adopted in England as early as the Magna Carta (1215) but not adopted in continental Europe until the Enlightenment; second, the sanctity of property and of an owner's right to use his property as he saw fit; and third, the role of legal codification.[13]

Codification had been a central feature of civil law since the late Roman Empire, and Spain's thirteenth-century *Siete Partidas* (Seven Parts) became a core component of Spain's colonial legal system and remained influential in the former Spanish colonies, including Louisiana, well into the 1800s.[14] After the United States acquired Louisiana, it found civil-law sensibilities deeply rooted in the region, and American officials were forced to introduce common law cautiously and slowly. As the first American territorial governor of Louisiana, Claiborne gradually instituted jury trials and other Anglo-American criminal-law procedures but did not interfere with existing substantive law. Between 1820 and 1825, Edward Livingston and other Louisiana jurists created civil- and criminal-law codes that included common-law elements, but the legislature was careful to preserve large portions of the civil law in the new codes.[15]

Mississippi also adhered to the codification model, but its path was considerably different from Louisiana's. In 1790, Congress enacted the Southwest Ordinance providing a system of government for all American territory south of the Ohio River. The ordinance, though not itself a code, was the first step in Mississippi's codification process.[16] It was an outgrowth of the Northwest Ordinance fashioned by Thomas Jefferson and James Monroe in 1785 in order to provide a governmental system for the unsettled lands north and west of the Ohio River and bind them permanently to the new nation. The Northwest and Southwest Ordinances created a colonial system not seen before in the world, one which provided for gradual but systematic introduction of American government into the new territories and for their eventual admission to full membership in the American union. The ordinances provided for three stages leading to statehood. In the first, the president would appoint a territorial governor, a secretary, and a three-judge Supreme Court; the governor and judges would form a legislative council that could adopt "such laws of the original States . . . as may be necessary and best suited to the circumstances of the district."[17] In the second stage, after a territory acquired at least 5,000 free male inhabitants, settlers would elect representatives to a legislature that could create laws of its own and would not be confined to selection of laws from other states. In the third stage, a territory could apply for admission to statehood when its population reached 60,000, with additional conditions for admission to be added in Congress's discretion.[18]

The Northwest and Southwest ordinances did not create a system of substantive laws but they addressed several important areas of law. They created a bill of rights protecting freedom of religion, trial by jury, the right not to be deprived of liberty or property without due process of law, and sanctity of contract. They also included a navigation clause providing that all navigable waters in trans-Appalachian America would be "common highways and forever free" for public use. The only significant difference between the two ordinances was that the Northwest Ordinance prohibited slavery in territories to which it applied; the Southwest Ordinance did not.[19] The ordinances worked reasonably well in practice and when Congress turned its attention to creating and organizing the Mississippi Territory in 1798, it incorporated the Southwest Ordinance into the act of organization.[20]

Sargent's Code, Mississippi's first comprehensive code, followed the civil-law codification tradition—but unlike the *Partidas*, which was the product of a long-established social order, the code reflected the new territory's remoteness from the centers of American population and power. Mississippi's territorial officials were authorized to create a body of laws derived from other states, but Sargent could not act until at least two of the new territorial judges were present. One judge, Peter Bruin, was a longtime Natchez resident, but the other judges had to make the long journey from the East, and Sargent was not able to achieve a quorum until January 1799. Sargent faced additional difficulties. No statute books of other states were available in the territory; Sargent had only his own book of Northwest Territory ordinances to rely on, and his colleagues, whose attendance in Mississippi Territory was spotty, provided little help. Sargent's personality also posed an obstacle. His New England upbringing and military experience inclined him to insist on rigidly upright conduct and strict order and made it difficult for him to accept the often informal and violent nature of the frontier and the need for flexibility in administering frontier law.[21]

During 1799 and 1800, Sargent and his colleagues crafted a series of laws that were not as comprehensive as the *Partidas* but had important points of similarity. Like the *Partidas* authors, Sargent devoted a substantial part of his work to framing a centralized governmental system and allocating its powers, with a particular eye toward public safety. The first portions of Sargent's Code established a territorial militia; other portions established a territorial system of general courts and probate courts, and Sargent later added provisions for county officers and taxation to support local law enforcement.[22] Like the *Partidas*, the code addressed criminal law at length: it set forth a basic compendium of crimes including homicide, infliction of lesser injuries, and robbery and theft. The code also addressed two crimes particularly common on the frontier: arson and unlawful assembly and riot. Settlers assembling in groups of three or more for any unlawful purpose were subject to heavy fines and whipping, and local officials were authorized to form posses to disperse them. Arsonists were subject to whipping, imprisonment up to three years, and forfeiture of all their property.[23] Like the *Partidas*, the code included a law regulating slavery in detail, albeit one reflective of the fact that at the end of the eighteenth century slavery was already more extensive and more economically important to Mississippi than it had ever been to medieval Spain and the Spanish colonies.[24]

There were also important points of difference. The *Partidas* contained an entire section on canon law, regulating the role of the Catholic Church in Spain and its colonies. Sargent's Code did not address religion at all: any connection between church and state was antithetical to American law and was prohibited by the Northwest and Southwest ordinances. The code paid less attention than the *Partidas* to private civil and commercial matters. It included a law outlining basic requirements for marriage but it did not address the balance of power between husband and wife or the right to control family property and income. The code created procedures for litigating debt-related disputes in the courts but did not address contract law further, and it made no reference to inheritance rights, a subject to which the *Partidas* devoted considerable attention.[25] Conversely, Sargent addressed several subjects omitted from the *Partidas* that were relevant to frontier Mississippi if not medieval Spain. For example, the code included a law closely regulating taverns and liquor sales. It also prohibited the sale of alcohol to Indians and the purchase of certain meat products from Indians, presumably because the meat might come from stolen livestock.[26] Sargent and his colleagues restricted the entrance of "Foreigners of Infamous character" into the territory, and they enacted a law authorizing Sargent to impose quarantines and provide assistance upon outbreaks of yellow fever and other diseases, although outbreaks of disease in frontier Mississippi were rare.[27]

Several parts of Sargent's Code elicited widespread opposition, which illuminated the nature of Mississippi's frontier culture as much as the code itself. Many settlers viewed the code's elaborate scheme of local courts and officials, particularly the probate courts, as excessive and autocratic, not least because Sargent was able to increase his power by controlling appointment of local judges and court officials. The broad reach of Sargent's criminal code and its many harsh penalties grated on the sensibilities of settlers who wanted maximum freedom and minimal regulation. Unlike Sargent, they accepted a certain amount of violence and disorder in everyday life as a matter of course. Many established planters and merchants supported Sargent's efforts to impose order quickly and forcefully, but others resented his efforts and his blunt way of exercising power. After Jefferson replaced Sargent in 1801, the territorial legislature repealed some portions of the code and modified others, particularly those concerning state and local government, in order to placate Sargent's opponents and meet the needs of a growing territory.[28]

Law and Order on the Mississippi Frontier

Mississippi Territory was a land of opportunity. As one early settler observed, there was "money in great plenty to be made here by agriculture & with superior Talents, a man must rise."[29] But it was also a land whose inhabitants favored direct action and plain speaking over reflection. They expressed their feelings through fights as well as frolics, resorting freely to violence when they felt that their safety or their honor was threatened. Defense of personal honor was important above all else. A man who had been intentionally insulted but did not defend himself, to the death if necessary, became an outcast in his community. Planters, merchants, and other members of the elite carried out the code of honor through duels; other settlers used less formal but no less deadly forms of combat.[30]

Figure 1.1. Governor Winthrop Sargent. Courtesy of the Archives and Records Services Division, Mississippi Department of Archives and History.

The culture of honor and violence, together with an underlying suspicion of all authority, permeated Mississippi's legal system. During the territorial era, residents regularly petitioned Congress to remove officials who had incurred their displeasure and to overturn official acts. They complained about Sargent and the manner in which he enacted his code, and they spoke out against malfeasance by territorial judge Bruin, which prompted Bruin to resign in 1809. The territorial legislature attempted to impeach Bruin's colleague Seth Lewis in 1803; Lewis pointed out that only President Jefferson could remove him, but rather than continue the battle he, too, resigned.[31]

Toulmin was a particular magnet for complaints. His early efforts to impose legal order in the Tombigbee District elicited cries of tyranny, and in 1810, a petition to Congress for his removal. Two years later, when district settlers attempted to secure a port for the region by invading Spanish West Florida and occupying Mobile, Toulmin, hoping to avert diplomatic disaster, notified federal authorities of their plan and instructed a local grand jury that invasion would be illegal.

Toulmin's actions elicited another removal petition, and when Toulmin encouraged a district grand jury to indict the movement's leaders, the jury defied him and one of the insurgents sued him for false imprisonment. A frustrated Toulmin predicted to President Madison that a full hearing on the petition against him "will satisfy Congress of the folly and madness of expecting that in the present state of our settlements, anything like real liberty or law should prevail over such a widely extended tract of country as the Mississippi Territory."[32]

The culture of honor and violence also spilled into the courtroom. In *The Flush Times of Alabama and Mississippi* (1853), jurist and author Joseph Baldwin described the business of frontier Mississippi courts: "The major part of criminal cases, except misdemeanors, were for killing, or assaults with intent to kill. They were usually defended upon points of chivalry. The iron rules of British law were too tyrannical for free Americans, and too cold and unfeeling for the hot blood of the sunny South."[33] Even judges were exposed to threats of violence. Reuben Davis, a prominent attorney and politician who served on the state's supreme court in the 1840s, recounted two occasions when unfavorable judicial rulings prompted immediate resistance and violence. After a state judge, one Howry, ruled against Davis on a point of procedure Davis felt "a perfect blaze of sudden fury": he drew a knife and moved to attack the judge. Other lawyers intervened, ordered the clerk to adjourn court and took the judge away for his protection. Later that day, Howry told Davis he had meant no insult but he refused Davis's demand for a further explanation of his ruling. Davis then struck and stabbed the judge, who responded by grabbing a hammer and hitting Davis. Other lawyers separated them; when court resumed that evening, both appeared, having put on extra clothing to conceal their wounds. Another judge was then called in and took over for Howry. Seven years later, when friends tried to repair the breach, Davis responded that "Howry was a gentleman, and that our difficulty was casual and without malice. Although it had been a death-struggle, it had been about almost nothing," and the two made up.[34]

In another case, federal judge Samuel Gholson peremptorily ruled against Davis on a point of evidence, denied his request to argue the point and told him to sit down. Davis refused and appealed to the courtroom crowd, warning Gholson that "[e]very man in this room will sustain me" against the judge's "monstrous tyranny and injustice" and that if Gholson tried to jail him for contempt of court, "I will hold you personally responsible." After the crowd "began to make audible movements and suppressed remarks of an angry nature," Gholson "saw [its] temper . . . and knew that he could not venture farther." Gholson reversed his ruling, and Davis won his trial. Davis thus made clear that at bottom honor took precedence over legal order, even within the legal profession itself.[35]

Mississippi accorded considerably less deference to its territorial judges than did most American territories, and this affected the operation of its courts. Its territorial supreme court experienced unusually high turnover, with judges holding office for little more than three years on average.[36] Longer-serving judges in other territories frequently played a prominent part in shaping their territories' politics and culture as well as law. For example, Henry Brackenridge of Louisiana, Augustus Woodward of Michigan, and James Doty of Wisconsin all wrote scholarly works, including studies of their regions. Woodward helped design Detroit's street system and establish the University of Michigan, and Doty established Wisconsin's capital and served as territorial governor and congressman after his time on the bench ended.[37] The only Mississippi judge who came close to this level of achievement was Toulmin, who wrote the *Mississippi Magistrates Guide* as well as a revised Mississippi code (1806). After the Tombigbee District was split off from Mississippi and incorporated into the new state of Alabama (1819), he helped prepare Alabama's first constitution and served in its legislature.[38]

Mississippians' anti-authoritarian streak would produce important legal reforms after statehood, but during territorial days, it prevented the talents of Mississippi judges, an important potential resource, from being fully exploited. Mississippi was not a legal wilderness: it had a well-established legal structure at statehood, and the amount of attention that territorial and early state legislatures gave to the court system showed that they considered law to be important. But anti-authoritarianism, as well as the culture of honor and violence, meant that Mississippi lawmakers would have to cope with countervailing forces much stronger than their counterparts in other states.

Sargent's Code was in large part a response to these forces. Creation of a trial court system, comprising quarter-sessions judges and local magistrates whose primary duty was to keep the peace, was one of Sargent's first priorities. Consequently, Mississippi's court system was unusually elaborate for a thinly settled territory. Laws prohibiting mobs from gathering and committing unlawful acts were common in frontier territories and states, but Mississippi's anti-riot law was draconian: it applied to groups of as few as three people and its penalties, including infliction of up to thirty-nine lashes and imprisonment up to a year, were among the harshest in the nation. The anti-riot law was a check against the culture of honor and violence, but at the same time other portions of the code tacitly accepted that culture, particularly in the context of private fights. Mississippians who "cut out or disable[d] the tongue, put out an eye, slit or bit[ ] the nose, ear or lip, or cut off or disable[d], any limb" during a fight were subject only to fines and comparatively short prison terms, and dueling was not outlawed until 1832.[39] In short, Mississippi lawmakers did their best to preserve basic social order but from the beginning they recognized that the taste for violence was too deep-rooted to eradicate completely. It required a modicum of legal accommodation, which they provided.

The challenge facing Mississippi territorial courts was compounded by uncertainty over the extent of their jurisdiction. When Congress created Mississippi Territory, it did not say whether the new territory's judges had the same powers as federal judges sitting in established states, or whether their decisions could be appealed to the US Supreme Court. Local officials divided: territorial Judge Thomas Rodney believed he and his colleagues had full power but George Poindexter, the territory's attorney general, did not. The dispute took on urgency in early 1807, when Aaron Burr arrived in Mississippi. Burr had served as Thomas Jefferson's vice president (1801–1805) but had recently and dramatically fallen from favor. After killing Alexander Hamilton in a duel, Burr had left for the West, shadowed by rumors that he was plotting a secession movement and formation of a new frontier republic of which he would be the leader. A faintly comic clash of wills ensued. Rodney, believing that his court had jurisdiction to try Burr for treason, urged Poindexter to indict Burr, but Poindexter refused. Burr, sensing that passivity would ultimately prove safer than resistance, enjoyed the hospitality of local planters while awaiting the outcome of the struggle. Rodney then made a presentment to a grand jury, which to his chagrin, refused to indict. Judge Toulmin supported Rodney but his other colleagues did not. Burr was later indicted and acquitted in a Virginia federal court. The issue of whether territorial courts had full federal judicial powers was not resolved until 1828, but by then it was moot in Mississippi, which had received a fully empowered federal district court at statehood (1817).[40]

Organizing the Land

Land ownership in early Mississippi rested on a confusing and often conflicting array of French and Spanish land grants, older states' cessions of western lands to the federal government, and Indian treaties. Spanish authorities made extensive grants to British and American pioneers during the late eighteenth century in order to encourage settlement of the Mississippi Valley, and a majority of early Mississippi planters held their lands by Spanish title. Georgia claimed title to all of Mississippi and Alabama under its colonial charter, and it complicated matters greatly in 1794 when speculators, through liberal use of bribery, induced its legislature and governor to grant them title to the "Yazoo lands" comprising most of central and northern Mississippi. Opponents promptly challenged the Yazoo grants, and title remained uncertain until the US Supreme Court upheld the grants in 1810.[41] Furthermore, at the beginning of the territorial era (1798), all Mississippi lands were still subject to Indian claims; the United States government had not yet made any treaties of cession with the Chickasaws, Choctaws, and other Indian nations that occupied portions of the territory.

Congress began the process of clearing up confusion when it enacted the Land Ordinance of 1785. The Land Ordinance created a survey system that would place a great geographic grid over lands west of the Appalachians including Mississippi, thus providing a uniform basis for land-title descriptions. A standard procedure quickly developed in which the federal government negotiated land cessions from local Indian nations, and, where needed, from older states and foreign nations. Surveyors would then move into the ceded lands, and when their work was complete, the federal government would open a land office and offer the lands for sale.[42] Spain ceded its claims to the Mississippi territory in the Treaty of San Lorenzo (1795); Georgia ceded its claims in 1802, and in 1814 Congress established a claims-resolution fund to clear up remaining disputes over titles based on the Yazoo grants. Titles became so confused that in 1803 Congress enacted a law presumptively confirming early Spanish and British titles. Congress also created a land commission, headed by Judge Rodney, that was able to resolve most remaining title conflicts by 1807. The commission freely used civil-law property rules to resolve disputes over titles acquired during the French and Spanish colonial eras, and Mississippi courts subsequently did the same.[43]

The Choctaws, who were the principal Indian nation in Mississippi, ceded the Natchez area to the United States in 1801 and a large area covering roughly the southern quarter of the state in 1805. There were no further cessions for more than a decade, due in part to artful negotiation and delay by the Choctaws and other Southern Indian nations, and in part to increasing Indian resistance as incoming white settlers pushed aggressively for more land. Cessions resumed after the Creek nation, which occupied most of Alabama, suffered a crushing defeat in the Creek War of 1813–14 at the hands of American troops led by Andrew Jackson. The Choctaws ceded a large portion of west-central Mississippi to the United States in the Treaty of Doak's Stand (1820) and much of northern Mississippi in the Treaty of Dancing Rabbit Creek (1830). The Chickasaw nation, whose tribal lands included the northernmost part of the state, ceded its lands in the Treaty of Pontotoc (1832). The newly acquired lands were surveyed quickly after cession; in addition to its original land-sales office at Natchez (1807), the United States opened offices at Jackson (1827), Columbus and Grenada (1833), and Pontotoc (1836).[44]

Since colonial times, American settlers had regularly gone ahead of government surveyors to settle on new lands, and the same was true in Mississippi.

During the territorial era, many squatters occupied the Yazoo lands and unceded Indian lands without waiting for treaties, surveys, and settlement of title disputes. Squatting was condoned both by the public and by lawmakers, who felt that the imperative of settling the frontier and binding it to the nation took precedence over strict enforcement of the niceties of title. When the 1814 Yazoo claims settlement prompted a new rush of squatters into central Mississippi, President Madison ordered them removed, but Toulmin persuaded the president that immediate removal would be impracticable and would cause hardship to settlers who had just planted crops. Madison suspended his order, and no further effort was made to evict the squatters.[45] When Congress enacted western land-sale laws in the early nineteenth century, it routinely inserted clauses granting squatters preemption rights. Typically, settlers who had squatted on a parcel of land for a certain period of time and who agreed to pay the established government price for their parcel were given first right to purchase the parcel. In 1841, Congress enacted a general preemption law that put an end to all debate over the propriety of squatting.[46]

There was little difficulty settling Spanish land titles. Spanish authorities in charge of grants to early Mississippi settlers were less prone to corruption and more diligent in their record-keeping than their counterparts in Louisiana and California, thus minimizing potential conflict over titles. The threat of conflict was further reduced when the United States agreed as part of the Spanish cession treaty to recognize all Spanish land grants made up to the time of the treaty (1795). Some disputes arose over whether particular Spanish grants predated the treaty, but the disputes were settled in the courts on a case-by-case basis with little controversy.[47]

Indian Relations in Mississippi: Bringing Order to Displacement

The Indian land cession process was more peaceful in Mississippi than in most frontier territories and states. From the earliest days of French and Spanish settlement, the Choctaws were more interested in trading with white settlers than fighting, perhaps because early white settlements were small and did not appear to pose a real threat. By the start of the nineteenth century, the Choctaws had incurred substantial debts to settlers, which made the land cession process easier than it otherwise would have been. The Creek War did not touch Mississippi directly, but it sent a clear message to the Choctaws and Chickasaws that the advance of white settlement was inexorable and that resistance would be futile.[48]

Federal and local officials made genuine efforts to leaven the inexorability of Indian displacement with a measure of due process. In *Johnson and Graham's*

Lessee v. McIntosh (1823), a decision issued soon after Mississippi became a state, federal Chief Justice John Marshall distilled these efforts into legal doctrine. Marshall was more sympathetic to Indians' plight than most Americans of his time, but even he accepted the fact that displacement was inevitable. "To leave [Indian nations] in possession of their country," he reasoned, "was to leave the country a wilderness."[49] The high value that the common law placed on property rights required that Indian nations be allowed to retain the rights to land they occupied, but Marshall held that they were incapable of transferring title to anyone except the federal government and that they would lose all rights of possession if they moved off the land.

In a similar vein, Congress and territorial officials made efforts to protect Indians from predatory conduct of white traders but did not try to end trading altogether. Between 1790 and 1802, Congress enacted laws requiring traders to be licensed and establishing a system of government trading posts to compete with private traders.[50] In 1799, Sargent addressed the damage that liquor sales were doing to Mississippi Indians: his code prohibited all such sales except those made with the governor's express permission.[51] In 1802, Congress authorized the president to regulate the liquor trade, and it later gave government agents broad authority to inspect Indian shipments of trade goods for liquor. But market forces proved to be stronger than reform impulses, and the protective laws proved difficult to enforce.[52]

Another difficult question was how to reconcile American and Indian concepts of crime in Mississippi and elsewhere. From the beginning, American lawmakers treated Indian tribes as partly (but only partly) sovereign nations. In the words of Chief Justice Marshall, they were "domestic dependent nations" in a "state of pupilage" to the United States. Indian legal customs were to be respected on Indian lands, but ultimately Congress had the power to override such customs by law.[53]

Initially, Congress was more concerned about the harm whites could inflict on Indians than about Indian crimes against whites. In 1790, it provided that crimes by whites would be subject to American law whether or not they took place on Indian lands, and in 1796, it passed a new act increasing the penalties for such crimes.[54] These laws also proved difficult to enforce, partly because many white settlers viewed Indians as natural enemies, not fellow Americans, and partly because Indian nations had very different concepts of crime than officials in Washington and Natchez. Under Indian custom, typically a homicide victim's family could choose either to accept an indemnity from the perpetrator's family or to kill the perpetrator or one of his family in retaliation. American law viewed retaliatory killings as murder, and territorial officials and courts throughout the American frontier prosecuted and convicted Indians for such killings, much to the nations' dismay.[55]

Local officials often used pardons to resolve this clash of cultures. For example, in 1810, after two Indians were convicted of murder in Toulmin's court, he requested and received pardons from both President Madison and territorial governor David Holmes. Holmes granted the pardons because he recognized that "to punish [the prisoners] under our laws might be attended with unpleasant consequences," but he instructed Toulmin to warn Mississippi Indians that they would be held accountable under American legal standards in the future.[56] Reuben Davis described a similar murder trial held in the early 1830s:

> After short deliberation a verdict of guilty was returned. The defendant was informed . . . that he would be hung. He was shocked at the mode of death, and made pathetic appeals against such an indignity, claiming his right to die like a warrior. The court had no power to interfere, and sentence was pronounced . . . When this was done, Pushmattahaw rose to his full height, and gave vent to a wild war-whoop, so full of rage and despair that it was terrible to hear. As there were many Indians present, there was for a time danger of attempted rescue.[57]

But a pardon was soon issued, and Davis later regretted that the matter had ever been prosecuted: "[T]ribal laws were still in force . . . [and] their peculiar system of government, however obnoxious to our ideas of justice, was regarded with reverence by the lawless people of their tribes."[58]

In another case, American law proved to be more lenient than Indian legal custom. After Atoka, a Choctaw warrior, accidentally killed a white settler in a bar brawl, he expected to be killed in return under Choctaw custom. Friends persuaded him to plead Choctaw jurisdiction as a defense in an American court. The justices invited several Choctaw chiefs to sit with them, and Atoka was acquitted of murder and released. Choctaw custom prevailed in the end, however, when shortly after the trial Atoka either killed himself or was killed by fellow Choctaws.[59]

The 1817 Constitution: First Steps toward a Pure (White) Democracy

Mississippi was a highly hierarchical society throughout its territorial period. The small population, concentrated in Natchez and adjacent river counties, was dominated by planters and merchants, most of whom had arrived just in time to take advantage of the cotton boom that began in the mid-1790s. Political factions were based more on family rivalries than on ideological differences, and unlike other frontier aristocracies, Mississippi's elite resisted admitting able men of humble origins into its ranks.[60] Territorial chief justice Seth Lewis (1800–1803) provided an example; he had been a laborer before studying law and rising to judicial office, and local leaders never accepted him despite his genuine legal ability. After enduring repeated criticism and calls for his removal over the course of three years, Lewis resigned and moved away from the territory.[61]

Dramatic demographic and political changes took place in Mississippi during the last years before statehood. The American victory in the Creek War effectively ended Indian resistance to white settlement, and the resolution of the Yazoo claims removed an important legal impediment to settlement of central Mississippi. The end of the War of 1812 eliminated all remaining British influence in the Gulf region and convinced Spanish authorities in West Florida to allow Tombigbee District residents free access to Mobile and the Gulf of Mexico. Settlers then poured into the hill and piney-woods regions of southern and central Mississippi, and after the Choctaws and Chickasaws relinquished their claims to northern Mississippi in the early 1830s, that region filled quickly as well.[62] The new waves of settlement would soon spell the end of the old hierarchy, but Mississippi statehood arrived before the change got fully under way.

After the movement for statehood began in 1815–16, Southern congressmen insisted that the eastern part of the territory, including the decidedly non-aristocratic Tombigbee District, be detached for future admission to the Union as an additional slave state. In the western part of the territory, which would become the new state of Mississippi, power still centered on Natchez and a handful of neighboring river counties, which supplied most of the delegates to the state's constitutional convention held in mid-1817. A majority of delegates were planters and lawyers, with a scattering of merchants and farmers. Many of the delegates were wealthy; many had served in territorial posts and would occupy high positions in the new state government.[63] Mississippi's first constitution was neither reactionary nor progressive. One Northern newspaper concluded that it was "so similar to the constitutions of many of the other states that its perusal does not excite much interest."[64]

The convention's handling of suffrage provided the most important example of its innate conservatism. Most pre-nineteenth-century lawmakers believed that government should be conducted by men of property and standing, and that suffrage and officeholding should be limited to that circle. They agreed with New York Chancellor James Kent, one of the nation's most prominent jurists, that universal suffrage was an "extreme democratic principle . . . productive of corruption, injustice, violence and tyranny," and that "the individual who contributes only one cent to the common stock, ought not to have the same power and influence in directing the property concerns of the partnership, as he who contributes his thousands."[65] At the time of American independence, most of the original states imposed stakeholder requirements, which typically limited suffrage to men who held specified minimum amounts of property. Some states required that voters pay taxes or perform militia service.[66]

States created after the end of the Revolution were less receptive to such views. Nearly all rejected stakeholder requirements for suffrage.[67] A few Mississippi convention delegates, mostly from outside the Natchez district, advocated elimination of all property and taxpaying qualifications for voting and officeholding, but future governor and senator George Poindexter of Natchez, "the master-mind and admitted leader of the Convention" and a temperamental conservative, forged a majority in support of limited restrictions. Congress had required voters for the territorial legislature to own fifty acres of land or property worth at least $100; the 1817 convention eliminated all property ownership requirements but required that voters pay taxes or perform militia service.[68] The convention was considerably more restrictive as to officeholding. State representatives were required to own land amounting to 150 acres or $500 in value; state senators, 300 acres or $1,000; and governors, 600 acres or $2,000.[69] Poindexter and his colleagues may well have felt that they were acting liberally—that any man who possessed ambition, energy, and a reasonable amount of luck surely could acquire enough property to qualify for office—but the convention did not submit that issue, or the constitution itself, to a popular vote before the constitution went into effect.[70]

The constitution was modestly progressive in several respects. By 1817, slavery was already a pillar of Mississippi's social and economic structure, and the slave population was growing rapidly. The slaveholding planters and merchants who controlled the 1817 convention could have bolstered their power by counting slaves as persons for legislative apportionment purposes, as the US Constitution did, but they chose not to: Mississippi's legislature would be apportioned based solely on white population.[71]

The convention also abolished imprisonment for debt. Use of imprisonment to force debtors to meet their obligations had been common in the United States since colonial times but had never proved effective. Starting in the mid-eighteenth century, the practice drew a growing number of critics, who argued that imprisonment only prevented debtors from earning money to pay their debts and inflicted needless suffering on their families.[72] The abolition movement gained widespread support west of the Appalachians during and after the Revolution. The prospect of imprisonment posed a threat to the supply of credit upon which cash-poor frontier economies depended. Perhaps more importantly, it cut against the vision of the West as a land of new opportunities and fresh starts, a vision that was a central force driving Western settlement. Most states formed after the Revolution inserted clauses in their constitutions prohibiting imprisonment for debt, and Mississippi followed suit. Debtors who turned over their assets to creditors would be exempt from imprisonment unless they fraudulently concealed assets.[73] The 1817 convention embraced the expansive vision of the West in another important way—it encouraged formation of banks to serve the needs of a state economy that was expected to grow rapidly, and it encouraged the state to take an active role in economic development. The new constitution authorized the legislature to subscribe for up to one-fourth of the stock of every bank it chartered.[74]

Implementing Statehood

Mississippi's economic and population growth during the first years of statehood fundamentally changed the state's social and political structure. The Natchez district grew only modestly, but within the space of fifteen years the regions to the north and east went from near wilderness to heavily settled areas that formed the state's new political center of gravity.[75]

In its first sessions, Mississippi's legislature modified the old territorial laws in order to implement statehood. Legislators established a three-member supreme court and a system of lower state courts, and they created the machinery for the other branches of state government.[76] They also sought to meet the new state's economic needs; their efforts provide an interesting picture of daily life in the new state and of its most pressing problems.

When Mississippi gained statehood, the United States was in the middle of a severe recession (1816–19) which caused particular suffering in the heavily credit-dependent West. The legislature enacted laws implementing the 1817 constitution's prohibition of imprisonment for debt.[77] It also enacted laws designed to relieve the burden on debtors in other ways, but the supreme court held that several of the laws violated clauses in the federal and Mississippi constitutions that prohibited impairment of contracts, including contracts to pay for goods and services. The legislature reacted by summoning the court's justices to explain their conduct, and it debated whether the court had the right to determine the constitutionality of state laws. After some talk of impeachment, the legislature contented itself with enacting a law requiring the court to put all future decisions in writing.[78]

In 1822, the legislature also enacted a comprehensive criminal code that addressed the prominent role violence played in the frontier Southwest. Some

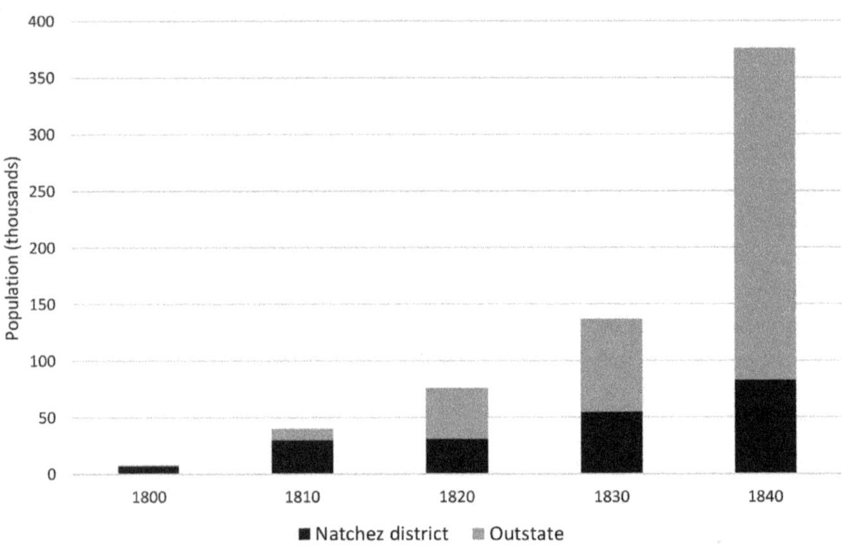

Figure 1.2. Mississippi's Growth, 1800–40

code penalties were harsh. Petty larceny and cattle theft were punishable by whippings up to thirty-nine lashes, and infliction of injuries to cattle and other property was punishable by imprisonment up to one year.[79] The legislature was particularly concerned about gambling, which, it said, "must be often attended with quarrels, disputes and controversies, the impoverishment of many people and their families and the ruin of the health, and corruption of the morals of youth." It prohibited gambling at taverns and racetracks and other public places, although the penalties were light. It required local sheriffs to seize and destroy gaming tables, and required professional gamblers to give large bonds to secure their good behavior.[80] Rowdiness on the Sabbath was also a concern: the legislature made disruptive behavior in church punishable by fine and prohibited all work on Sunday except works of charity or necessity.[81]

Early Mississippi legislatures were active, but their output did not match the proliferation of laws in older states during the 1820s and 1830s. States such as New York, Massachusetts, and Pennsylvania that were going through the first phases of the industrial revolution had need of laws addressing the changes the revolution had brought. During the 1820s and 1830s, Mississippi's economy grew rapidly but remained almost entirely agricultural. No detailed industrial or commercial laws were required. Likewise, the state's new supreme court steered a relatively tranquil course during its first years, apart from the temporary controversy over its decisions against debtor relief laws.

The court's main task during its early years was to search out and select legal tools for use in building a body of law for Mississippi. The justices were fortunate in that Mississippi had begun its statutory codification process very early. Many territories and states delayed codification until the accumulation of laws became so large that no one in the legal community could keep track of them all, but Sargent had ensured that Mississippi would have a code from the beginning of its existence. After Sargent left office, his code was regularly revised and updated by prominent jurists including Toulmin (1806), Edward Turner (1816), Poindexter (1822), and Anderson Hutchinson (1840). These codes made the court's job easier than it otherwise would have been.[82]

New state courts also had to decide which legal treatises and decisions of other courts they would use for guidance. Sometimes choices were dictated by judges' geographic and philosophical preferences, sometimes simply by what books were available. At the dawn of the nineteenth century, American courts relied heavily on English treatises and court decisions because there was very little American material available. The most popular treatise was Sir William Blackstone's *Commentaries on the Laws of England* (1765). Blackstone was popular because he wrote in a highly readable style and because the *Commentaries* covered many aspects of law in a single volume, useful features in a new nation whose judges had little formal legal training and where access to law books was often limited.[83]

After 1800, English influence slowly declined as American jurists produced an ever-increasing number of decisions and treatises. New York's Chancellor Kent, who served on his state's supreme court and as the state's chancellor, or highest equity-court judge (1798–1823), played a central role in the shift. When Kent began his judicial career, only a few volumes of American court decisions existed. Kent persuaded New York's legislature to authorize an official reporter who would compile and publish decisions of the state's appeals courts, and he selected his ally William Johnson for the job. Over the next twenty years, the two men used Johnson's reports to disseminate Kent's decisions and views to the nation, and they encouraged Kent's judicial colleagues to publish also. Many New York publishers maintained national networks of booksellers that included Southern cities such as Charleston, Savannah, and New Orleans. This ensured that lawyers and judges in almost all areas, including remote Mississippi, would have access to the latest New York decisions. As a result, by the time Kent left the bench New York's legal influence far exceeded that of any other state.[84] After his retirement Kent bolstered New York's dominance by publishing his *Commentaries on American Law* (1826), the first comprehensive American legal treatise, which remained influential for nearly a century.[85]

Early Mississippi Supreme Court decisions reflected these influences. During its first years, the court relied heavily on English cases and treatises, but by 1840, when New York's legal influence was at its peak, the court's use of English authority had declined sharply and its early reliance on civil-law treatises had largely ended. After the 1830s, the Mississippi court relied mainly on American cases. Not surprisingly, it cited its own decisions with increasing frequency as it built up a body of published case law, but it did not show any particular preference for Southern over Northern court decisions. The lack of regional emphasis is surprising at first blush, but it was consistent with trends in other states. Antebellum Southern judges were not blind to the growing differences and conflicts between the South and other parts of the nation, but their professional lives, like those of their Northern counterparts, were spent largely in isolation and reflection—reading and absorbing a common body of legal principles expounded by Kent and other legal authorities known to judges in all regions.[86]

The Mississippi court's adherence to a common judicial culture was reinforced by the increasing stability of its personnel. During the court's early years, judicial turnover was high; twenty justices served on the three-person court between 1817 and 1832. After that time, however, several justices, most notably Chief Justice William Sharkey (1833–51) and Justices Cotesworth Smith (1833–38, 1840–41, 1850–63), Alexander Handy (1853–67), and William Harris (1858–67), served for long periods and used their time on the court to integrate Mississippi into the evolving national judicial culture.[87]

The 1832 Constitution and the Triumph of Pure Democracy

As Mississippi settlement expanded outward from the Natchez district, many Mississippians came to view the 1817 constitution as a "dress that was well adapted for the infant, but is getting too short for the adult."[88] Beginning in 1825, legislators regularly introduced resolutions for a new convention, and in 1831 they prevailed: the legislature ordered that a convention be held the following year. The delegates elected to the 1832 convention differed considerably from their predecessors. There were many lawyers but fewer planters and merchants among them, and the Natchez district furnished a minority of the delegates, reflecting changes that had taken place in the state's population distribution.[89]

The convention movement was driven by a generalized desire for change rather than specific reform issues, but after the convention was called, issues surfaced in abundance. Natchez-district and outstate delegates divided over some issues, but not all. One of the most critical reforms, elimination of all

	1820	**1840**	**1860**
CASES CITED:			
English cases	53%	23%	24%
American cases	47%	77%	76%
Mississippi cases	0%	8%	17%
New York cases	17%	22%	13%
Other Northern state cases	12%	7%	20%
Southern state cases	11%	32%	22%
Federal cases	8%	8%	5%
TREATISES CITED:			
American treatises	0%	23%	57%
English treatises	79%	68%	43%
Civil-law treatises	21%	9%	0%

Figure 1.3. Sources of Law in the Mississippi Supreme Court, 1820–60

property- and taxpayer-based limitations on suffrage and officeholding, had broad support throughout the state. A few Natchez-district delegates tried to preserve a taxpayer requirement for state senate voters, but they failed by a wide margin.[90]

Another pioneering reform, popular election of judges, was highly controversial, but support and opposition did not divide along sectional lines. Under the 1817 constitution, judges were appointed by the governor and held office on a good-behavior basis (that is, for life unless impeached by the legislature for serious crimes) up to the mandatory retirement age of sixty-five. This was consistent with Anglo-American legal tradition: British judges had always been appointed by the Crown, and in 1700, Parliament had established the good-behavior tenure system in response to the Stuart kings' habit of removing judges whose decisions displeased them.[91] During the years after the Revolution, state judges were appointed by governors and legislatures, but early nineteenth-century Americans increasingly came to distrust the appointive system. Governors were viewed as being too subject to monarchical tendencies, and legislatures were viewed as vulnerable to faction and corruption. Local justices of the peace were elected in some colonies and in some states after the Revolution, but before 1832 no state had experimented with popular election of higher-level judges.[92]

It is unclear how the idea of making all judgeships elective arose in Mississippi, but it is not unreasonable to think that the idea arose out of

Mississippians' traditional wariness of authority. That wariness would lead naturally to a feeling that judges must be kept in check and must be accountable to the people, and that elections were the best means of achieving that end. Delegates to the 1832 convention divided into three camps: traditionalists who wanted to maintain an appointive system, "Whole Hogs" who wanted judges at all levels to be elected, and "Half Hogs" who favored election only of lower-court judges. Traditionalists, led by future governor John Quitman, argued that an elective system would result in selection of judges based on political loyalties rather than legal ability and decisions based on political rather than legal considerations. But after much debate, the Whole Hogs prevailed by a comfortable margin, and it was settled that judges at all levels would be elected for six-year terms.[93] Implementation of the new system went smoothly; fears of judicial partisanship proved largely unfounded, and by the 1840s, the elective system was universally accepted in Mississippi. Quitman explained the reason for his own change of heart when Louisiana's 1845 constitutional convention asked him for advice on the subject:

> [In 1832, w]e regarded [judicial elections] as a new and hazardous experiment, beautiful in theory, but dangerous in practice. Many of us . . . feared that popular excitements would find their way upon the bench . . . [But t]he experience and observation of nearly thirteen years, have convinced me, and many others who opposed the experiment, that our apprehensions were not well founded. . . . Our judicial stations have been filled with as much, if not more ability, learning and weight of character than formerly. . . . I believe no instance has yet occurred of the election of a judge, in our state, upon mere party questions.[94]

At the same time, the convention made all county offices elective.[95]

Another of the convention's innovations was an anti-dueling clause. Though accepted in practice, dueling had been widely condemned in principle since the late eighteenth century. By 1820, it had largely died out in England and the northern United States, but it persisted in the South, where the culture of honor and violence remained strong. Opponents had made an unsuccessful effort to insert an anti-dueling provision in Mississippi's 1817 constitution; in 1832, they renewed their campaign and secured approval of a clause authorizing the legislature to enact "such laws to prevent the evil practice of dueling as they may deem necessary" and disqualifying duel participants (including seconds) from holding office.[96] Mississippi was one of the first states to enact a constitutional anti-dueling provision,[97] but it was on the front end of a national wave of anti-dueling sentiment. During the next twenty years, six other Southern states[98] and eight Northern and Western states[99] enacted similar constitutional provisions. Like Mississippi's, most such provisions authorized the legislature to enact anti-dueling laws and barred duelists from holding office; a few states also denied duelists the right of suffrage. The anti-dueling clause did not greatly diminish Mississippi's culture of honor and violence, but it was a marker of general support for the rule of law, and it sent a signal that many in the state believed it was necessary to move away from that culture in order to modernize.[100]

The 1832 convention did not ignore Mississippi's recent economic growth and change. Constitutional provisions dealing with finance demonstrated the new political strength of outstate Mississippi. Credit systems were essential to frontier and agricultural states as well as industrial states. That was particularly true of Mississippi, which was heavily dependent on New Orleans and the world markets it served to provide the funds needed to grow Mississippi cotton, to maintain the plantations and slave labor that produced the cotton crops, and to provide buyers once the cotton was harvested and baled.[101] In 1817, the state had made the Bank of Mississippi a public bank, sponsored by the state, in an effort to create a stable local credit source, and it had issued bonds to provide capital for the new bank. During the 1820s, the bank was accused of making loans to favored members of the Natchez-district elite, and in 1830, the legislature, now dominated by outstate lawmakers, created a rival Planters' Bank to finance purchases of newly available cession lands in central and northern Mississippi.[102]

The Natchez-outstate rivalry over state support of banks came to a head in the convention. Outstate delegates secured a provision prohibiting the state from borrowing money through bond issues or otherwise unless two consecutive legislatures agreed, but they made an exception for a proposed $1.5 million loan to Planters Bank.[103] Outstate delegates also favored state subsidy of turnpikes, canals, and other improvement projects, most of which would likely run through their communities and improve local economic prospects, but Natchez-district interests secured a small victory by persuading the convention to require the support of two-thirds of each house of the legislature for any such subsidy.[104]

The new constitution marked the culmination of a decades-long journey that white Mississippians had taken toward a democratic society, although that society was still quite rough around the edges. Control of state politics and law had shifted from the Natchez planter and merchant elite to a broad base of yeoman settlers distributed throughout the state. That base was not united in all things, but it was united in a determination not to return to a society controlled by gentlemen in any way. All suffrage restrictions had been removed and an assertive egalitarianism permeated the state's legal system. Those who sat in judgment over the people would be answerable to them through judicial elections, and the culture of honor and violence would hover over the court system, available for use in the courtroom as needed. The social and legal disruptions rising elsewhere in the industrial revolution's wake seemed far away. The only challenge Mississippi's cotton economy faced was the happy one of accommodating steady growth, which, in 1832, showed no sign of abating.

Many white Mississippians felt their state was setting an example to the nation as a successful experiment in democracy, and that it had the potential to further expand that democracy. But in their pride they overlooked another pillar of Mississippi life, one that was already undermining the democratic vision and that would send the state down an entirely different path after 1832. That pillar, the state's system of slavery, and the path it took are the subjects of the next chapter.

CHAPTER TWO

Prescribed Spheres: The Legal Path of Slavery in Mississippi

Unconditional submission and obedience to the lawful commands and authority of the master is the imperative duty of the slave, as well as the undoubted right of the master. . . . [U]pon its proper observance the happiness and welfare of both races, in that relation, necessarily depend.
—Justice William Harris (1860)[1]

Isaac Ross was one of the more enlightened members of Mississippi's early planter elite. After fighting in the American Revolution and building a prosperous plantation in South Carolina, Captain Ross moved to Mississippi in 1808, settling at Prospect Hill near Port Gibson. By 1830, he owned more than 5,000 acres of land and 150 slaves. Like many planters who came of age during the Revolution, Ross had private doubts about the morality of slavery. In the early 1830s, he helped establish the Mississippi branch of the American Colonization Society, which aimed to resolve the dilemmas of slavery by freeing slaves and providing them a new life in Africa.[2] In 1834, as Ross's health declined, he faced a conundrum—what to do about his own slaves when he died? His answer ignited a legal controversy that lasted more than a decade and illuminated the shifts then taking place in Mississippi's approach to slavery.

Mississippi's 1822 slave code prohibited Ross from manumitting (that is, freeing) his slaves in Mississippi, so he directed that all but a disfavored few be offered the chance to go to Liberia at his expense under the Colonization Society's auspices. When Ross died in 1836, a battle broke out between the

Colonization Society, which supported his wishes, and his grandson and executor Isaac Ross Wade, who wished to overturn the will and retain the Ross slaves for himself.[3] The dispute forced Mississippi's supreme court to confront for the first time the question whether the state's 1822 anti-emancipation law applied to manumission of slaves by sending them to freedom outside Mississippi. In *Ross v. Vertner* (1840), the court angered Wade and many other slave owners by holding that the law did not apply. The anti-emancipation law was designed to prevent "the dangers of too great an increase of free negroes" who might "sow[ ] the seeds of mischief, of insubordination, perhaps of revolt, amongst the slaves in their neighborhood," said Justice James Trotter, but it did not foreclose manumission altogether. Freed slaves would not pose a threat to Mississippi if they left the state after emancipation.

The court's decision did not end the war between Wade and the Colonization Society or the larger debate over manumission. Wade and his allies demanded that the legislature retroactively prohibit manumission of slaves by will, and Wade threatened to retain the Ross slaves by force if necessary. In 1842, the legislature prohibited all future manumission of slaves by will and provided that slaves already freed must leave the state within one year or forfeit their freedom. Only the efforts of Dr. John Ker, a state senator and leader of the Colonization Society, prevented the law from being made retroactive so as to apply to the Ross slaves.

Wade and his fellow executors then delayed making travel arrangements for Liberia. They hoped that if they waited long enough, the Ross slaves, not having left the state within a year of the 1842 law's passage, would lose their freedom and would pass to Wade and other family members. In 1845, Wade's house at the Ross plantation burned down in a fire set, it was rumored, by slaves angered by his efforts to block their freedom. Exasperated Colonization Society officials finally sued Wade in order to enforce Captain Ross's wishes, and in 1846, an equally exasperated court rejected Wade's stratagem. Justice Alexander Clayton condemned Wade for his "breach of trust and perversion of power," suggesting that manumission restrictions might be an unconstitutional infringement of slave owners' absolute right of property in their slaves.[4]

For the Ross slaves, it was a happy ending because most of them finally went to Liberia in 1848–49. But as the nation moved along the path to civil war, Mississippians became increasingly protective of slavery and ever more hostile to legal paths to freedom. Mississippi's supreme court backed away from Justice Clayton's challenge to anti-manumission laws and in *Mitchell v. Wells* (1859), Clayton's successors affirmed that the door to further emancipation would remain shut. Justice William Harris criticized the court's Ross decisions as a departure from the state's true policy of preventing emancipation in any form, a departure engineered by "avowed public enem[ies]" of slavery. Manumission, said Harris, was "at war with the interests and happiness of both races." Mississippi's "climate, soil and productions, . . . habits, manners and opinions . . . *require slave labor.*"[5]

The gradual hardening of the slave system was a central theme of antebellum Mississippi law. But there was always a strain of ambivalence in the state's slave laws. Maintenance of racial superiority and control was always the paramount goal, but planters' and lawmakers' approaches to slavery were also driven by economic needs—overly harsh treatment of slaves might reduce their productivity—and even by occasional humanitarian concerns. These competing impulses surfaced repeatedly as Mississippi lawmakers and judges confronted the many legal problems that slavery raised. Could Mississippi constitutionally restrict slave owners' freedom to dispose of their own property by manumission? Should it restrict the interstate slave trade, which supplied labor that the state needed but introduced unknown, potentially dangerous slaves into Mississippi society? Should slaves be allowed some degree of economic and social freedom when they were not working for their owners? Should the state protect slaves from abusive treatment through its criminal laws? Despite Mississippi's place at the heart of the American cotton belt, as well as its heavy dependence on slavery in order to maintain that position, it governed slaves with a slightly lighter hand than some of its sister states. But as war approached and the deep South drew together, their legal paths converged.

The Path to the 1822 Slave Code

Slaves were present in Mississippi from its earliest days of settlement, but the French Code Noir and Spain's slave code, which prevailed at least nominally until the late 1700s in the Mississippi country, reflected a sensibility quite different from that of the British colonies to the east. The primary object of all slave codes was to maximize slaves' economic productivity while maintaining strict white control, but French and Spanish colonial officials found it easier to accommodate slaves' humanity than did their British counterparts. The Code Noir imposed strict limits on slaves' economic freedom; slaves could not sell goods they produced on their own time without their owner's permission and they could not sell sugar cane, a key French colonial crop, at all. But the code recognized slave family relationships, even interracial ones, in a way that British law did not. Slave owners who formed relationships with slave women could free such women by marrying them. Owners could not force slaves to marry or breed, and splitting up slave families with young children through sale was prohibited. The code imposed no restrictions on manumission, and freed slaves were given legal rights fully equal to those of whites.

Spain's *Siete Partidas* created a highly paternalistic slave system. Like the Code Noir, it allowed slaves no economic independence but it created mutual obligations of support between slaves and their owners. Slaves were required to preserve their owners from harm, and owners were enjoined not "to strike [a slave] in an unnatural or cruel manner, or cause him to perish by hunger." Owners could freely manumit their slaves, even marry them, but freed slaves were obligated to show deference to their masters for life. [6]

In British America, South Carolina's 1740 slave code, enacted in the wake of the Stono slave rebellion, became a model for other southern colonies. Unlike its civil-law counterparts, the South Carolina code focused on restriction of slaves' personal freedom more than their economic freedom. The Code Noir and the *Partidas* imposed some limits on slaves' freedom of movement and assembly, but the South Carolina Code went much further, allowing whites to break up slave meetings, to punish slaves who showed disrespect or defiance, and to impress other slaves to help administer punishment. Whites who killed or maimed slaves without justification were subject only to fines. Slaves were strictly prohibited from learning to read and write, from hunting, from keeping boats for their own use, and from assembling or traveling without white supervision or white permission. A white presence was required on plantations at all times. Even clothing was regulated, with slaves restricted to certain types of coarse cloth that served both as identification and as a badge of submission. But in keeping with the common-law tradition of trial by jury, the code created an elaborate system providing for criminal complaints against slaves, to be heard and adjudged by local magistrates and planters.[7]

Like other aspects of civil law, the influence of the Code Noir and the *Partidas* slave code quickly faded as Mississippi became Americanized. Mississippi's earliest planters were sufficiently remote from the capital at New Orleans that they could bend the civil law to meet their own needs. Desire for economic productivity and efficiency was uppermost in their minds; the Code Noir and the *Partidas* demonstrated at least a modest concern for slaves' personal welfare, but early planters had virtually none.[8]

When Winthrop Sargent introduced American law to Mississippi in 1799, he borrowed heavily from the South Carolina code. Under Sargent's Code, slave assemblies and seditious speech were punishable by severe whipping and confinement. Slaves were not allowed to keep guns without a special license, and they were not allowed to keep dogs or horses at all. Their right of movement was severely restricted; they were not permitted to travel without a pass from their owner or other authorities. Slaves could not visit friends and relatives on neighboring plantations for more than two hours without their owner's permission, and no more than five slave visitors at a time were permitted under any circumstances. Sargent proclaimed his desire for a "humane policy . . . to protect this useful but degraded class of men" and his code prohibited whites from inflicting "cruel or unusual" punishment on slaves, but, as in South Carolina, violators were subject only to small fines. Excesses against slaves committed in the name of order would not be handled through imprisonment. The code contained economic restrictions as well; slaves were not permitted to trade without their owner's consent, and planters were not allowed to hire their slaves' labor to others. [9]

Sargent soon retired from Mississippi's political scene, but his code provided an enduring template for Mississippi slave law. Territorial legislators made some adjustments to the code as the territory filled up, mostly in response to economic fluctuations and wartime crises. For example, fear of slave insurrection increased when the War of 1812 created a very real threat of British invasion and provided to slaves the hope of escape to the British lines and freedom; the legislature responded by providing for summary trials of slaves suspected of insurrection (1812).[10] Statehood provided an occasion to revisit Mississippi's slave laws. Delegates to the 1817 constitutional convention made no attempt to create a detailed slave code, but they addressed several issues that would command state legislators' attention during the decades to follow.

One issue was whether slave owners would be allowed to manumit their slaves. During the Revolutionary era, the number of American manumissions had increased for several reasons. The profitability of slave labor had declined as wheat and corn production replaced tobacco farming, and a surprising number of Eastern slaveholders concluded that the rights of liberty and equality proclaimed in the Declaration of Independence could not logically be limited by color. Many late eighteenth-century southerners considered slavery to be a regrettable or even injurious institution and viewed the prospect of its end with equanimity. Some states, most notably Virginia, eased or eliminated colonial-era restrictions on manumission in response.[11] But Mississippi was a thousand miles from the Revolution's intellectual centers, and it was at the center of the cotton boom that was restoring slavery's profitability. From the beginning, Mississippians deemed slavery essential in a way that the East did not. Nevertheless, many Eastern immigrants to Mississippi, such as Isaac Ross and John Ker, brought their misgivings with them, and when a national movement began in the late 1820s to eliminate slavery by sending American slaves to colonize west Africa, Ross, Ker, and other respectable Mississippians gave it a presence in the state.[12]

The 1817 convention approached manumission elliptically. It did not create a constitutional *right* to manumit slaves but it did authorize the legislature to *permit* owners to manumit their slaves, provided they did not do so in order to defraud creditors or to avoid the expense of caring for aged or disabled slaves. The new constitution also authorized the legislature to free slaves who had "rendered to the State some distinguished service," and to require owners to treat their slaves "with humanity."[13]

Soon after the new state's supreme court was created, it indicated it would take a comparatively liberal approach to freedom. In *Harry v. Decker* (1818), the court addressed the issue of whether slaves who traveled with their owners to free states thereby became free. During the early nineteenth century, Northern and Southern courts alike held that if a slave owner sojourned in a free state for a substantial period of time without a definite intent to return South, his slaves became free; but if he merely traveled across a free state to get from one slave state to another, they did not. The *Harry* court followed that rule, holding that a group of slaves who had resided in Indiana for many years before being returned to Mississippi were free. Justice Joshua Clarke went further, stating that "slavery is condemned by reason and the laws of nature" and that it could only exist where explicitly permitted by statute. "In matters of doubt," said Clarke, it was "an unquestioned rule, that courts must lean in *favorem vitae et libertatis.*"[14]

In 1822, Mississippi's legislature enacted a comprehensive slave code that would remain in effect throughout the antebellum period. The 1822 Code addressed manumission in response to the 1817 constitution's directive, and it took a hard line in response to the *Harry* decision. Slaves could be freed only by will, and even then only if the legislature found that they had performed a "meritorious act for the benefit of such owner . . . or some distinguished service for the benefit of the state." Black Mississippians could seek freedom as the slave Harry had done, but freedom suits were discouraged: if they lost, they and their sponsors would be required to pay their owner's legal fees. The new code did not restrict the interstate slave trade but it prohibited free blacks from immigrating to Mississippi. Those who did so would be subject to heavy fines and if they could not pay, they would be sold into slavery.[15]

The emphasis on restriction of personal liberty that had characterized the South Carolina code and Sargent's Code continued in the 1822 Code. The new code prohibited slaves from assembling in groups of more than five or assembling for worship without white supervision. They could not travel off their home plantation without a pass and could not use firearms, even for hunting, unless their owner obtained a license from a local magistrate.[16] Slaves who conspired to rebel would be put to death, and those who fought with their owners were subject to severe physical punishment unless they were acting to protect their own lives.[17] A patrol system was formed to monitor slave movements

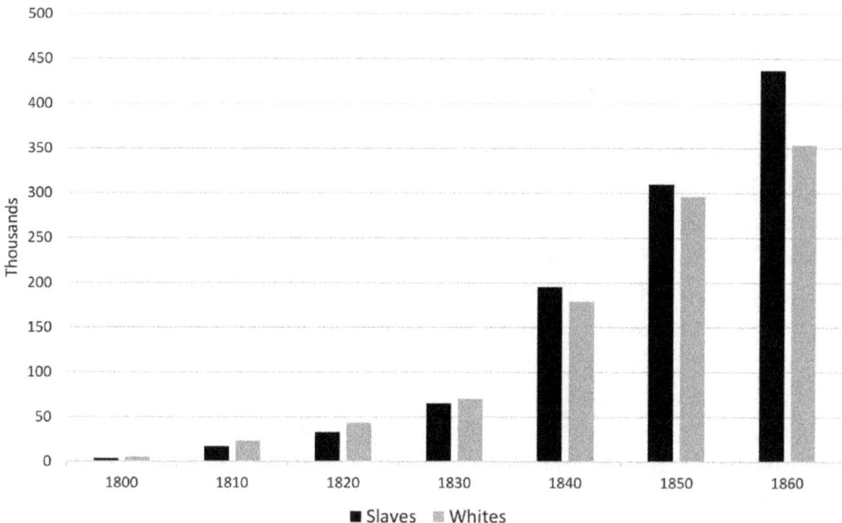

Figure 2.1. Slave and Free Population, 1800–60

and administer on-the-spot whippings for suspicious behavior, with planters and most militia members being required to perform patrol service. Blacks, both slave and free, were prohibited from meeting in groups to learn to read and write.[18] The code by no means neglected economic restrictions, as slaves could not trade, work for wages, or cultivate cotton for their own account, and they were not allowed to possess cattle, horses, sheep, or pigs.[19] Punishments for violating both liberty and economic restrictions were harsh, typically up to thirty-nine lashes.[20] A reaction to Revolutionary-era efforts to soften slavery was underway, and it remained to be seen whether the reaction would deepen.

The Interstate Slave Trade

The transatlantic slave trade began in the early 1500s and steadily expanded over the next two hundred years in response to settlement of the Americas and development there of crops well-suited to slave labor such as tobacco, rice, and sugar cane. In the late eighteenth century, as the horrors of slaves' treatment during their "middle passage" from Africa to North America received increasing publicity, a movement arose to ban the international slave trade. It drew support not only from opponents of slavery but from many slave owners who believed they could meet their labor needs entirely from the new generations of slaves being born in the United States. The nation's founders struck a compromise in the federal Constitution, giving the international slave trade a twenty-year grace period but requiring that it terminate in the United States in 1808.[21]

The termination provision created a dilemma for Mississippi. As 1808 approached, the territory's cotton production was expanding and demand for additional slaves was growing rapidly. Northern and eastern Mississippi would soon open to white settlement, which would further increase demand. Mississippi planters acceded to the loss of international sources of slave labor but recognized that they would have to import slaves from other Southern states on a large scale. Many white Mississippians were ambivalent, caught between economic need and fear that unfamiliar slaves would bring unrest and rebellion with them. The state's legal approach to the slave trade reflected that ambivalence and oscillated throughout the antebellum years.[22]

Mississippi began by imposing only mild restrictions on the interstate trade. In 1808, the territorial legislature allowed interstate slave trading but required traders to procure certificates of good character for their slaves from whites who had known them. An exception was made for white immigrants who brought slaves with them; presumably they would not in bring slaves who were rebellious or otherwise dangerous.[23] The 1817 constitution made the immigrant exception permanent but otherwise gave the legislature full power to restrict the interstate slave trade as it saw fit. The state's first legislators felt no need to do so, but during the late 1820s, Mississippians became increasingly uneasy about the trade. Commercial slave traders, a direct reminder of the brutal underside of slavery that many preferred to ignore, were now a prominent presence in the state and many sister states were beginning to restrict interstate slave traffic. In 1828, Governor Gerard Brandon urged the legislature to limit or end the trade. Slavery, he argued, "has invariably operated oppressively on the poor classes of every community . . . and excludes from the State, in proportion to the number of slaves, a free white population, through the means of which alone, can we expect to take rank with our sister States." Justice Trotter agreed, noting that the interstate trade had produced frauds and "scenes . . . shocking in many instances to our feelings of humanity," as well as "the introduction of slaves from abroad of depraved character, which were imposed upon our unsuspecting citizens by the artful and too often unscrupulous negro trader."[24]

A tipping point was reached in 1832. Mississippi's new constitution prohibited interstate slave trade effective the following year and provided that the immigrant exception would end in 1845, but voters and lawmakers soon had second thoughts. An effort to repeal the constitution's slave-trade restrictions failed only narrowly and the legislature declined to provide any penalties for violation of the restrictions until 1837, when it formally criminalized the interstate slave trade and required planters moving to Mississippi to certify that they intended to use their slaves for work, not sale. The legislature's delay created a minor constitutional crisis. When hard times came to Mississippi in the mid-1830s, many planters who had purchased slaves on credit from out-of-state traders tried to avoid their obligations by arguing that under the 1832 constitution, such transactions were illegal and void. In *Green v. Robinson* (1840), Mississippi's supreme court agreed, but soon afterward the US Supreme Court held in *Groves v. Slaughter* (1841) that contracts with out-of-state slave traders entered into before the 1837 legislative ban were enforceable. Notwithstanding the high court's decision, Mississippi's supreme court adhered to the position it had staked out in *Green*, thus creating a situation where slave traders who tried to enforce their pre-1837 promissory notes in federal court succeeded, but those who resorted to Mississippi state courts failed.[25]

As the cotton economy recovered in the early 1840s, unpleasant memories of slave traders faded and Mississippi planters had a change of heart. Once again, they feared that the increase of the domestic slave population through childbirth would not be sufficient to meet their needs. In 1846, voters ratified a constitutional amendment repealing the 1832 ban and reopening the interstate slave trade. Doubts about the trade lingered, but no further trade restrictions were enacted during the slavery era.[26]

Manumission: The Struggle between Social Control and Property Rights

The struggle over manumission exemplified by the *Ross* cases was not limited to Mississippi but took place throughout the South. Some states, most notably Virginia, placed no limits on manumission other than ensuring that it would not be used to avoid payment of an owner's debts.[27] After an 1831 rebellion in which slaves led by Nat Turner killed several dozen whites and terrorized southside Virginia, there was a general tightening of slave laws throughout the South. Several upper-South states that had formerly followed Virginia's liberal model shifted to systems similar to the one Mississippi had created in the 1822 Code and the *Vertner* case; manumission by will would be permitted only if the freed slaves promptly left the state so as not to increase the local free-black population.[28]

Some Deep South states tried to prohibit manumission altogether. Georgia did so in 1801, and in 1820, South Carolina provided that only its legislature could emancipate slaves.[29] But South Carolina chief justice John Belton O'Neall had a different view, and for nearly thirty years he jousted with his state's legislature over manumission. In *Frazier v. Executors of Frazier* (1835), O'Neall persuaded his colleagues to create an exception to South Carolina's 1820 anti-manumission law that echoed *Vertner*. The purpose of South Carolina's law, O'Neall reasoned, was to prevent an increase in the state's free-black population, not to limit owners' right to free their slaves. Thus, owners could free their slaves if the freed slaves left the state and did not return. O'Neall's opinion in *Frazier* influenced the Mississippi justices who decided the *Vertner* case; after their decision attracted criticism, Justice Trotter added a supplement defending the decision and citing *Frazier* as support.[30] O'Neall was admired by Southern jurists who did not view manumission as a threat to the slave system, but he was anathema to William Harris and others who believed the threat was real.

Harris exemplified Mississippi's and the South's abandonment of ambivalence over slavery in the late antebellum era. Spurred by their increasing dependence on cotton, by steadily increasing Northern hostility to slavery beginning in the 1830s, by the Nat Turner rebellion and by rumors of slave rebellion in central Mississippi in 1835,[31] Mississippians increasingly defended slavery as a positive good and vowed to defend it at all costs. In 1826, the legislature had viewed slavery as a "national evil," albeit one which, "however much we may regret it: circumstances over which we could have no control have rendered . . . inevitable." By 1837, however, it considered slavery to be "the very palladium of [our] prosperity and happiness." Likewise, in 1831 Mississippi politician and orator Seargent S. Prentiss had written that slavery was a "necessary evil," but five years later, he described it as "a blessing . . . authorized both by the laws of God and the dictates of reason and philanthropy." Harris fully subscribed to the latter view, and when he joined the state's supreme court in 1858, with intersectional tension reaching new heights and war approaching, he hoped to overturn the court's ambivalent approach to manumission. Harris's colleague Alexander Handy, a moderate in the O'Neall style, opposed Harris. Between 1858 and 1860, the two justices waged a duel over the meaning of slavery which Harris, the more faithful mirror of the times, won.[32]

Shortly before Harris joined the court, Handy set the stage for their debate in *Shaw v. Brown* (1858). James Brown had taken his two sons from an interracial relationship, Francis and Jerome, to the North and had freed them and settled them in Indiana, where they remained. James then returned to Mississippi and left his estate to his sons at his death. Other relatives argued that under the recently decided *Dred Scott* case, Francis and Jerome were not citizens and therefore did not have a right to inherit; furthermore, allowing them to inherit would contravene Mississippi's 1842 anti-*Vertner* law.

Speaking for the court, Handy rejected both arguments. If James had intended that his sons return south, said Handy, the 1842 law would have nullified their free status and as slaves they would not have been allowed to inherit, but the evidence indicated that James intended them to leave Mississippi permanently. Handy conceded that Francis and Jerome were not citizens, but he noted that Indiana allowed all free persons to inherit and he concluded that Mississippi should defer to Indiana policy as a matter of comity. "Otherwise," he reasoned, "conflicts between the States . . . would be continual and irremediable, and the 'perfect Union,' designed to be established by the Constitution, would be the most frail of human compacts." The 1842 law's purpose was to reduce the number of free blacks in Mississippi, not to prevent manumission or deny manumitted slaves all rights. Thus, allowing the sons to inherit would not contravene state policy.[33]

Harris engineered a change of course soon after he joined the court. In *Heirn v. Bridault* (1859), Harris and Chief Justice Theophilus Smith sided with a deceased planter's white daughter in her will contest with Marcelette Marceau, a free black Louisianan with whom her father had cohabited after her mother's death. Harris assumed that Marceau had lived in Mississippi in contravention of the state's 1822 code which prohibited free blacks from entering the state; thus, he concluded, under state policy Marceau could have no property rights whatever. Harris minced no words. Mississippi law, he said, was based on "the great principles of self-preservation, which have induced civilized nations in every age of the world to regard [blacks] . . . as wholly incapable, morally and mentally, of appreciating or practicing, without enlightenment, the principles and precepts of the Divine and natural law." Handy protested that there was no proof that Marceau had intended to reside in Mississippi and therefore, under the *Shaw* case, she was entitled to inherit.[34]

The climax came in *Mitchell v. Wells*, decided at the same time as *Heirn*. Harris and Handy used *Mitchell* to fully air their competing views on slavery and interstate comity, and historians have often cited *Mitchell* as a leading example of Southern courts' late antebellum-era embrace of slavery as a positive good. *Mitchell* presented a situation similar to that in *Shaw*: Nancy Wells, a slave whose planter father had taken her to Ohio, freed her, and provided for her in his will, claimed her inheritance upon his death. Harris and Smith rejected Wells's claim. Harris proclaimed that "our policy is to prevent emancipation," not merely to reduce the state's free black population. He condemned his predecessors' decisions in the *Ross* cases as "the crowning error of . . . misconceptions of our public policy" and concluded that the 1842 anti-*Vertner* law had effectively ended any obligation the court might have to observe Northern laws favoring freedom. Harris was not content to rest on legal reasoning alone: Mississippi's "climate, soil, and productions, and the pursuits of her people, their habits, manners, and opinions," he said, "all combine not only to sanction the wisdom, humanity, and policy of the system thus established by her organic law and fostered by her early legislation, but they *require slave labor*." [35]

Harris then turned to the question of whether, under the doctrine of comity, Mississippi should recognize Ohio law which allowed Nancy to inherit. Since the mid-1830s, many Northern courts had abandoned the old consensus over the sojourn doctrine that Harris's predecessors had followed in the *Harry* case. A turning point had come in *Commonwealth v. Aves* (1836) when Massachusetts Chief Justice Lemuel Shaw held that his state's policy against slavery meant that any slave who set foot on Massachusetts soil would instantly become free, regardless of whether her owner intended to sojourn in Massachusetts or quickly pass through. Other Northern states including Ohio had followed Shaw's lead, and more would soon follow.[36] Harris may also have been mindful of Northern states' increasing resistance to enforcement of federal fugitive slave laws: Wisconsin's supreme court had declared such laws unconstitutional in 1854 and soon would openly defy the US Supreme Court's reversal of its decision, and in 1858, Ohio's supreme court had nearly followed Wisconsin's lead.[37] Harris served notice that Mississippi would respond in kind. In denouncing Ohio, a state "afflicted with a negro-mania, which inclines her to descend . . . in the scale of humanity," he used language that vividly evoked the South's deepest fears of loss of racial hierarchy and identity:

> Suppose that Ohio, still further afflicted with her peculiar philanthropy, should determine to descend another grade. . . . and claim to confer citizenship on the chimpanzee or the ourang-outang (the most respectable of the monkey tribe), are we to be told that "comity" will require the States not thus demented, to forget their own policy and self-respect, and lower their own citizens and institutions in the scale of being, to meet the necessities of the mongrel race thus attempted to be introduced into the family of sisters in this confederacy?[38]

Handy responded with an equally vigorous dissent. He argued that the 1842 anti-*Vertner* law did not bar owners from taking slaves North and emancipating them there, and that the law did not preclude comity toward Northern states that granted their free black residents the right to inherit. Handy carefully couched his argument as a defense of slave owners' rights rather than the rights of freed slaves. To "unsettle a rule of property and private right declared, reiterated and established," he said, would be "scarcely less deplorable than abolitionism." Handy concluded with a plea to restore comity as an essential part of the Union, and he replied to Harris's denunciation of Ohio in language strikingly similar to that which Chief Justice O'Neall would use the following year in counseling moderation.[39] "If [Northern] courts of justice have been prostituted to the purposes of fanaticism and lawlessness," said Handy, "that is no reason why we should descend from our elevated position, which should be superior to such influences." But Harris prevailed: there would be no more bequests to freed slaves and no more manumissions of any sort during the remaining years of slavery.[40]

Defining the Boundaries of Submission

The question of how far an owner could go in disciplining his slaves was intertwined with questions about the meaning of slavery itself. Were slaves to be considered property subject to an owner's absolute control? Were they human beings who should receive full protection from the law? Or did they have an intermediate status? Southern judges, legislators, and their constituents had to weigh considerations of humanity, economic interest, and social order as they struggled to answer this question. North Carolina justice Thomas Ruffin provided the most famous formulation of the dilemma in *State v. Mann* (1829): "The end [of slavery] is the profit of the master, his security and the public safety," said Ruffin. "The power of the master must be absolute, to render the submission of the slave perfect. I most freely confess my sense of the harshness of this proposition . . . But in the actual condition of things, it must be so."[41] But Ruffin's colleagues and most southern lawmakers, including Mississippi lawmakers, were unwilling to go that far.

Mississippi planters recognized that considerations of humanity and economic interest were not mutually exclusive. Indulgent management of slaves would reduce productivity, but so would overly harsh treatment. Accordingly, Mississippi legislators placed statutory checks on disciplinary abuses while preserving owners' broad discretion in matters of slave control, and they continued the British tradition of providing trials and at least nominal due process to slaves charged with infractions against their masters. Sargent's Code and the 1822 Code prohibited cruel and unusual punishment of slaves in general terms; the 1822 Code also provided that slaves charged with murder, larceny, and other serious crimes would be tried by a jury, and it authorized courts to appoint counsel to defend them.[42] The code allowed slaves and free blacks to testify in cases where slaves were defendants but not in cases against owners, and as one Northern critic noted, "[w]ithout the testimony of the slave . . . a law of this nature may be regarded as nugatory."[43] However, some protections granted to white criminal defendants were applied to whites and slaves equally; for example, Mississippi's supreme court consistently excluded slaves' confessions from use at their trials where the confessions had been coerced.[44]

Many Southern whites believed that at least some enforcement of white behavioral boundaries was desirable, and as a result, owners occasionally were prosecuted for killing and maiming slaves or for other egregious violations of those boundaries. Mississippi's supreme court encouraged that effort. In *State v. Jones* (1821), the court affirmed that owners could be held liable for murder of their slaves. "[I]t would be a stigma upon the character of the state," said Justice Clarke, "if the life of a slave could be taken with impunity . . . He is still a human being, and possesses all those rights, of which he is not deprived by the positive provisions of the law." Twenty years later, the court went further, affirming in *Kelly v. State* (1844) that slaves had the right to fight back if their owner or another person put their life at risk. Justice Joseph Thacher, speaking for the court, criticized Ruffin's suggestion in *Mann* that owners had absolute power over their slaves; he noted that North Carolina had never adopted a statute prohibiting cruel and unusual punishment, as had Mississippi. But Thacher also made clear that what constituted cruel and unusual punishment was a question for the jury—one as to which all-white juries would surely give the benefit of the doubt to slave owners in all but the most exceptional cases.[45]

In cases involving abuses by overseers and persons other than a slave's owner, local authorities often decided to forego criminal prosecution and leave owners to their civil remedies. For example, in *Trotter v. McCall* (1853), Trotter hired out a pregnant female slave (whose name is not given in the case report) to McCall, who treated her "in a very cruel manner" that caused severe injuries and apparently cost the slave her child. Mississippi's supreme court held that McCall's abuse gave Trotter the right to terminate the contract of hire and recover from McCall the slave's lost economic value resulting from her injury, but nowhere in its opinion did the court express concern for the slave or address the morality of McCall's conduct.[46] Was the court's failure to view the injuries from the slave's perspective a failure of empathy, or a deliberate policy decision? In 1859, Justice Harris suggested it was a matter of policy when he and his colleagues held that a male slave could not be prosecuted for rape of a slave child because the slave code did not provide penalties for rape. Harris stressed that slaves had no rights except those granted by statute, and he derided his predecessors' statements in *Jones* and other cases that the law favored humanity toward slaves as "unmeaning twaddle" contravening "the rigor of the common law." This was too much for the legislature; the following year, it made rape of girls under age twelve a criminal offense punishable by death or whipping. [47]

As the Civil War approached, the court retreated from its earlier tone of moderation in slave-discipline matters as in manumission matters. Justice Harris again served as the messenger of change. In *Oliver v. State* (1860), George

Oliver's slave John used a stick to push corn into a sheller, a task that Oliver had assigned to another slave. Oliver then wrested the stick away from John, striking and killing him. Harris and his colleagues reversed Oliver's conviction for manslaughter, emphasizing that John was larger than Oliver, had recently been disciplined for disobedience, and, according to witnesses, had a "very vicious and savage look" as he struggled with Oliver for the stick. Harris noted that owners could still be liable for murder if they deliberately killed slaves without provocation, but he affirmed that owners could use all force necessary to compel obedience, including deadly force: "Unconditional submission and obedience . . . is the imperative duty of the slave," he warned.[48]

It is difficult to say how effectively these laws and decisions promoted the goal of complete submission. There is evidence that master-slave relationships were often flexible. Slaves who were treated harshly could retaliate through work slowdowns, pilferage, and covert destruction of property, and many slave owners recognized that negotiation and small concessions to the slaves' well-being would prove more profitable than a quest for absolute submission. "I have never known anyone to succeed in getting hands to pick well who drove by the lash," commented one planter in the early 1840s. "This should be the last alternative." In order to improve morale and productivity, owners sometimes granted slaves more economic freedom and freedom of movement than the letter of the law allowed; trusted slaves could hunt, fish, and roam their plantation neighborhoods with little supervision if they did not push too far. Planters did not hesitate to train talented slaves, hire them out and even allow them to work for themselves on a limited basis where that brought the owner more profit than field work would have.[49]

The patrol system provided the best example of the gap between the law and social reality. Many slaves were able to avoid patrollers with relative ease and even regarded avoidance as a game, but white Mississippians showed little interest in strengthening the system. They regarded patrolling as "a necessary annoyance and a burden of community service to be avoided during normal times." Nevertheless, the legal boundaries set by the 1822 Code and supreme court decisions remained omnipresent, always available for strict enforcement if a slave pushed against them too hard.[50]

Mississippi and the Antebellum Struggle over Federalism

In the 1850s, as Northern hostility to slavery intensified and Southern states grew ever more protective of the institution, the debate over slavery became entwined with another long-standing debate over the proper balance of power between states and the federal government. Southern courts, whose members belonged to a legal culture shared by judges throughout the United States, tended to be more sympathetic to federalism than their constituents.[51] Mississippi's supreme court proved to be no exception.

The state-rights debate originated in colonial-era disputes over what degree of autonomy the British crown should allow American settlers. The Revolution provided a definitive answer to that question, but the debate then shifted to the issue of whether the new nation should form a strong central government or remain a loose confederation of states. During the federal Constitutional Convention and the ratification debates that followed (1787–88), Alexander Hamilton championed the federalist view that the new national government was a direct creation of the American people, not of the states, and that the federal judiciary should have final say as to whether state and federal laws complied with the new federal Constitution. Hamilton did not address the right of secession directly. He did not have to because the concept of a perpetual national union was at the very core of federalism.[52]

Antifederalists argued that state courts had a concurrent right with federal courts to determine the constitutionality of laws, but they did not address who should have the final say in cases of conflict until 1798–99, when the Kentucky and Virginia legislatures, in memorials authored by Thomas Jefferson and James Madison, respectively, invoked a right of state interposition as grounds for opposing the unpopular Alien and Sedition Acts recently enacted by Congress.[53] "[A]s in all other cases of compact among parties having no common judge," Jefferson argued, "each party has an equal right to judge for itself, as well of infractions, as of the mode and measure of redress."[54]

Clashes between the federal government and states in both North and South arose regularly during the antebellum years. In 1817, Virginia chief justice Spencer Roane vehemently denounced the US Supreme Court's reversal of his decision upholding Virginia's Revolutionary-era policy of confiscating land from British royalists and he urged interposition, but his state reluctantly submitted.[55] Other state judges were more circumspect. In 1823, the Supreme Court struck down a Kentucky law that required Virginians holding colonial-era titles to Kentucky lands to pay Kentucky squatters the value of the squatters' improvements as a condition of retaining title to the land. Kentucky governor Joseph Desha and other state officials urged defiance of the high court's decision but soon afterward, Kentucky's highest court counseled deference to the high court and the controversy abated.[56] In 1834, after a legislatively sanctioned South Carolina convention nullified an unpopular 1828 federal tariff and required state officials to swear an oath of allegiance to the state over the federal constitution, the state's supreme court, with Chief Justice O'Neall again leading the way, held that South Carolinians also owed allegiance to the federal government and that the oath violated South Carolina's constitution.[57] In the 1850s, Georgia chief justice Joseph Lumpkin, an ardent defender of slavery, adopted a Hamiltonian view of federalism, holding that federal treaties and laws took precedence over Georgia laws and that the federal government was a creation of the American people, not the states.[58] But as war approached, an increasing number of southerners agreed with Lumpkin's colleague Henry Benning that "neither the Government of the United States, nor any department of it, can give this Court an order"—or give any state an order.[59]

No clashes of this magnitude arose in Mississippi. The legislature adopted a resolution opposing the 1828 federal tariff, but it also opined that South Carolina had acted rashly and proclaimed "that this State owes a duty to the Union, above all minor considerations" and "[t]hat she prizes that Union less than liberty alone."[60] The closest the Mississippi Supreme Court came to colliding with federal authority was its resistance of the US Supreme Court's decision in *Groves* that the state's constitutional prohibition of slave importation was ineffective without implementing legislation. Mississippi chief justice William Sharkey stated bluntly that *Groves* was wrongly decided and declined to follow it, but he took pains to show his respect for the federal high court. "A decision emanating from a court so justly entitled to our highest respect, one whose decisions are received as an authoritative," he said carefully, "demands of us that we should review our own decisions, and reconsider this question with the utmost possible scrutiny."[61]

Mississippi's deference to federalism frayed as Northern antislavery sentiment grew.[62] Mississippians raised an alarm when Congress enacted the Compromise of 1850, a series of laws designed to defuse sectional tensions through concessions to both North and South.[63] Compromise opponents persuaded Mississippi's legislature to call a special convention to consider if the Compromise's concessions to antislavery forces were grounds for secession. After a bitter fight, Unionist delegates narrowly prevailed. They proclaimed that "no secession can . . . take place . . . which will not virtually amount . . . to a civil revolution," but they also stated that any failure to enforce the Compromise's concessions to the South and any further effort to cabin slavery would justify secession. Harris, who was a convention delegate, signed a separate report rejecting Hamiltonian federalism and arguing that the federal Union was nothing more than a compact of the states.[64] Shortly after the convention Henry Foote, a leader of the Unionist faction, defeated Jefferson Davis, a state-rights supporter, for the governorship, but that was the high-water mark of Unionism in the state. Foote's party soon disintegrated and Unionist sentiment continued to erode throughout the 1850s.[65]

Curiously, increasing sectional tensions did not impel Mississippi to tighten its slave laws significantly during the last years before the Civil War. Only a few minor restrictions were added; limits on slaves trading on their own account were modestly tightened in 1850, and the rule requiring slaves away from their plantation to have close white supervision was strengthened in 1861.[66] After Harris joined the supreme court in 1858, he freely criticized Northern hostility to slavery but he avoided talk of secession. The US Supreme Court's decision in *Dred Scott v. Sandford* (1857), declaring that American blacks had no rights of citizenship and that Congress could not restrict slavery in the territories, gave Harris hope that the federal government would protect Mississippi's slave culture.[67] White Mississippians viewed Abraham Lincoln's election to the presidency in November 1860 as the death blow to that hope, and concluded that secession was now the only path by which the institution could be saved.[68] At the end of that year, Justices Harris and Handy took leaves of absence from the supreme court to serve as envoys to Georgia and Maryland, tasked with persuading those states to join Mississippi in a new Confederacy to preserve slavery.[69] The justices' legal colleagues and their Mississippi constituents also turned from balancing considerations of humanity and economic interest within Mississippi's slave system to preparing for a war that would put slavery's very survival at issue.

Slavery had been central to Mississippi's world from the beginning, but doubts about the proper parameters of slavery had also been constantly present. Planters who crossed the color line and developed feelings for (or a sense of guilt over) their black consorts and black children; reform-minded planters such as Isaac Ross and John Ker; and slaves and free blacks such as Marcelette Marceau, Francis and Jerome Brown, Nancy Wells, and George Oliver's slave John, all had steadily pushed the boundaries of custom. By doing so, they had forced Mississippi's legislature and supreme court to consider just how rigidly slaves should be controlled and the extent to which planters' property rights in slaves, ranging from rights of discipline to rights of manumission, should be curtailed in order to promote social order.

A streak of ambiguity ran through the lawmakers' responses. Sargent's Code and the 1822 Code regulated slaves thoroughly and harshly, but the legislature did not respond to the slave-rebellion scares of the 1830s with a new wave of restrictions. The supreme court's decisions in *Harry* and *Vertner* sealed a compact under which manumission was allowed on condition that freed slaves leave the state. When the legislature enacted an anti-*Vertner* law in 1842, it repudiated that compact and sent a signal that doubts about the merits of slavery would no longer be publicly tolerated, but the supreme court balked. The court refused to make the 1842 law retroactive, and for a time it continued to honor claims and rights of free blacks who observed the old compact by leaving Mississippi. The old compact finally collapsed in the late 1850s, along with Mississippi federalism. William Harris's arrival on the court was both a contributing cause and a reflection of that collapse. Harris made it his mission to serve notice that henceforth Mississippi would accord no rights of any sort to freed blacks, and he carried the day over Alexander Handy, who provided a continuing voice for moderation but lacked the finesse that South Carolina's O'Neall had employed in his effort to preserve Unionism and a small window of possible freedom for slaves.

No one knows whether Justices Harris and Handy, when they left Jackson in early 1861 on their missions to Georgia and Maryland, thought about what would happen to Mississippi's world if the war were lost. That world crumbled quickly. Slavery took a back seat in the supreme court and the legislature to war-related issues; the court did little business during the war, and by the spring of 1865, the South's fight to preserve slavery had led to slavery's demise. Harris, Handy, and other Mississippi lawmakers now faced the task of overcoming the entrenched expectations generated by a slave-based social order that had existed for more than a century, and of building a new legal system of race relations, one in which black Mississippians could give voice to their expectations. That task, described in chapters to follow, has accounted for much of Mississippi's subsequent legal history.

CHAPTER THREE

Flush Times, Hard Times: Law, Jacksonism, and a Cotton Economy

The new country seemed to be a reservoir, and every road leading to a vagrant stream of enterprise and adventure. Money, or what passed for money, was the only cheap thing to be had. . . . To refuse [credit]—if the thing was ever done—were an insult for which a bowie-knife were not a too summary or exemplary a means of redress. . . . The stampede towards the golden temple became general; the delusion prevailed far and wide that this thing was not a burlesque on commerce and finance.

—Joseph G. Baldwin (1853)[1]

Thomas Hadley and Piety Smith came to Mississippi by paths common to many of the young state's inhabitants. Piety's father liked what he saw of Mississippi when he fought with Andrew Jackson in the Creek War, and he moved his family there from Kentucky in 1820. Thomas's family moved to the Natchez region from South Carolina at about the same time. Both families prospered, and after Thomas and Piety married in 1831, they led a life similar to other couples who competed for wealth and political power in antebellum Mississippi—with a single exception. In 1839, they persuaded the state legislature to enact the nation's first married women's property law.[2] The law is a milestone in the history of American women's rights. It is also important because its origins and aftermath illustrate several central themes of antebellum Mississippi life and law.

In the mid-1830s, Thomas helped found the Mississippi Importing &
Exporting Company, a cotton-trading agency that was one of the state's first
corporations. He also won election to the state senate, and Piety tried to
increase his political influence by turning their Jackson home into a boarding-
house catering to legislators. The Hadleys had prospered during the cotton and
land boom of the early 1830s, but in 1836, the federal government restricted use
of paper currency to pay for land purchases, dealing a hard blow to Mississippi
and other states whose economies depended on paper and credit. As economic
depression loomed, the Hadleys, like many other Mississippians, found themselves financially overextended. Efforts by Thomas and his legislative colleagues
to generate capital by creating a new state-sponsored bank, the Union Bank,
proved unsuccessful. Thomas was accused of securing bank loans for his business on preferential terms, and his finances tightened to the point that he was
forced to ask his colleagues to enact a law relieving him from liability on earlier
guarantees he had given for loans to construct the governor's mansion.[3]

As 1839 approached, Thomas and Piety began to worry about what would
happen to their family if a crash came. Like other common-law states,
Mississippi followed the marital-unity doctrine; all property that a wife brought
to her marriage passed to her husband, and her rights in it ended. This offended
Piety's entrepreneurial spirit. Furthermore, she had expectations of receiving
land, slaves, and other assets from her father at his death, assets that would
go automatically to Thomas and from there directly to his creditors. But the
Hadleys saw a way out. They had briefly lived in Louisiana, a civil-law state
in which wives and husbands both enjoyed rights in property brought to and
acquired during their marriage. Mississippi's Chickasaw nation observed a
similar rule, one which Mississippi's supreme court had recently enforced.[4]
Some Jacksonians were beginning to argue that married women's property
laws should be enacted, either "debt-free" laws sheltering assets that wives
brought to the marriage from their husband's creditors or "separate-estate" laws
that allowed women to retain outright ownership of such assets. Neighboring
Arkansas Territory had recently enacted the nation's first "debt-free" law.[5]

Thomas and Piety went to work. In the Mississippi Senate chambers,
Thomas appealed to his colleagues' sense of fairness and to economic realities; absent a social safety net, wives of improvident and indebted husbands
should at least be allowed to keep their own property secure from creditors
for use in supporting the family if all else failed. Tradition has it that at the
Hadley home, Piety repeated these arguments to her legislative boarders and
perhaps even hinted that she would withhold her cooking until they came
round. The Hadleys' strategy worked. In 1839, Mississippi's legislature enacted

the nation's first separate-estate law, providing that "any married woman may become seized or possessed of any property . . . in her own name, and as of her own property."[6]

The Hadleys did not stay to savor their victory. Hard times continued and in 1841, like many other financially distressed Mississippians, they migrated to Texas, which, like Louisiana, had adopted a community property system. They never returned to Mississippi, but they left a double legacy: the married women's property act, which would soon be emulated in other states across the nation, and the examples they provided of the intersection of law and culture during Mississippi's antebellum flush times and hard times.[7]

Two central features of antebellum American law were the sprawling reform movement associated with Andrew Jackson, which began well before Jackson's presidency (1829–37) and continued for more than a decade after he left office, and the efforts of lawmakers to accommodate the economic changes being wrought by the industrial revolution. Jacksonian legal reform unfolded in three phases: an early period (1815–30) that featured efforts in many states to abolish imprisonment for debt and to extend suffrage to all white adult males; a middle period (1830–40) in which Jacksonians sought to curtail concentrated power, most notably that of banks, and to ensure that legislatures retained broad authority to regulate corporations; and a late period (1840–51) that featured a broad variety of reforms including married women's property rights, enactment of homestead exemptions, popular election of judges and imposition of limits on states' ability to finance canals, railroads, and other instruments of America's new commercial and industrial economy.

Mississippi occupied an anomalous position in the Jacksonian reform movement. It steadfastly supported Jackson and took the lead in implementing many Jacksonian reforms, but its reaction to banking and corporate reform was mixed. Mississippi was a predominantly agricultural state, but it did not fit the Jeffersonian-Jacksonian ideal of a society dominated by self-sufficient farmers and local merchants and mechanics. Mississippi planters were firmly integrated into an international marketplace that ran from Mississippi plantations to factors in New Orleans and Mobile, and thence to textile mills in New England, Great Britain, and beyond. Mississippians needed credit to sustain their place in that market, and that could only be supplied by banks.[8]

But Mississippians turned against banks with a vengeance during the depression of 1837–40. They did so not because they wished to tame concentrated economic power, but because Mississippi banks had failed to uphold their promise of easy credit and prosperity. Other states that had incurred heavy debt due to imprudent subsidies of banks and internal improvements gradually repaid those debts through retrenchment and tax increases. Mississippi chose instead to repudiate its obligations and phase out most state banks. Mississippi planters thereafter relied on factors, not money markets, for their capital needs.[9] Mississippi also played little part in the Jacksonian debate over legislative control of corporations. Fewer entrepreneurs sought incorporation in Mississippi than in more industrialized states, and when regulation was deemed necessary, legislators and judges almost unanimously assumed that the legislature's power to regulate was plenary. Mississippi law thus presented a unique combination of adherence to and deviation from the Jacksonian reform framework.

Early Jacksonian Reform

The core principles of Jacksonism were equality of opportunity for all and resistance to the industrial revolution's tendency to produce aggregations of wealth and power, which Jacksonians viewed as a threat to democracy and to America's founding ideals. Andrew Jackson distilled those principles in his 1832 message defending his veto of a Congressional re-charter of the Bank of the United States. "In the full enjoyment of the gifts of heaven and the fruits of superior industry," Jackson explained, "every man is equally entitled to protection by law; but when the laws undertake to add to these natural and just advantages . . . the humble members of society . . . who have neither the time nor the means of securing like favors to themselves, have a right to complain of the injustice of their Government."[10] That view resonated deeply with the small planters and farmers who settled Mississippi's newly opened lands in the 1820s and 1830s, and soon came to dominate state politics through force of their numbers. But as Mississippi's 1817 constitution demonstrated, the view had taken root even before they came.

Two of the earliest movements associated with Jacksonian reform were suffrage expansion and abolition of imprisonment for debt. As noted in an earlier chapter, at the end of the American Revolution most of the original states had limited suffrage to persons holding substantial land or wealth in keeping with the common law's emphasis on protection of property rights. But the new trans-Appalachian states created after independence had different views; they either limited suffrage restrictions to a taxpaying requirement or abolished property-holding and taxpaying restrictions altogether,[11] and the older states eventually followed.[12] Mississippi's 1817 constitutional convention came close to establishing universal white male suffrage; in the end, it abolished territorial-era property requirements and imposed only a taxpaying requirement, procured by the efforts of George Poindexter and other members of the early Natchez aristocracy. Fifteen years later, with the aristocracy's political power greatly diminished, the 1832 convention completed the transition to full white male suffrage.[13]

The movement to abolish imprisonment for debt had its origins in colonial times, but did not gain widespread support until the early nineteenth century. In 1817, Martin Van Buren, who would soon become a Jacksonian stalwart and would eventually succeed Jackson as president, made a crucial contribution by leading a successful campaign for complete abolition of imprisonment for debt in New York. But the movement succeeded mainly because frontier states such as Mississippi were heavily dependent on credit and favored easing debtor's burdens as much as possible. Mississippi's 1817 convention was one of the first to elevate protection from imprisonment to constitutional status.[14]

The Middle Period: Banks

The American industrial revolution introduced business enterprise on a scale never before seen. Unlike the small shops and smithies of the pre-industrial age, the mines, textile mills, factories, canals, and railroads that arose during the new age required large work forces and immense amounts of capital in order to operate successfully. It soon became clear that traditional business forms such as sole proprietorships and partnerships were not well-suited to these tasks, and beginning about 1800 the modern corporate form arose to fill the need.

Incorporation enabled entrepreneurs to attract investors and capital more easily, to share their risk with others, and to limit their liability for corporate debts to the amount they invested in their companies.[15] But many Jacksonians feared that the growth of corporations would concentrate wealth and power in the hands of a few, thus creating a fundamental threat not only to the Jacksonian vision of a decentralized, agrarian America, but to the American democratic experiment itself. Corporations received individual charters from state legislatures, and entrepreneurs who had substantial economic and political influence often received more favorable terms than those who did not. "Every special act of incorporation," argued William Leggett, a New York newspaper editor and leading Jacksonian intellectual, "is, in a certain sense, a grant of a monopoly . . . There is no single object can be named, for which, consistently with a sincere respect for the equal rights of men, a special charter of incorporation can be bestowed."[16] Jacksonians viewed banks as the most egregious embodiment of the evils of concentrated capital. Most corporations at least produced tangible goods of some worth, but banks appeared to do no more than manipulate paper and foment financial crisis. Banks' "direct and inevitable tendency," Leggett argued, was to "create artificial inequalities and distinctions in society" and to "foster a spirit of speculation, destructive of love of country."[17]

Jackson made non-renewal of the Bank of the United States's federal charter a centerpiece of his presidency. In the end, he succeeded in destroying the bank, but in many states his supporters were not willing to go that far with state banks. They recognized the risks inherent in a financial system whose currency consisted mainly of promissory notes issued by state banks, but they also realized that credit was essential to growth, particularly in frontier states such as Mississippi where specie (gold and silver coin) was in short supply, and that banks with all their faults were the best vehicle for supplying credit.[18]

Mississippi supplied a vivid example of Jacksonian ambivalence toward banks. The young state relied on and supported banks from its inception, turning against them only after excessive state investment in Mississippi's banking system led to a crushing public debt burden in the wake of the 1837 depression. Shortly after statehood, the legislature re-chartered the Bank of Mississippi, which had been relatively well managed and had provided a stable source of credit during territorial days, as a public bank under a clause in the 1817 constitution allowing the state to purchase up to one-fourth of the stock of every bank it chartered. The constitution's banking provisions and the legislature's decision to re-charter, which came at the beginning of an era in which the cotton economy and its need for credit expanded dramatically, sent a message that Mississippi lawmakers intended to take an active role in managing the state's economy.[19]

But cracks soon appeared. Beginning in the mid-1820s, the bank came under attack for its supposed preference of the Natchez district in making loans. In 1830, the legislature, now dominated by members from newly settled northern and eastern Mississippi, created a new bank, the Planters Bank, in order to break the Bank of Mississippi's monopoly. Delegates to the 1832 constitutional convention trimmed the state's involvement in banking modestly; they prohibited the state from borrowing money or backing loans taken out by others unless such action was approved by two consecutive sessions of the legislature. However, the convention made an exception so that the state could make a final loan of $1.5 million to the Planters Bank.[20]

During the flush times of the late 1820s and early 1830s, the legislature also encouraged Mississippians to look to the private sector for credit needs. It issued charters for dozens of private banks that freely granted credit and issued promissory notes, often without sufficient cash reserves to back their obligations. "Men of this day," politician and judge Reuben Davis opined many years later, "would be appalled at the recklessness with which business was transacted then," a recklessness ultimately "ruinous in its consequences." The road to ruin began with President Jackson's 1836 order to federal agents to accept only specie, not bank notes, in payment of public-land purchases. Federal land sales had peaked in Mississippi during the previous two years, but many purchasers could not procure the specie now needed to make installment payments. Foreclosures became endemic, although sheriffs often declined to sell foreclosed lands for fear, in Davis's words, of "the full fury of a [popular] storm that, once let loose, would spend itself in irresistible destruction."[21]

In 1837, as the national depression got underway, the legislature intervened once more. It chartered another new bank, the Union Bank, in an effort to provide a fresh source of capital and credit to Mississippians, and it authorized the state to issue $15.5 million in bonds to be used by the new bank to secure its commitments. The 1838 legislature gave the Union Bank charter a second approval as required by Mississippi's constitution, but lawmakers quickly concluded they had given the bank too much for too little. Ten days after the second approval, they enacted a supplemental law authorizing the state to raise an additional $5.5 million to be paid to the bank in exchange for bank stock, thus giving the state a direct stake in the bank.[22]

The Union Bank quickly ran into trouble. It was accused of favoritism in its loan practices toward its directors and their associates, and it fell victim to a downturn in cotton prices that reduced planters' ability to repay their loans. The bank's slide toward failure raised the specter that the state would be saddled with heavy debt on the bonds it had issued under the 1837 law, and that it would realize nothing in return. Other states faced similar problems, some due to failed investments in banks and others due to failed investments in canals and railroads. Most such states reluctantly raised taxes and cut back on expenses in order to meet their bond obligations, believing that austerity was preferable to loss of financial reputation and of the ability to obtain credit in Eastern and international markets. Other states and municipalities tried to avoid their debt obligations by arguing that the obligations were invalid under constitutional provisions limiting state spending for banking and internal improvements or imposing caps on state debt, but courts in most states rejected the challenges. Mississippi took another, more drastic path when it rejected a tax increase and opted instead to repudiate its debt.[23]

The repudiation movement began in early 1841, when Governor Alexander McNutt advanced a novel constitutional argument. McNutt reasoned that the supplemental 1838 Union Bank law had sufficiently modified the 1837 law that it was really a new law, one that also required a second ratification. Because it did not receive a second ratification, the state's bond obligations were invalid and the state could not be compelled to pay. McNutt appealed to his constituents' touchy sense of independence and honor, proclaiming that Mississippians were not so "degenerate as to submit to heavy taxation to pay a claim not contracted in accordance with their supreme law."[24] The 1839 legislature had refused to repudiate the Union Bank bonds, but after McNutt took his stand, repudiation became the central issue of the 1841 state election. Pro-repudiation forces prevailed, and subsequent legislatures consistently refused to fund payment of the bonds.[25] Union Bank bondholders grumbled, but in the end few took action to enforce their rights. Mississippi's credit in capital markets all but vanished, but legislators preferred to face that penalty rather than voters' wrath.

More than a decade later, after a Union Bank bondholder finally decided to press for payment, Mississippi's supreme court registered a dissent from repudiation and rejected McNutt's theory of invalidity in *State v. Johnson* (1853). Chief Justice Theophilus Smith held that the 1838 law did not change the essential terms of the 1837 law and did not itself require a second passage because it did not involve borrowing. Smith also proclaimed for good measure that the state should pay its bond obligations like any other contract obligation.[26] Mississippi legislators and their constituents were unmoved; the legislature continued to refuse to appropriate money for bond payments, and in 1854 Justice William Yerger lost his campaign for reelection, largely due to his vote in *Johnson*.

In 1840, prior to repudiation, the legislature had laid the foundation for banking's demise in Mississippi by requiring existing banks to phase out all of their small-denomination notes and to replace them with specie within a short period of time, on penalty of losing their charters. Very few banks could comply due to the general lack of specie, and every Mississippi bank that had existed in 1840 went out of business during the next two decades. Thus it was that Mississippi finally joined the Jacksonian anti-bank movement via a highly unusual path. Repudiation sentiment never faltered; at the end of Reconstruction, Mississippi inserted a clause in its constitution formally prohibiting payment of the Union Bank bonds, thus definitively overturning the supreme court's *Johnson* decision, and the clause was renewed in the 1890 constitution. Pride and frustration had triumphed over economic pragmatism.[27]

The Middle Period: Corporate Regulation

Another debate over corporate privilege, one in which Mississippi adhered more closely to the Jacksonian pattern, was the extent to which corporations should be subject to regulatory laws enacted after they received their charters. In *Trustees of Dartmouth College v. Woodward* (1819) the US Supreme Court, then dominated by Chief Justice John Marshall and other federalist judges who believed that attacks on corporate privilege would injure the national interest, held that corporate charters were contracts with the legislature and that application of subsequently enacted laws to a corporation without its consent would unconstitutionally impair those contracts.[28] The *Dartmouth College* decision raised serious fears that states would never be able to regulate corporations effectively, but Jacksonians eventually managed to circumvent the dilemma. Beginning in the 1830s, many states enacted anti-*Dartmouth* statutes and constitutional clauses providing that charters would be issued only to corporations that agreed to be bound by future laws. These laws did not violate the *Dartmouth* doctrine because it had long been legally established that state legislatures had near-absolute power to set conditions of incorporation.[29]

Jacksonian jurists, who by the 1830s were beginning to supplant federalist judges on American courts, also weakened the *Dartmouth* doctrine by making clear that they would allow legislatures more regulatory leeway than their predecessors had. In *Proprietors of Charles River Bridge v. Proprietors of Warren Bridge* (1837), the Charles River company, which had received a charter in 1780 to build a toll bridge connecting Boston and Cambridge, challenged the Massachusetts legislature's 1828 decision to grant the Warren company a franchise to build a second bridge nearby. The Charles River proprietors had spent huge sums to build and maintain their bridge and the new charter, which provided that the Warren Bridge would eventually become toll-free, would effectively destroy their revenue stream and their business. Chief Justice Roger Taney, recently appointed by Jackson to succeed Marshall after the latter's death, upheld the Warren Bridge franchise. In an indirect but clear rebuke to Marshall, Taney explained that "[w]hile the rights of private property are sacredly guarded, we must not forget that the community also have rights, and that the happiness and well being of every citizen depends on their faithful preservation." A franchise would not be considered exclusive unless the company's charter stated in "plain words that it was intended to be done."[30]

Mississippi's legislature did not enact a general anti-*Dartmouth* law or insert anti-*Dartmouth* clauses in the corporate charters it granted. Its failure to do so was not due to latent sympathy for the *Dartmouth* doctrine: antebellum Mississippi's rocky relationship with banks demonstrated that it was hardly deferential to corporations. At bottom, lawmakers simply did not feel a need for anti-*Dartmouth* provisions: because Mississippi was an agricultural state with little industry, there were fewer incorporations in Mississippi than elsewhere. The legislature issued its first commercial charter in 1820 to the Pearlington Company, a land development company, but during the next four decades the pace of commercial incorporation was slow, due in part to the hard times after

1837 and the rise of intersectional tensions and the prospect of war in the late 1850s. Turnpike, bridge, and steamboat companies were the first business corporations to appear. They were joined by insurance companies, railroads, and a handful of manufacturing companies in the 1840s and 1850s, but throughout the antebellum era a majority of corporate charters were for charitable and social organizations such as schools and colleges, militia units, and fraternal lodges.[31]

Perhaps a more important reason for Mississippi's lack of interest in anti-*Dartmouth* clauses was that the state's supreme court consistently cabined the *Dartmouth* doctrine and viewed the legislature's regulatory power expansively. The most dramatic example came in the case of *Payne v. Baldwin* (1844).[32] During the 1830s, Mississippi was awash in promissory notes given to banks, which customarily were repayable in the bank's own currency. Debtors counted on the right to repay in the bank's own currency because that currency often depreciated over time, thus giving them an advantage when their promissory notes came due.

As the 1837 depression deepened, many banks sold their notes to Eastern financiers who demanded that debtors pay in specie, and in 1840 Mississippi's legislature responded by prohibiting banks from selling or assigning their promissory notes to others.[33] The banks protested that this interfered with their constitutional right to dispose of their property as they saw fit, but in *Payne* the Mississippi Supreme Court disagreed and upheld the 1840 law. Chief Justice William Sharkey paid nominal deference to the *Dartmouth* doctrine but affirmed Mississippi's guiding rule: "As these [banking] laws are alterable at the pleasure of the legislature," said Sharkey, "the corporation cannot claim exemption from the effect of these alterations, unless by express stipulation the legislature has consented to grant such exemption."[34]

In a related case, *Planters Bank v. Sharp* (1844), the court held that the 1840 law's prohibition of note transfers was absolute, even where a transferee sought payment only in the bank's own notes. Sharkey, who dissented, protested that this went too far because the 1840 law was intended to provide protection only against creditors who sought payment in specie. Both decisions went too far for the US Supreme Court: in 1848, it reversed them, holding over Chief Justice Taney's dissent that the power to dispose of property, including promissory notes, was a fundamental right of all corporations that could not be impaired by the legislature, even where that right was not specified in a corporation's charter.[35]

The Mississippi Supreme Court reluctantly acceded to the federal high court's decision but ten years later, in an era of markedly sharpened states-rights sensibility, it changed course. In *McIntyre v. Ingraham* (1858), the court held that the 1840 law applied to all promissory notes issued after its enactment and reasoned that *Sharp* applied only to notes issued before the law's

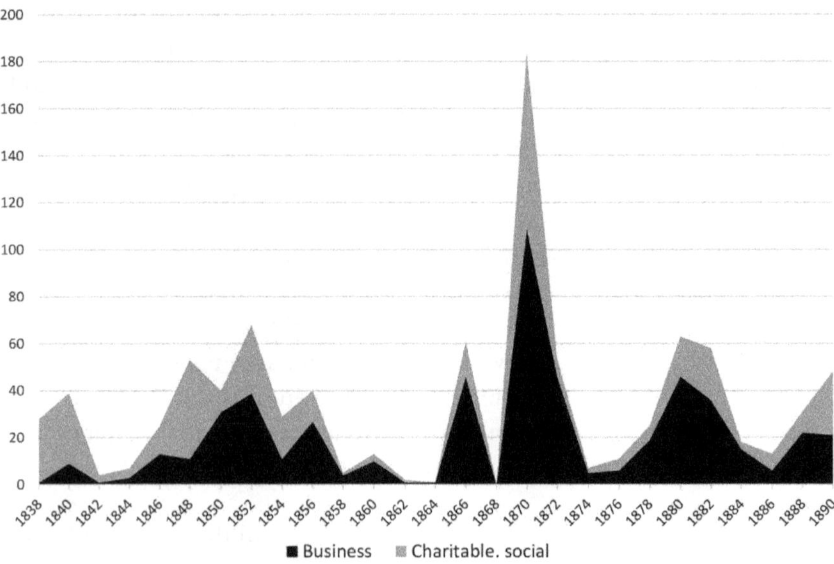

Figure 3.1. Mississippi Incorporations, 1838–90

enactment—a conclusion that the federal high court likely would have rejected. Justice Handy warned the justices at Washington against "revers[ing] the settled law of this State as declared by its constituted tribunal, in relation to the rights vested under its own laws . . . [N]o such dangerous and anomalous power," said Handy, "was ever intended to be conferred upon that court."[36]

Mississippi's supreme court also reaffirmed its vision of broad legislative power in several cases involving an 1843 law that allowed insolvent banks to dissolve but authorized their trustees to collect outstanding debts as part of the winding-up process. In *Commercial Bank of Rodney v. State* (1845), the court rejected an argument that the 1843 law contravened a common-law rule that obligations to a bank terminated at its dissolution. Justice Clayton looked back ruefully on Mississippi's flush times when he announced the court's decision upholding the law: "[E]xcessive issues of [bank] paper have been made—inflation—depreciation and insolvency have followed, and then comes legislation . . . to save a few planks from the wreck." And in 1856 the court decided its own version of the *Charles River Bridge* case, holding that the legislature had the right to issue a second franchise for a ferry across the Yalobusha River at Grenada even though it had granted a franchise for a nearby ferry only seven years before. "The retention of the [franchise] power by the State, is for the public benefit," said Justice Handy, and "is never held to be precluded of its exercise, except by a plain and manifest intention."[37] Thus,

Figure 3.2. Chief Justice William L. Sharkey. Courtesy of the
Archives and Records Services Division, Mississippi Department
of Archives and History.

Mississippi established a firm tradition of deference to legislative regulation
of corporations, a tradition that would be revisited at several later points in
the state's legal history.

Late Jacksonian Reforms

Mississippi was an irregular participant in the Jacksonian crusade against
banks and concentrated corporate power, but it was leader, indeed a pioneer,
in three movements that were hallmarks of the late Jacksonian era: popular
election of judges, married women's property rights, and homestead exemptions. The three movements found early success in Mississippi because each
appealed in different ways to Mississippians' overarching suspicion of aristocracy and authority and their desire to take action against the hard times
that started in the late 1830s.

An elective judiciary. As has been seen, in 1832 Mississippi became the
first state to provide for popular election of judges at all levels. More than a
decade would go by before other states followed suit and Jacksonians fully

articulated the intellectual rationale for an elective judiciary.[38] There was debate in Mississippi's 1832 constitutional convention about judicial selection, but its details are obscure; the only ready evidence consists of John Quitman's comments more than a decade later that opponents feared that "popular excitements would find their way upon the bench."[39] William Leggett and other early Jacksonian theorists paid little attention to judicial selection mechanisms; it was not until 1848 that retired Ohio supreme court justice Frederick Grimke took up the issue in his treatise *Considerations on the Nature and Tendency of Free Institutions.* Grimke's argument was simple: "If the principle of responsibility [to the people] is the hinge on which republican government turns," he reasoned, then "it does not appear clear why a thorough application should be made of it in some instances, and an imperfect one in others."[40]

But Grimke the intellectual was seconding conclusions that others in the political arena had already reached. The elective-judiciary movement reignited in mid-1840s when New York (1846), Iowa (1846), and Wisconsin (1848) all held constitutional conventions that debated and approved popular election of judges. During those conventions, opponents argued that an elective system would produce judges beholden to the parties that nominated them and got them elected, judges who would make decisions based as much on political as legal considerations. Supporters retorted that judicial appointments were not free of political considerations either, and that opponents underestimated the people's willingness to support independent judges. They argued that an elective judiciary was essential to the Jacksonian ideal of increased popular participation in government. "Every man," said one Wisconsin delegate, "should be made to feel that he is a citizen, a part of the state, and that a portion of its sovereignty resides in him," and a New York delegate argued that a popularly elected judge would "carry into his study a knowledge of everyday life, instead of the frigid, technical maxims of the dead, and the wire-drawn subtilities of the law."[41] It is likely that similar arguments framed the debate in Mississippi's 1832 convention.

Married women's property laws. Married women's laws were not a formal part of Andrew Jackson's reform program and did not receive much attention from Leggett, Grimke, and other Jacksonian intellectuals, but the movement for such laws arose during Jackson's presidency and was consistent with the core Jacksonian themes of equal opportunity and hostility to concentrated power. The common-law marital-unity doctrine, holding that "the very being or legal existence of the woman is . . . incorporated and consolidated into that of the husband: under whose wing, protection and cover, she performs everything," was a basic part of British and American law prior to 1800. Under that doctrine, women effectively surrendered to their husbands all control and ownership of property they brought to the marriage.[42]

The common law provided some devices to help women in the higher echelons of society, most notably marital trust rules that enabled landed families to give their daughters use of family estates while assuring that control would remain in the family. Phoebe Calvit, one of Natchez's early settlers and a woman of unusual determination, provided a striking example. She and her husband William divorced while Natchez was still under Spanish rule and, as required by civil-law community property principles, she received a substantial portion of the marital property, including a house, in her own name. She required Ebenezer Dayton, her next husband, to sign a prenuptial agreement preserving her home and other property as her own. Calvit was not done with defending her rights: when John Moore sought possession of her home under a British land grant, she won her case against him in the trial court only to have Mississippi's territorial court overturn the decision because her parol (verbal) testimony of ownership was not admissible under the common law. Undaunted, Calvit criticized territorial chief justice Seth Lewis, an attack which played a role in his resignation soon thereafter, and she helped persuade the legislature to create a new system of equity courts that could accept parol evidence. Calvit's example notwithstanding, for most Mississippi women marriage meant a real loss of liberty and power.[43]

The married women's property movement was driven in part by an idealistic desire to expand the rights of women. During the debate over Mississippi's 1839 law, Thomas Hadley spoke of protecting "the certain possession of property to which they have so just a claim" and of "secur[ing] to them the product of their own labor," and he rebutted traditionalists who argued that "female delicacy forbids their participation in the turmoils and strife of business."[44] But the primary driving force in Mississippi and other states that adopted such laws was more practical. During the early nineteenth century, alcoholism had become a common response to social and economic stresses created by the industrial revolution. Husbands who succumbed to drink often descended into poverty; in the process, they expended their wives' assets to satisfy creditors and eventually left their families destitute. The specter of destitution was not limited to alcoholics: it was omnipresent in an entrepreneurial, risk-taking economy, and as Mississippians learned in the late 1830s, personal disaster could strike at any time regardless of one's personal virtues.[45] The 1839 law's authors hoped that by sheltering property that wives brought to the marriage from their husbands' creditors, they would provide a rudimentary safety net for the family in the event of economic disaster and would reduce the state's burden to care for paupers. During debate, one of the Mississippi law's opponents worried about "[t]he injury to be inflicted by this bill, upon creditors" in that "the credit of Mississippi is, in all conscience, low enough already."[46] But in a state that would soon choose to resolve its debt crisis by repudiating its bonds rather than raising revenue to pay them, his argument was not enough to carry the day.

Mississippi's legislature continued to take a progressive attitude toward married women in later years. In *Grand Gulf Bank v. Barnes* (1844), the supreme court interpreted the 1839 law narrowly, holding that it "was designed to guard [married women's] property from any liability for the debts and contracts of the husband" and "reaches no further." The court's conclusion was not entirely accurate. Mississippi's 1839 law was not a "debt-free" law: it was a stronger "separate-estate" law which provided that "any married woman may become seized or possessed of any property . . . in her own name, and as of her own property."[47] The 1846 legislature responded to *Barnes* by giving wives the right of control over all revenue generated by their slaves and other property. It also modified the common-law rule that a wife could not contract in her own name by granting wives the right to contract jointly with their husbands for the hiring of overseers, purchase of supplies, and other activities related to management of slaves. Thereafter, the court construed married women's property laws more liberally.[48]

In 1857, the legislature again expanded married women's contract rights, allowing wives to contract for all aspects of managing their separate property and general family matters. In 1871, it eliminated all remaining restrictions on married women's right to contract, allowed them to operate businesses in their own name, and confirmed that their property rights extended to wages and business income as well as property. Married women's rights reached a high point in 1890, when members of a convention called to create a post-Reconstruction constitution inserted a clause prohibiting the legislature from "creat[ing] by law any distinction between the rights of men and women to acquire, own, enjoy, and dispose of property of all kinds, or their power to contract in reference thereto."[49]

There was a striking divergence among Southern states on this point. Mississippi and other cotton states were among the first to enact married women's property laws, but older Southern states along the Atlantic seaboard were among the last to do so; they did not follow suit until Reconstruction.[50] Mississippi's experience suggests that concerns about economic security in states just emerging from frontier status, heavily dependent on credit, and highly sensitive to market changes, played an important role in generating married women's property rights laws, and that a cultural sense of independence and fluidity played an equally important role. In states where tradition was thin and economic improvisation was essential, legal openings for women appeared sooner than elsewhere.[51]

Homestead exemptions. The homestead exemption movement was another legal movement that took root in newer states with more fluid societies. It had originated long before the Jacksonian era: many American colonies had exempted basic items of personal property from attachment by creditors in order to order to encourage their inhabitants to take the risks necessary to create a civilization in the wilderness and to create a rudimentary social safety net. But the idea of expanding exemptions to include homesteads was a product of the early nineteenth-century frontier. In 1820s Texas, Stephen Austin and other colonizers tried to attract American settlers by promising that their new homes would be exempt from seizure. The promise proved effective, particularly during the hard times of the late 1830s and early 1840s. Many Mississippians and others who had failed in their search for prosperity on the cotton frontier moved to Texas in order to make a fresh start with a guarantee that come what might, they could always keep a portion of their land as their own. After Texas won its independence from Mexico, it enacted the first American homestead exemption law (1839) and later became the first state to elevate the exemption to constitutional status (1845).[52]

The homestead exemption movement spread rapidly outward from Texas. The National Reform Association, dominated by liberal Jacksonians, promoted the movement in many parts of the nation and by 1860 the vast majority of states had homestead exemptions.[53] Mississippi enacted one of the earliest and broadest exemption laws in 1841: planters and farmers could keep up to 160 acres of their land, and town residents could keep their homes up to a value of $1,500. The law came at the high tide of Mississippi's debt-repudiation movement and it represented, at least in part, an effort to induce financially distressed residents to stay rather than go to Texas. Even creditors were not entirely unhappy with the new laws. Many hoped that the homestead laws, combined with earlier personal-property exemption laws, would give debtors the tools and assets they needed to recover, which in turn would enable them to pay their debts and would save the trouble and expense of foreclosure.[54]

Jacksonian Aftermath: Railroad Subsidies and General Incorporation Laws

Mississippi's antebellum legal history was defined by what did not happen as well as what did happen. Mississippi conspicuously failed to participate in two important movements of the late antebellum era: a prolonged debate over the wisdom and constitutionality of governmental subsidies of railroads and other internal improvements, and a movement to replace the system of individual corporate charters with general incorporation laws. Mississippi's inaction was due mainly to its antebellum emphasis on agriculture and its delay in joining the industrial revolution. After 1865, as the state sought to build a more diversified economy from the ashes of war, it became a participant in both movements, a shift endorsed by Reconstruction and post-Reconstruction governments alike.

Railroad subsidies. Most early nineteenth-century Americans believed that transportation networks were vital to the new nation's prosperity and even its survival, but they disagreed about the extent to which government should promote those networks. Beginning in the 1780s, state governments regularly experimented with canal and turnpike subsidies, with mixed results. New York's Erie Canal, completed in 1825, was the greatest success of the era, prompting Midwestern states to shift much of their commercial traffic from St. Louis and New Orleans to New York. The canal ultimately turned a substantial profit and inspired a new wave of projects and subsidies in other states. Yet, for every successful project, there was a canal or turnpike that failed to realize expectations and saddled its sponsoring state with debt, sometimes disastrously so. The pattern repeated itself with the advent of railroads in the early 1830s.[55]

Southern states, like states in other regions, varied in their approaches to internal improvements. Some states, notably North Carolina and Georgia, subsidized improvements enthusiastically and even undertook direct construction of rail lines. Others limited themselves to indirect support, most commonly by making land grants that were contingent on completion of a specified portion of a projected canal or rail line and by allowing municipalities and private citizens to subscribe for stock in canal and railway companies. The 1837 depression administered a sharp check to the subsidy movement and caused many investors to question whether railroad subsidies were a proper purpose of government.[56] Despite this, and despite the fact that most railroads were privately owned corporations, courts in nearly all states held that railroads served a public purpose and therefore were legitimate objects of public bounty. "If [railroad building] be public it makes no difference that the corporation which has it in charge is private," Pennsylvania justice Jeremiah Black explained in 1853. "A railroad is a public highway for the public benefit . . . because travel and transportation are cheapened by it to a degree far exceeding all the tolls and charges of every kind."[57]

Nonetheless, a wave of popular reaction set in at the end of the Jacksonian era. Between 1837 and 1851, thirteen states enacted new constitutions. Nearly all set limits on state debt in order to avoid a repetition of the past canal and railroad financial crises,[58] and seven states explicitly prohibited state aid to corporations.[59] But few of the new constitutions addressed municipal railroad subsidies, and most state courts that considered the issue held that in the absence of an explicit prohibition, municipal subsidies were permitted.[60]

Mississippi stood apart from both the early rush to subsidies and the later reaction against them. Mississippi lawmakers, mindful of the damage that bank failures and debt repudiation had done to the state's reputation, refused to subsidize railroads. The legislature chartered many railroads in the 1840s and 1850s but made clear that they would have to find their own financing. The most successful Mississippi lines were short lines designed to transport cotton and other crops from interior plantations to local river ports. They had little difficulty attracting necessary capital from local investors, and the Illinois Central, the state's main north-south line, was able to secure private financing based on a large land grant from Congress. As a result, the constitutionality of state and municipal subsidies was largely an academic question in Mississippi. Nor did the state feel a need to amend its constitution to limit state and municipal debt: lawmakers' willingness to repudiate government obligations, shown in the Union Bank affair, eliminated any political pressure to do so.[61]

The situation changed dramatically after the Civil War, both in Mississippi and nationally. Between 1868 and 1870, the supreme courts of several upper Midwestern states went against past precedent and held that state and municipal railroad subsidies were unconstitutional. Iowa justice John Dillon and Michigan chief justice Thomas Cooley, who as young men had imbibed Jacksonian suspicion of corporate power, reasoned that railroads, like other private corporations, existed primarily to make money for their shareholders. Railroads' benefit to the public was incidental, they said, and taxation for the purpose of subsidizing a railroad would impair the property rights of all taxpayers who opposed the project. Dillon and Cooley were well known in legal circles throughout the nation, and Cooley had just published a treatise, *Constitutional Limitations*, which later became the most influential American constitutional treatise of the late nineteenth and early twentieth centuries; thus, their anti-subsidy decisions commanded attention.[62] No other state courts adopted Cooley's or Dillon's reasoning, but the two judges helped fuel a feeling that America's increasingly mature railroad system was in less need of public help than formerly, and public resentment over railroad rate discrimination would soon generate a movement to expand state railroad regulation.[63] During the 1870s, many state legislatures enacted laws further limiting state and municipal subsidies and imposing debt ceilings. The decisions of Cooley and Dillon also provided powerful support for those laws.[64]

Mississippi traveled from the age of subsidy to the age of regulation by a distinctively Southern path. The Civil War badly damaged the state's rail network, but it also demonstrated how vital that network was to the war effort and to the state's future. As a result, postwar Mississippi lawmakers gave a degree of attention to railroad building that their antebellum predecessors had not.[65] But they continued to be ambivalent about subsidies. Memories of the failed prewar experiment in state bank subsidy remained fresh, and in the aftermath of war there were many competing demands for public funds and too little money to meet them all. During Reconstruction, Mississippi's legislature freely chartered new railroads and in some cases provided aids, such as tax exemptions, that did not make direct demands on the public treasury. The only notable instance of direct aid was the Subsidy Act of 1871, in which the legislature offered $4,000 per mile to any railroad that would construct twenty-five miles of line by mid-1872 and complete its entire line by mid-1875. The act was intended to help William Mann's Mobile and Northwestern Railroad, which was projected to run across the entire state from Mobile to Memphis, but the act and Mann's project were soon engulfed by charges of bribery and unconstitutionality. In the end, the road was a failure and no state money was ever paid out.[66]

Mississippi's Reconstruction constitutional convention (1868) prohibited all state internal-improvement subsidies, but it authorized municipal subsidies if approved in a referendum by at least two-thirds of voters. In 1872, the legislature added a requirement that municipalities providing subsidies through bond issues must commit to pay the bonds in full within twenty years and must levy sufficient annual taxes to pay interest and build up a redemption fund, but the law was repealed two years later.[67]

In *Hawkins v. Board of Supervisors of Carroll County* (1874), Mississippi's supreme court exemplified the state's postwar ambivalence: it cabined the state's municipal aid law by holding that subsidies must be approved by two-thirds of a municipality's qualified voters, not merely two-thirds of those voting. Justice Horatio Simrall affirmed that railroads could be subsidized because they served a public purpose but he also expressed sympathy for the old Jacksonian concern, most recently expressed by Cooley and Dillon, that there was an element of unfairness about taxing subsidy opponents to support what was, after all, a private corporation. "It would not be safe, wise or prudent," said Simrall, "to push the power beyond the line already established in usage, legislation and judicial sanction . . . The power is dangerous, and greatly liable to abuse . . . [although] it is also true that a wise, cautious and prudent use of county credit may result in public good."[68] In 1890, Mississippi's post-Reconstruction constitutional convention underscored the state's tradition of caution by explicitly prohibiting state land donations and other forms of state and municipal aid for internal improvements.[69]

Mississippi enjoyed substantial postwar railroad growth, but that growth was due to the late nineteenth-century trend to consolidate railroads into national networks, rather than governmental support. Collis Huntington, one of the builders of the Central Pacific and Union Pacific lines in the West and of the Chesapeake & Ohio in the East, competed with the Illinois Central to purchase and consolidate financially stressed local lines in Mississippi and in the end the Illinois Central, operating from Chicago, became the state's leading rail line.[70]

General incorporation laws. Mississippi also joined in another reform movement, the replacement of individual corporate charters by general incorporation laws. That movement originated during the Jacksonian era but did not come to fruition in most states until after the Civil War. Despite their suspicion of corporate power, Jacksonians did not wish to abolish corporations; they merely wanted to ensure that entrepreneurs large and small could incorporate on equal terms. In 1834, William Leggett proposed that legislatures "pass one general law, which will allow any set of men. . . . to form themselves into that convenient kind of partnership known by the name of corporation."[71] The bank controversies of the 1830s sparked nationwide sentiment for general incorporation laws. Another motivating factor, particularly in industrializing states, was that legislatures simply could not keep up with the ever-increasing demand for individual corporate charters.

Nevertheless, the general incorporation law movement proceeded slowly and incrementally. As early as the 1810s, a handful of states enacted general incorporation laws limited to manufacturing companies, and during the 1840s and 1850s other states expanded the catalog of general incorporation laws to include banking, insurance, and telegraph companies and companies in other specialized sectors. Beginning in 1845, some states inserted clauses in their constitutions explicitly authorizing general incorporation laws; by 1875, nineteen states had such provisions. In that year, New Jersey became the first state to adopt a true general-law model when it amended its constitution to prohibit all individual charters except in limited circumstances. Many other states soon followed New Jersey's lead.[72]

During the antebellum era, Mississippi took no action to encourage general incorporation laws. There was little support for developing industry on a large scale, and the legislature had little difficulty handling the comparatively modest demand for corporate charters. But immediately after the Civil War ended, demand for charters rose dramatically. Mississippians viewed new industrial and commercial enterprise as the state's best hope to rise from wartime destruction, and promotion of commercial enterprise would create a need for more corporate charters. Sentiment for general incorporation laws grew accordingly and in 1871 the legislature enacted Mississippi's first limited general incorporation law, one that applied to ice plants and waterworks. In 1879, when Judge Josiah A. P. Campbell prepared a revised code of laws at the legislature's request, he inserted a clause requiring that corporations be formed under general laws except where that was impractical.[73]

The legislature continued to enact individual charters as businesses sought to exploit Campbell's impracticality exception in order to obtain individual advantage, but pressure for effective general laws continued to grow. The general-law movement achieved final victory at Mississippi's 1890 convention, when delegates inserted provisions in the state's new constitution prohibiting individual charters unless they were essential to achieve a corporation's business purpose, and requiring the legislature to enact general incorporation laws. The 1890 convention also enacted the state's first anti-*Dartmouth* clause explicitly reserving to the legislature the right to modify corporate charters at any time, through enactment of reform laws or otherwise.[74]

By 1890, Mississippi was edging toward the American economic mainstream. The state was still heavily agricultural, and cotton was still an important crop, but the Civil War and the ruin it brought had spurred the state to move toward a mixed economy in which forestry and industry would also play important roles.[75] Mississippi law reflected this shift, but the law's eccentric antebellum course in economic matters left a permanent imprint that took several different forms. The Mississippi Supreme Court's early, and ready, acceptance of the legislature's power to regulate business and the court's cabining of the *Dartmouth* doctrine, reflected in cases such as *Payne* and *McIntyre*, created a climate sympathetic to regulation, one that continued after the war and that helped lay the groundwork for the economic reforms that would come during the Progressive and New Deal eras. The state's early embrace of expanded property rights for married women paid dividends after the war, as the grievous toll the war exacted from men of military age forced many Mississippi women to take a more active role in enterprise than they would otherwise have done.[76]

Mississippi's ill-fated experiment with bank subsidies left a double imprint. The state's decision in the early 1840s to repudiate its bank bond obligations did long-term damage to its credit and standing in financial markets but the decision, together with the limited local supply of capital, reinforced the state's conservative approach to railroad subsidies and arguably forestalled further financial crises: Mississippi was able to avoid the new round of crushing debt suffered by some sister Southern states that subsidized railroads aggressively during and after Reconstruction. One might ask whether Mississippi's approach inhibited the development of a state rail network after the war, but that is doubtful.

Even if Mississippi lawmakers had wanted to embark on an aggressive subsidy program, they simply did not have sufficient resources to do so. Outside capitalists supplied that need when they determined that the Mississippi market had recovered sufficiently to justify such expenditures. In the end, Mississippi's core legal values of ready acceptance of corporate regulation and belief in separation of government from business finance proved to be blessings, albeit mixed ones. Those values would change shape during the vast economic changes of the twentieth century, but they would never entirely disappear.

CHAPTER FOUR

Legal Legacies of War and Reconstruction

Events of such vast magnitude and influence now and hereafter have gone into history within the last ten years, that the public mind is not yet quite prepared to consider them calmly and dispassionately. To the judiciary, which ought at all times to be calm, deliberate and firm, especially so when the public thought and sentiment are at all excited beyond the normal tone, is committed the high trust of declaring what are the rules of conduct and propriety . . .

—Justice Horatio Simrall (1873)[1]

Horatio Simrall and Isaiah Montgomery have largely been relegated to historical obscurity and are unknown to most Mississippians, but their lives, perhaps better than any others, exemplified the profound social and legal changes that the Civil War and Reconstruction brought to their state and the complex ways in which Mississippians of both races responded to those changes.

Like Piety Smith Hadley, Simrall was a member of a prominent Kentucky family who decided to try his luck in the frontier Southwest. In the early 1840s, Simrall moved to Vicksburg, where he established a successful law practice and formed a close attachment with the Whig Party, as well as planter and merchant interests. The approach of war created a dilemma for Simrall, who was committed to the social order of the slaveholding South but was a Unionist at heart. In 1857, he returned to Kentucky, but when war finally came he cast his lot with the Confederacy, serving in a provisional Confederate government that General

76

Edmund Kirby Smith established during his short-lived invasion of Kentucky in 1862. When Smith's forces retreated south, Simrall returned to Mississippi.[2]

Simrall kept a low profile for the rest of the war but then re-entered the public arena. Throughout the Reconstruction era, he carefully steered a course between those who wished to preserve as much of the antebellum order as possible and those who believed that the relationship between the races in Mississippi must be transformed. As a member of the Restoration constitutional convention called in 1865 to restore Mississippi to the Union, Simrall persuaded diehard Confederate loyalists to accept the demise of slavery and the indissolubility of the Union. The following year, as a member of the legislature, he warned his colleagues that if they restricted black Mississippians' rights excessively they would risk Northern criticism and Congressional sanctions, but he then helped draft a harsh Black Code and helped persuade his colleagues to resist ratification of the Thirteenth Amendment to the federal Constitution that formally abolished slavery.

Both actions aroused Northern ire; in response, Congress enacted a series of Reconstruction Acts in 1867, ending the restoration phase and inaugurating the military phase of Reconstruction.[3] The acts placed Mississippi and other former Confederate states under military rule and instructed commanders to protect the rights of all Mississippians regardless of race, to suppress violence, and to compile a new roll of voters limited to those who had not supported the Confederacy.[4] Simrall now decided he would rather "take [his] state from her isolation and hitch her onto the car of [economic] progress" than continue to resist federal authority, and he gravitated to a group of native prewar Unionists led by James Alcorn of Coahoma County, who favored acceptance of Congress's conditions for an end to military rule and a meaningful measure of civil rights for newly freed slaves.[5]

In 1868, in order to end military rule and regain full representation in Congress under the terms of the Reconstruction Acts, a new convention prepared a constitution that not only guaranteed black Mississippians the right to vote as required by Congress but excluded ex-Confederates from the franchise. The exclusionary clause was too much even for many Unionists, and voters narrowly rejected the new constitution. Moderate Unionists then asked Simrall to go to Washington and persuade federal authorities to allow a separate vote on the exclusionary clause. Simrall was successful, and in early 1869, voters rejected the clause but approved the remainder of the new constitution, and a domestic phase of Reconstruction replaced military Reconstruction.[6]

A coalition of white Unionists and newly enfranchised black voters elected Alcorn governor, and Alcorn rewarded Simrall with an appointment to the state's newly constituted supreme court.[7] Simrall and his new colleagues faced a daunting task. They had to decide what civil and political rights Mississippi must extend to its black citizens; in addition, they had to decide whether to recognize any acts of the Confederate state and national governments as legitimate. The justices steered a middle course: wartime governmental acts and contracts would be enforced unless they directly aided the Confederate war effort, but debts payable in Confederate money would be scaled down to reflect the steady depreciation of that currency during the war.[8] The justices also rejected most requests to nullify acts of Mississippi's Restoration government (1865–67) and its military government (1867–69): to do so would ignore the realities of the era and would encourage anarchy. They also rejected challenges to several Reconstruction civil rights measures, most notably an 1873 law prohibiting hotels, theaters, and other places of public accommodation from engaging in racial discrimination.[9]

Isaiah Montgomery's life was just as complex as Simrall's. Montgomery and his parents were favored slaves of Joseph Davis, Jefferson Davis's brother, who operated a large plantation at Davis Bend near Vicksburg. Joseph Davis was a follower of Robert Owen, a utopian socialist who founded and inspired model communities in Great Britain and America based on principles of communal ownership and mutual aid. When Davis applied the Owenite model to his plantation, he gave the Montgomery family a degree of freedom of action and responsibility unprecedented among Mississippi slaves. As Union troops approached Davis Bend in 1862, Davis fled and the Montgomerys took his place. Davis quietly sold the plantation to them after the war, making Isaiah Montgomery one of the most prominent Delta residents of either race. At the beginning of military Reconstruction, Montgomery's father was appointed justice of the peace for Davis Bend, thus becoming the first black judicial official in American history.[10]

In late 1874 and early 1875, conservative Democrats used Republican disunity, together with election fraud and violence, to regain control of Mississippi's legislature and bring the state's domestic Reconstruction era to an end. When Simrall's term on the supreme court expired in 1878, he returned to his law practice and private life and he remained a Republican. Montgomery also remained loyal to the Republican Party, but like most black Mississippians he lived a dual life in order to reconcile his desire for survival with his need for self-respect. Publicly he took a conciliatory attitude to white conservatives, espousing Booker T. Washington's philosophy of black self-help and acquiescence to white supremacy, but at the same time he quietly expanded his plantation holdings and helped discontented freedmen emigrate from Mississippi while opposing such emigration publicly. In 1887, Montgomery founded the all-black community of Mound Bayou in an effort to replicate the Owenite teachings of his former owner.[11]

Montgomery's and Simrall's paths crossed in 1890 when both returned to the public stage for a final act. Mississippi whites had firmly reestablished political control of the state, but many were tired of the continuing need to resort to fraud and violence in order to suppress black votes. They wanted to ensure white political supremacy, but they worried that direct disfranchisement of black Mississipians would rekindle the wrath of Congress. A new constitutional convention was called in 1890 in order to address the dilemma; Simrall and Montgomery were the only Republican delegates in a body of 134 members, and Montgomery was the sole black delegate. Surprisingly, both men contributed to the suffrage-restriction plan devised by the convention, a plan that served as the basic model for black disfranchisement throughout the South for the better part of a century.[12]

Simrall was a Republican but he was also an old-time Whig at heart, one who believed in government by gentlemen and was skeptical of broad-based suffrage regardless of race. He was asked to help lead the convention's suffrage committee; the committee ultimately devised an elaborate set of suffrage restrictions including a poll tax and a requirement that voters demonstrate literacy or an understanding of the constitution; this did not violate the letter of the US Constitution but guaranteed that many poor whites as well as nearly all Mississippi blacks would be excluded from suffrage.[13]

As the vote on the proposed restrictions drew near, Mississippi blacks and their dwindling band of white supporters hoped that Montgomery would bear witness against the restrictions. But their hopes were disappointed: Montgomery endorsed the restrictions in the hope that they would help end racial conflict in the state. He reasoned that the restrictions did not eliminate blacks' "high privilege" of voting but "only lifted it to a higher plane," and he trusted that "the two great races shall peaceably travel side by side, each mutually assisting the other [to] mount higher and higher on the scale of human progress"—sentiments that Booker T. Washington surely would have approved. "Is our sacrifice accepted?" Montgomery asked white delegates. "Shall the great question be settled?" Perhaps Montgomery's Washingtonian sentiments were sincere, or perhaps he regarded the convention as a part of his dual life: suffrage restrictions could not be stopped, and more progress could be achieved by surface cooperation and private racial self-betterment than by acts of protest and witness.[14]

Like Montgomery's and Simrall's lives, the legal path of Reconstruction and its aftermath in Mississippi was marked by constant shifts. The Reconstruction era posed unprecedented legal challenges that had to be resolved with little time for reflection and refinement. A slave system that had served as a social and economic pillar of Southern life for nearly 250 years was utterly destroyed in the space of four years, in a war that also took the lives of nearly one-quarter of white Southern males and wrecked the region's economy. White

Figure 4.1. Isaiah T. Montgomery. Courtesy of the Archives and
Records Services Division, Mississippi Department of Archives
and History.

Mississippians knew, and most accepted, that the old concept of black persons
as property was gone. What was less clear was whether they were now obligated
to accept blacks as fully empowered fellow citizens. The Confederacy's demise
also gave rise to many other legal questions. Were returning soldiers liable for
damage they had done during the war? Were laws enacted by Confederate
legislatures valid, and were contracts payable in Confederate money enforceable? Likewise, at the end of Reconstruction, newly ascendant conservatives
had to consider whether they would challenge legal reforms enacted during
Reconstruction, whether any of those reforms were worth preserving, and
how far they could go in curtailing black Mississippians' civil rights without
rekindling Northern wrath and reaction.[15]

In the end, Reconstruction measures promoting political and social equality
among the races were pulled down but a residue of laws guaranteeing basic civil
rights remained in place. Those laws were seldom enforced—the racial caste
system that arose after Reconstruction and the white custom that enforced

it were too powerful—but the laws remained on the books, and the federal Fourteenth and Fifteenth amendments served as a continuous reminder to Mississippi conservatives that there were legal limits beyond which they could not go. Eventually, the Reconstruction laws that survived would provide a legal nucleus for the second great civil rights movement of the mid-twentieth century.

Law and the Lost Cause: The 1865 Constitution and the *ab initio* Debate

The first and most basic postwar challenge that whites in Mississippi and other Southern states faced was acceptance of the end of the Confederacy and of slavery. Slavery had begun to crumble even before the end of the war; thousands of slaves escaped to the Union lines as those lines advanced south, and it gradually became clear that slavery would die in the upper South regardless of the war's outcome. Some states began the process of repudiating slavery even before the war ended. Border states Maryland and Missouri enacted new constitutions in 1864 and early 1865 abolishing slavery, as did governments formed in Union-controlled portions of Arkansas and Louisiana with encouragement from Abraham Lincoln's administration. In upper-South states, where pockets of Unionist sentiment persisted throughout the war, Unionists attempted with some success to take power at war's end by denying suffrage to those who had served the Confederacy and those who would not take an oath of loyalty to the Union. Many Southern whites viewed the war's result as a divine judgment against slavery; others grudgingly accepted slavery's demise as the product of superior Union force, and a few clung to hope that slavery could survive the war.[16]

The situation was different in Mississippi. Most of the state's Unionists readily supported the Confederate cause after secession and although Union forces occupied large portions of Mississippi from 1863 on, the state's Confederate government continued to function throughout the war. At war's end, Andrew Johnson, the new president, allowed Mississippi's existing state government to remain in place subject only to the requirement that it abjure further rebellion and accept the end of slavery. But even those modest conditions proved too much for some Mississippians. Congress had approved the Thirteenth Amendment abolishing slavery in February 1865 but it had not yet been ratified by the states. Furthermore, when Mississippi's constitutional convention convened in August a few delegates held out hope that the amendment would never go into effect. Others complained that voluntary abolition of slavery would amount to a confession of guilt, a "stigma upon the graves of your sons that mark the fields of a thousand battles." Delegate Hampton Jarnagin stated that he had "no hesitation in recording my vote" to abolish slavery, but wanted to "record . . . how it was brought about . . . Mississippi was abolitionized."[17]

Former supreme court justice William Yerger, the leader of the convention's Unionist faction, criticized such attitudes and warned that resistance would do more harm than good. "Why . . . ignore facts, and contend for constitutional rights and constitutional guarantees, that we have no more power to grasp, than we have to grasp the rays of the moon?" he asked. "Why do this, knowing that we place an argument in the mouth, and a weapon in the hands of those who wish not only to strike down the institution of slavery, but to strike down the social and political superiority of the whites?" Delegate E. J. Goode also counseled realism: "There was a wager of law, as well as of battle," he said, "and . . . the question was decided against us." In the end Jarnagin's middle position prevailed: the convention abolished slavery but added a clause stating that it did so due to the fortunes of war.[18]

The convention also considered the closely related issue of whether secession had affected Mississippi's status as a state. Early in the war, Massachusetts senator Charles Sumner had introduced the *ab initio* doctrine. By seceding, he argued, the Confederate states had forfeited their status as states of the Union and should be treated as territories at war's end, eligible for readmission only after the federal government had refashioned Southern culture based on free-labor principles. Few in the North were willing to go that far, but a closely related issue, namely, the legitimacy of Confederate state governments and the laws they enacted, became a subject of intensive debate within American legal circles after the war.[19] Treating all wartime laws and acts as valid might lend the rebellion an air of legitimacy, but blanket nullification of wartime transactions could upend postwar recovery and lead to social and economic chaos.

During the years immediately after the end of the war, Unionist-dominated legislatures and courts in several upper-South states adopted *ab initio* and used it to punish unreconstructed ex-Confederates. They refused to grant amnesty to Confederate veterans for wartime acts, thus exposing them to lawsuits for damage they had done during military campaigns. They also refused to uphold Confederate-era business transactions, thus giving wartime debtors an advantage over their creditors.[20] Mississippi did not go that far: its Unionists were fewer in number, and they wisely used their postwar window of opportunity to increase their own support rather than try to destroy their opponents. Mississippi's first postwar legislature extended amnesty for wartime acts to both Confederate and Union veterans. The state's domestic-Reconstruction court later extended amnesty to civilians who had committed acts in defense of home and family that would have been illegal in peacetime, and it gave amnesty a broad scope because, as Justice Simrall explained, "[i]t is not to be expected . . . that those who acted under military orders were at all times discreet and forbearing." Without amnesty, wartime passions would be rekindled and postwar efforts to build a new society on the ashes of the old, already difficult, would be made more so.[21]

Mississippi's supreme court firmly rejected other manifestations of *ab initio* throughout Reconstruction. In *Hill v. Boyland* (1866) the Restoration-era court made clear that simply "[b]ecause the government of the United States detained Mississippi in the Union by coercion of arms, . . . [it] does not follow that Mississippi thereby became extinct as a state." No "sound public policy," said Justice Harris, "could be promoted by holding, contrary to the fact, that the citizens of this State were in a state of anarchy among themselves, without rights, without laws . . . for the regulation of their private, internal, local affairs, during the progress of the war." But Harris indicated that an exception would be made for governmental acts that directly promoted the Confederate war effort: they would not be sanctioned or enforced. Most Southern courts adopted the same rule both during and after the Restoration period.[22] This exception must have been painful to Harris since he had been the state's chief legal defender of slavery before the war, had served as its envoy to promote the Confederacy's cause, and had witnessed the wartime destruction of a way of life he held dear. The fact that he tried to accommodate the legal changes the war brought attests to the power of the national judicial culture that arose in America during the late eighteenth and early nineteenth centuries.[23]

The court devoted much time to defining the scope of the exception during the Restoration and domestic-Reconstruction eras. Even though Confederate currency had provided the financial foundation for the rebellion, Mississippi's justices held that wartime transactions payable in Confederate dollars would not be overturned unless they involved the supply of Confederate armies or other activities that directly supported the war effort.[24] Wartime laws temporarily suspending lawsuits against Confederate soldiers and allowing litigants extra time to file lawsuits due to the disruptions of war were upheld,[25] as were wartime criminal laws and tax foreclosure sales.[26] But the military-Reconstruction court held that a conscript's contract to pay for a substitute was not enforceable,[27] and in one of its first decisions the domestic-Reconstruction court held that treasury notes issued by Mississippi's Confederate government could not be used to pay postwar taxes. The Restoration justices probably would have reached the same decision but their domestic-Reconstruction successors used more condemnatory language, even flirting with *ab initio*. Wartime currency, said Chief Justice Ephraim Peyton, "enabled [Mississippi] more effectually to aid the Confederate government in the prosecution of a sanguinary war, waged expressly for the purpose of subverting the government of the United States." The court did not pronounce all wartime laws invalid, but Peyton suggested that it could have done so because the failure of Mississippi's wartime legislators to take an oath of loyalty to the United States provided grounds for invalidation.[28]

In early 1869, the US Supreme Court effectively put an end to both the *ab initio* controversy and disputes over the validity of Confederate government acts. In *Texas v. White* (1869), it held that the nation was "an indestructible Union, composed of indestructible states": the rights of rebellious states and their citizens were suspended during the period of rebellion, but the states never lost their status as members of the Union. The court also adopted the rule exemplified in *Boyland*: acts of Confederate governments "necessary to peace and good order among citizens" were valid, but acts "in furtherance or support of rebellion . . . or intended to defeat the just rights of citizens" were void.[29]

In *Thorington v. Smith* (1869), the court also adopted a middle path with respect to disputes over transactions involving Confederate currency. The Confederate dollar started the war nearly at par with federal currency, but as the South's military fortunes declined it also declined correspondingly. By early 1865, a federal dollar would purchase nearly one hundred Confederate dollars. Soon after the war, many states adopted "scaling" statutes that required debtors to pay wartime obligations in United States currency but reduced their payments to reflect the Confederate dollar's depreciation. For example, a debtor who had promised to pay $100 in Confederate currency in 1865 could now pay his debt with a single federal dollar.[30] A handful of Southern courts declared all transactions involving Confederate currency void,[31] but most Southern courts, including Mississippi's Reconstruction-era courts, approved scaling as an appropriate recognition of economic and political realities, and in *Thorington* the federal high court agreed.[32]

Challenging Reconstruction: The McCardle and Yerger cases. Many Mississippians who had accepted the war's result changed their attitude with the advent of military rule, and two Mississippi newspaper editors, William McCardle and Edward S. Yerger, nearly brought down military Reconstruction. Both men had long been firebrands, and after military rule came to Mississippi they consistently denounced General Edward O. C. Ord, the local commander, and urged resistance to his rule. In late 1867, Ord ordered that McCardle be imprisoned for sedition and disturbance of public order. McCardle then petitioned for a writ of habeas corpus, arguing that the Reconstruction Acts were unconstitutional because they authorized imposition of military rule upon civilians, thereby violating civilians' right to due process of law. The US Supreme Court had recently ruled that the wartime military arrest and trial of an Indiana lawyer who opposed the Union war effort violated his constitutional due process rights, and Congressional Republicans became concerned that the court would reach a similar result in McCardle's case, which would sharply limit the military's ability to maintain order in the South. They enacted a law depriving the court of jurisdiction over appeals from lower courts in habeas cases, and in 1869 the Court reluctantly returned McCardle's case to Mississippi authorities, who, recognizing the close call they had had, dropped all charges against him.[33]

Soon afterwards Yerger, who had a history of mental illness, called out the military mayor of Jackson for seizing his property to satisfy a tax bill and stabbed him to death. When military authorities arrested Yerger and prepared to try him before a military court, he, like McCardle, sought a habeas writ from the Supreme Court. This time Congress did not try to block the court from acting; it was now satisfied that the court would not try to overturn military Reconstruction, which in any case was drawing to a close as other former Confederate states enacted new constitutions and fulfilled their obligations under the Reconstruction Acts. The court concluded it had jurisdiction over Yerger's petition and it confirmed that the military had no authority over civilian crimes. Mississippi officials then handed Yerger over to the state's civilian courts, newly restored to full authority under the 1869 constitution. Yerger was not re-tried but was released.[34]

Perhaps inspired by Yerger's case, Mississippi's supreme court became increasingly less deferential to Unionist principles as domestic Reconstruction progressed. In *Welborn v. Mayrant* (1873), the court refused to enforce a military tribunal's decision overturning an arbitration award against a black plaintiff; the tribunal believed that the defendant, who was white, had taken unfair advantage of him. Justice Jonathan Tarbell issued a lengthy dissent: he defended the military-Reconstruction government, arguing that it had restored order during a troubled time and had accomplished much good, including promotion of civil rights and sharecroppers' right to receive a fair portion of their agricultural production. People were now "settling down to their usual avocations, and generally accepting the situation, and forgetting their losses," said Tarbell, who warned that his colleagues' decision would throw into doubt thousands of military decisions upon which the social order had rested and continued to rest. But Tarbell was unable to stem the tide. In 1876, after Reconstruction had ended in Mississippi and Tarbell had left the court, Simrall pronounced the end of judicial support for *ab initio* and other "incongruous theories . . . put forward by jurists and judges" at the close of the war. "The times," he said, "were not then propitious for calm and unimpassioned juridical discussions." Mississippi did not accept those theories, and it never would.[35]

Civil Rights During the Restoration Period:
Mississippi's Black Code

The second great challenge that Mississippians faced at the end of the war was the creation of a new legal edifice to replace the state's slave code, a code that had been a keystone of Mississippi's economy and society since territorial days but had been swiftly and utterly destroyed by the Civil War. Before the war, debates over slave law had centered on whether slaves should be treated purely as chattel or as partly human for purposes of establishing legal rights and restrictions. Emancipation had indisputably eliminated black Mississippians' chattel status, but whites were far from prepared to recognize blacks as full equals and, thus, fully human. There were a variety of rights to consider. One category was civil rights, which in the mid-nineteenth century meant the basic right to move about freely, to own property, to enjoy the fruits of one's own labor, and to seek legal relief for wrongs committed by others. The other categories were political rights, including the right to vote, hold office, testify in court, and serve on juries; and social rights, including the right to mix in public places and marry regardless of race. At war's end, most white Mississippians genuinely accepted the end of slavery but were firmly opposed to anything approaching political and social equality for blacks, and many were reluctant to extend even basic civil rights to their new fellow citizens. They reasoned that former slaves had never known freedom and were not ready for its responsibilities, but at a more basic level it was difficult for them to shed fundamental beliefs about black inferiority that had built up over the past century. [36]

In the fall of 1865, the first postwar legislature enacted a series of laws, collectively known as the Black Code, that revealed how deep the resistance to change was. The code granted black Mississippians only limited property rights and prohibited them from leasing or purchasing land, except in urban areas where authorities could keep a close eye on them. They were allowed to marry and slave marriages were legally recognized, but the code prohibited interracial marriage, which would be punished by life imprisonment. Many legislators wanted to retain the antebellum rule that blacks could not testify against whites under any circumstances. Initially they prevailed, but after warnings by Simrall and Restoration-era Governor Benjamin Humphreys that such a ban would invite federal retaliation, the legislature relented and allowed black testimony against whites in limited situations. Circuit judge (and future Mississippi Supreme Court justice) Josiah A. P. Campbell paved the way for acceptance of the new rule by allowing black testimony in all cases in his court; he believed that no black witness could deceive "a jury of white men with all their knowledge of negro character." [37]

The code also required all blacks to find employment by the beginning of 1866 and to furnish proof of employment, typically labor contracts with local planters, to local officials. It provided a small measure of protection to black workers: labor contracts must be in writing and must be read and explained to workers before they signed. But the code also imposed work requirements that were disturbingly reminiscent of slavery. Black workers who quit could be arrested and returned to their employer; rival planters who enticed workers away from their current employer would be subject to stiff penalties; and any worker who was found to have quit without good cause would forfeit past wages due.[38]

The code included apprenticeship and vagrancy laws that particularly aroused Northern anger. Mississippi's apprenticeship law provided that black children whose parents "have not the means or who refuse to provide for and support said minors" could be apprenticed to "competent and suitable persons"; former masters were given preference, and children who attempted to leave their custody would be subject to punishment. The vagrancy law contained similar provisions for adults: persons who "neglect[ed] their calling or employment," did not support their families, had "no lawful employment" or were "found unlawfully assembling themselves together" were considered vagrants, as were persons who could not pay an annual poll tax. Black vagrants were subject to fines of $50, a large sum well out of reach for nearly all freedmen, and those who could not pay would be hired out until the fine was paid.[39]

The code reflected white Mississippians' belief that it was imperative to plant and harvest quickly in order to avoid further economic disaster; their belief that Mississippi's economic system would collapse without a prompt resumption of black labor; and their fears that newly freed blacks would equate freedom with the right to be idle—sentiments shared by many state and federal officials. "To work is the law of God, and the only certain protection against the pauperism and crime of both races," Governor Humphreys proclaimed. "The Negro . . . is free to choose his own labor and make his own bargain. But he should be required to choose some employment that will insure the maintenance of himself and family."[40] But the code had far too many echoes of the old slave code to survive Northern scrutiny. The 1865–66 legislature reinforced Northern suspicions by enacting collateral laws that forbade blacks to possess firearms and ammunition without permission of local officials, imposed penalties on those who provided liquor to blacks, and imposed criminal penalties on any blacks "committing riots, . . . seditious speeches, insulting gestures . . . [or] disturbance of the peace." These provisions, too, were carryovers from the old slave code.[41]

Mississippi was not the only former Confederate state to enact a draconian black code during the Restoration period but it was the first to do so, and its Code encouraged other Southern states to resist the new order. Northern reaction was swift. The *Chicago Tribune*, a leading national voice for Republicans, warned in December 1865 that "the men of the North will convert the State of Mississippi into a frog pond before they will allow such laws to disgrace one foot of soil in which the bones of our soldiers sleep and over which the flag of freedom waves." US Supreme Court justice Samuel Miller openly criticized Mississippi's Code and other black codes, stating that they "do but change the form of slavery."[42] Mississippi's 1865–66 legislature further inflamed Northern opinion by refusing to ratify the Thirteenth Amendment after Simrall's committee recommended against ratification. The Committee argued that the Amendment's enforcement provisions would open the door to increased federal power and to violation of Mississippi's rights as a sovereign state. It proclaimed that Mississippi wished "to withdraw the negro race from national and state politics," and it openly opposed federal efforts to promote blacks' civil rights.[43]

Some Mississippi lawmakers attempted to soften the code's effect. In 1866, the Restoration court held that black children could not be apprenticed unless their parents were notified and given a hearing, despite the lack of hearing provisions in the statute,[44] and when the next legislature convened in late 1866, lawmakers recognized that they had gone too far in provoking Congress. They made belated efforts to repair the damage by repealing the apprenticeship law, repealing the code's restrictions on black property ownership and black testimony, and by allowing blacks to serve on juries, but they refused to ratify the Fourteenth Amendment. Simrall argued that the Amendment "confers on Congress large and undefined power, at the expense of the reserved rights of the State" and that it "tends to create distrust and jealousy between the white and black races, and perpetually to disturb and keep alive these evil passions."[45] But Congress had had enough, and Military Reconstruction soon began.

Considerations of Humanity: Military and Domestic Reconstruction (1867–75)

Military Reconstruction presented an unprecedented but fragile opportunity for changes in Mississippi's legal system. White Mississippians never seriously entertained extension of suffrage to blacks during the Restoration period, but after Congress made clear that that would be a condition of return to civilian rule, many whites quickly concluded that it would be better to accept suffrage and compete with Republicans for black support than to resist.

The 1869 constitution. The first order of business was to call a constitutional convention in compliance with the federal Reconstruction Acts. Federal authorities compiled a list of voters, including eligible black men but excluding whites who could not take the loyalty oath prescribed by the Reconstruction Acts. Mississippi's first biracial electorate chose a body of convention delegates dominated by white Unionists. Many of the delegates had never held public office before. A few political veterans, including present and future Justices Simrall, Peyton, and Tarbell, were elected. Black delegates comprised about one-quarter of the convention, but Montgomery was not among their number, and unlike some Reconstruction conventions, no powerful voices emerged from their ranks.[46]

The convention got off to a rocky start. The state's conservative press attacked its legitimacy, a tactic that only drew moderate and radical Republican delegates closer to each other, and efforts in early sessions to provide relief to debtors and destitute families in a year of particular economic distress were rejected by General Alvan Gillem, who had replaced Ord as Mississippi's military commander and had veto power over measures not strictly related to the new constitution.[47]

Delegates then turned to the suffrage issue. There was near-universal agreement that suffrage should not be restricted by race, but the issue of whether ex-Confederates should be proscribed from voting was considerably more controversial. Radical Republican delegates proposed a measure requiring voters to affirm that they had not aided the Confederacy and that they accepted "the civil and political equality of all men." Moderates, who hoped to build a long-term coalition that included centrist whites, proposed that disqualification be limited to ex-Confederates who had taken prewar oaths to defend the US Constitution and had violated their oaths. Some delegates proposed education and property requirements that would disfranchise large numbers of blacks and whites alike. After much debate, the convention adopted a compromise that combined limited disqualification of ex-Confederates with the equality-of-all-men oath, an oath that many white Mississippians were unwilling to take.[48]

The constitution acknowledged Mississippi's "paramount allegiance . . . to the Government of the United States" and required officeholders to swear allegiance to the United States Constitution as well as the state constitution, thus rebuffing earlier state-rights arguments against the Thirteenth and Fourteenth Amendments.[49] The convention also placed some civil rights provisions in the new constitution, albeit not a comprehensive civil rights program. It provided that all males were eligible for the state militia, overturning an 1865 law that had limited membership to whites, and it also addressed calls for a clause prohibiting racial discrimination in hotels, restaurants, theaters, and other places of public accommodation. Delegates were not willing to approve a comprehensive accommodations clause but they did prohibit infringement of the right to travel on public conveyances.[50] The convention also abandoned the elective judiciary system in favor of an appointive system in order to prevent conservatives from gaining an extra source of power in counties where they were strong. The convention also gave constitutional protection to married women's property rights for the first time.[51]

Republican delegates used the constitution to implement another reform close to their hearts: they created a statewide common-school system that would educate all Mississippi children for at least four months per year, and they provided a permanent source of education funding from lands donated to the state by the federal government and from court fines. Many Northern states had included common-school provisions in their constitutions in the early nineteenth century, but the common-school movement took hold more slowly in the antebellum South, whose agricultural orientation and hierarchical structure created little pressure for universal education and self-improvement. The new constitution's educational provisions had distinct racial overtones: many whites equated universal education with racial leveling and believed that educating black Mississippians would undermine their value as agricultural workers.[52]

The constitution's suffrage restrictions aroused white conservatives who had gone along with the convention movement in hopes of placating Congress. They particularly feared that strict enforcement of the equality-of-all-men oath requirement would exclude them from political power for many years. When the constitution was submitted to voters for approval, conservatives turned out in force in a referendum marred by violence and fraud, and the constitution was narrowly rejected. White moderates, dismayed by the prospect of indefinite military rule, asked Simrall to go to Washington and see if an accommodation could be reached. Much depended on whether Ulysses Grant, the newly elected president, would insist on restrictive suffrage for unreconstructed whites. When Grant indicated he would not, Simrall and Congressional Republicans reached a compromise: if voters rejected the restrictive suffrage clause but approved the remainder of the Constitution, and if Mississippi ratified the new Fifteenth Amendment forbidding racial discrimination as to suffrage, Congress would approve the constitution without the restrictive suffrage clause and would readmit Mississippi to representation. Both sides kept their part of the bargain, and at the end of 1868, the constitution went into effect without the clause. Military Reconstruction ended and a brief period of domestic Reconstruction began, managed by a biracial Republican coalition that would fall six years later.[53]

Mississippi's first domestic-Reconstruction legislature spent more energy undoing Restoration-era laws than enacting new racial reforms. It promptly repealed the remnants of the Black Code, including the most noxious features of the 1865 vagrancy law, and it revised the state's apprenticeship law to provide additional procedural safeguards. Parental consent would be required for all apprenticeships, and apprentices could seek release for good cause at any time. The legislature ratified the Fourteenth Amendment, thus overriding its predecessor, as well as the Fifteenth Amendment. It also implemented several provisions of the 1869 constitution: racial discrimination would not be allowed in the state militia or on public transportation, and for good measure, lawmakers confirmed that Mississippi blacks had the right to serve on juries.[54]

The legislature also turned to a new problem: the rise of the Ku Klux Klan and other groups that formed to terrorize blacks and their white allies. Such groups first appeared about 1868 and their use of violence increased rapidly, particularly in areas where blacks and whites were roughly equal in number—that is, where blacks had a real chance to exercise political power but whites had sufficient numbers to prevent them from doing so. By 1870–71, the problem had become so serious several Southern states enacted anti-Klan laws. Mississippi's law was one of the strongest, in that it prohibited the use of masks and disguises in public, imposed severe criminal penalties on masked persons who demanded entrance to homes or committed assaults, authorized law enforcement officers to form posses to apprehend such offenders, and authorized the governor to offer rewards up to $5,000 for their capture. But the effectiveness of such laws was limited and Klan growth continued.[55]

In 1871, with Klan violence and civil disorder increasing throughout the South, Congress enacted a law defining Klan activities as civil rights violations in order to bring federal power to bear on the problem. Federal prosecutors in northern Mississippi used the new law vigorously and were able to obtain a substantial number of convictions, but the convictions had little effect because the local federal district judge, Robert Hill, handed out uniformly light sentences—typically a $25 fine and an order that the convicted Klansman post a $1,000 bond as security for future good behavior. Hill, a conservative Unionist appointed to his position by Andrew Johnson in 1866, took peace as his primary goal, rationalizing that "it is not the severity, but the certainty of punishment that prevents crime."

Some Klansmen were willing to plead guilty, and some Mississippi jurors were willing to convict. Convictions were regarded as badges of honor, not a stigma, and so long as the penalties were nominal, guilty pleas and convictions were viewed as an inexpensive means of placating Washington. Hill surely understood that harsher penalties would have resulted in more trials and fewer convictions. Prosecutors occasionally pushed for more convictions and harsher sentences but when they did so, Mississippi's culture of honor and violence quickly resurfaced. In 1871, Lucius Q. C. Lamar, a future US senator and US Supreme Court justice, rebuked a federal marshal for criticizing local citizens and demanded his arrest. When Judge Hill failed to censure the deputy, Lamar took matters into his own hands: he assaulted and badly injured the deputy, who met a mysterious and violent death soon afterward. When Lamar was arraigned before Hill, he threatened that the streets would "swim in blood" if he were punished; Hill contented himself with disbarring Lamar in his court, but reinstated him the next day after Lamar's temper cooled. Klan violence in Mississippi declined in earnest only when Reconstruction and black political power in the South ended.[56]

The other major reform measure of the domestic-Reconstruction era came in 1873, when the legislature enacted a broad accommodations law prohibiting racial discrimination in public places including hotels, restaurants, streetcars, and railroad cars. The movement for accommodations laws had begun in 1870 when Senator Sumner introduced an accommodations bill in Congress. His bill attracted controversy even among Republicans, many of whom supported full racial equality when it came to basic civil and political rights but believed that racial mixing in public places could only be achieved by changes in people's hearts and minds, not by statutory imposition. Opponents also suspected that accommodations laws might be unconstitutional: the common law prohibited discrimination by innkeepers but considered most other businesses to be essentially private, such that their owners had a property and liberty right to decide whom they would serve.[57] The Fourteenth Amendment had not changed the common law: it prohibited discrimination by states but not by private persons. Congress finally enacted a watered-down version of Sumner's bill in 1875, but in 1883, the US Supreme Court declared it unconstitutional for the reasons the bill's opponents had given.[58]

In the meantime, however, Mississippi had followed a different path. Governor Alcorn had signaled his opposition to a broad accommodations law in 1870 (although he approved an 1870 accommodations law limited to public transportation), but he left for the US Senate in 1871. Ridgely Powers, his successor as governor, was more receptive to a broad law.[59] The 1873 accommodations law was quickly put to a constitutional test. When Ham Carter, a black legislator who had helped write the law, was refused a seat in the whites-only section of the Angelo Theater in Jackson, state prosecutors brought charges against George Donnell, the theater doorkeeper. Donnell challenged the law's validity, arguing that "it is as unwise as it is unconstitutional for the legislature. . . . to attempt to control those matters of taste." Mississippi attorney general Joshua Morris responded that the law was a legitimate exercise of police power, designed to minimize racial friction created in the course of enforcing the Fourteenth Amendment. The law, said Morris, "takes away the question [of civil rights] from the mob, and transfers it to the courts." The domestic-Reconstruction court sided with Morris. Justice Simrall, who wrote the court's decision, had his doubts about racial equality but he firmly believed in enforcement of duly enacted laws. He concluded that theaters were sufficiently public in nature that they could be regulated and that the state's regulatory power extended to anti-discrimination measures. Although the law survived, it was widely ignored and only sporadically enforced.[60]

During its brief tenure, the domestic-Reconstruction court also addressed other racial issues. Several of its cases were legacies from the manumission disputes of the 1840s and 1850s. When former slaves whose masters had freed them and had provided legacies for them sought to collect those legacies after the war, rival claimants argued that they could not collect because the court had prohibited manumission by will in *Mitchell v. Wells* (1859). The domestic-Reconstruction court firmly rejected that argument; it returned to the pre-*Mitchell* rule allowing freed slaves to inherit if they left Mississippi and, going one step further, stated that with slavery's end, it would be absurd to require black legatees to leave the state in order to inherit.[61] The court also held that children of interracial couples were entitled to inherit from their parents, reasoning that despite the legislature's Restoration-era ban on interracial marriage and the 1868 convention's failure to deal with the subject directly, the Reconstruction constitution's clause legitimating all informal prewar marriages included interracial marriages. "As a question of policy or propriety, people may differ," said Justice Tarbell, but he and his colleagues refused to adopt a narrow construction limiting the clause to prewar slave marriages. Mississippi was unusual in this respect: most Southern states preserved and enforced antebellum miscegenation laws during and after Reconstruction.[62]

Reconstruction's Aftermath: Bourbonism and the Straight-Out Era

In 1873, the Reconstruction coalition was able to elect Adelbert Ames governor, but Ames, an unapologetic Radical Republican, had difficulty holding the coalition together. Ames encountered further trouble when a national recession struck Mississippi in early 1874, creating an agricultural crisis and, in particular, a crisis over the state's lien laws. One of Mississippi's most pressing postwar problems was how to integrate newly freed black laborers and white farmers displaced by the war into its agricultural system. Few were able to purchase their own farms, and after brief experimentation with a wage system, sharecropping became the main compensation system for farmers of both races. Landlords and local merchants would advance tools, seed, and supplies to tenant farmers in return for a share of their crop. In times of poor harvests, the question of who had first priority in the crop became a pressing one. Mississippi's 1867 legislature granted liens to both landlords and suppliers; the 1867 law did not give either group priority, but in 1872, the domestic-Reconstruction court interpreted the law to favor suppliers. The 1874 legislature tried to provide relief by modifying the law to favor sharecroppers and it also enacted a law staying foreclosure proceedings, but Ames, an economic conservative, vetoed both measures.[63]

As the recession deepened and relief failed to materialize, vigilantism and racial violence rose, and centrist whites moved steadily out of the Republican coalition into the conservative camp. The legislature's enactment of a law in early 1875 creating new militia units to combat vigilantism only led to more violence and centrist disaffection. President Grant refused to intervene, and in the fall 1875 elections, which were marred by extensive violence and fraud, conservative Democrats gained control of the legislature. In early 1876, Ames resigned the governorship rather than face certain impeachment, and domestic Reconstruction came to an end in Mississippi.[64]

The problem of consolidating power. The Bourbon conservatives who now controlled the state[65] did not immediately move to repeal all Reconstruction laws. Memories of military Reconstruction and federal action against the Klan remained fresh. Conservatives feared that Northern hostility and federal intervention would resurface if they repeated the mistakes of their Restoration predecessors, and the Fourteenth and Fifteenth Amendments remained in place as potential checks on new state laws designed to keep black Mississippians in a subordinate position. At the end of the Reconstruction era, several Southern states quickly replaced or extensively amended their constitutions to eliminate undesirable Reconstruction-era reforms, but Mississippi did not. Instead, Bourbons focused on reinforcing their control of the electoral system. The 1876 legislature authorized the governor to appoint local registration boards in each county; board members were given broad discretion to hear challenges and reject voter applications, and voters were given only a narrow window of time during which to register.[66]

The new system, combined with frequent ballot-box tampering and other forms of election fraud, proved useful not only for suppressing black votes when necessary, but also for suppressing white votes when intramural divisions arose within the now-dominant Democratic Party. Those divisions soon became significant. The state's legislative apportionment favored black-belt counties in the Delta and west Mississippi over the more rapidly growing white-majority counties in east and south Mississippi. Thus, Bourbon black-belt planters and merchants, who favored a measure of accommodation of their black neighbors in order to preserve labor peace, commanded ever-more disproportionate influence in the legislature as the black vote dwindled.[67] Smaller-scale farmers who made up the bulk of white Democrats had very different concerns. Railroad development and formation of cooperatives to reduce the cost of agricultural supplies were matters of vital interest to them but little interest to black-belt elites, who already had the railroads and financial networks that they needed. Grangerism, Populism, and other agricultural reform movements that shaped politics in much of the central United States from 1870 to 1900 never commanded strong support in Mississippi: the Bourbons convinced whites of all factions that Democratic Party unity was essential to preserve white rule in Mississippi, and white solidarity became the core theme of Mississippi politics.[68]

Nevertheless, economic discontent and resentment of black-belt dominance also became enduring themes in east and south Mississippi. In 1881, the Bourbons only narrowly avoided defeat at the hands of a coalition of white-belt Greenback sympathizers and remnants of the old Republican coalition, and thereafter the use of fraud and "bulldozing"—intimidation and selective use of violence against blacks and recalcitrant white voters—became a common feature of Mississippi elections. Bourbons became increasingly uncomfortable with that reality. "It is no secret," said Bourbon leader and district judge J. J. Chrisman in 1890, "that there has not been a full vote and a fair count in Mississippi since 1875—that we have been preserving the ascendancy of the white people by revolutionary methods . . . until the whole machinery for election was about to rot down."[69] In the late 1880s, Bourbons began casting about for ways to ensure white electoral supremacy without resorting to violence or fraud. The matter became urgent after 1888, when renewed public concern in the North about Southern suppression of black votes helped Republicans recapture control of the federal government and new civil rights measures were introduced in Congress. After some hesitation, Mississippi's legislature decided it was time for a new constitution and it called for a convention to be held in 1890.[70]

The 1890 constitution. The 1890 convention was closely divided between black-belt and white-belt delegates; the latter group insisted that allocation of political power among whites must be addressed as well as preservation of racial supremacy. Simrall and US Senator James Z. George, who had briefly served on the state's supreme court at the beginning of the Bourbon era, were asked to bring their legal expertise and federal experience to bear on the problem of how to effectively limit black suffrage without running afoul of the Fourteenth and Fifteenth Amendments and Congress's 1869 instruction to Mississippi, as a condition of readmission, that it must not restrict black voting rights in future. Simrall disposed of the Congressional instruction in a report setting forth his longstanding position that Mississippi had never really been out of the Union, which was indissoluble, and that accordingly Congress had no right to dictate conditions of readmission. Navigating around the federal amendments was more difficult. Simrall, George, Josiah Campbell (now a member of Mississippi's supreme court), and others devised provisions, racially neutral on their face, that they believed might be used to control black suffrage. But there was another problem: some of the provisions, particularly a poll tax and literacy requirements, might also disqualify poor and illiterate whites.[71]

After a lengthy and often contentious debate, a grand compromise was reached on suffrage and legislative apportionment. A proposal made by Simrall to limit voting to those who had resided at their voting address for at least a year, designed to screen out the many sharecroppers of both races who migrated from farm to farm, was adopted. Voters were also required to register at least four months in advance of an election, to pay a two-dollar poll tax, and to demonstrate to local election officials that they could read or understand any section of the new constitution. It was believed that the "understanding" clause would give local officials a tool to exclude otherwise-qualified black voters where necessary in order to ensure continued white supremacy.[72] White-belt delegates continued to grumble that the new restrictions would hurt them as much as blacks, but they had no alternative plan likely to pass constitutional muster and in return for their assent to the suffrage plan, they received important concessions on legislative apportionment. New assembly districts were added and existing districts were redrawn so that white-belt counties gained more than a dozen new seats. The convention also provided that in order to be elected, governors must receive both a majority of the popular vote and a majority of "electoral votes" computed by giving each county votes equal to the number of assembly seats it held, which would go to the candidate who carried the county.[73]

Looking back several years after the convention, delegate J. S. NcNeilly concluded with satisfaction that the suffrage and apportionment provisions, together with the convention's decision to retain an appointive judicial system, made "[s]tate government upon the foundation of white electorates . . . lawful, complete and secure." But McNeilly regretted the concomitant reduction of the white vote, made necessary by the federal requirement that laws be racially neutral on their face. Mississippi, he concluded, had "exchanged an organic malady for a functional disorder . . . a dessicated for a diseased electorate."[74] The first voter list compiled after the convention showed that the number of registered white voters had fallen from approximately 120,000 to 68,000 and that the number of black voters had fallen to 6,800. Contemporary observers noted that as many blacks as whites qualified to vote under the "understanding" clause, possibly because black voters were given "understanding" tests more frequently, and that the poll-tax requirement proved to be the most effective suppression device for both races.[75]

Mississippi's 1890 constitution provided a model for the rest of the South. When South Carolina, the next state to adopt a disfranchising constitution, did so in 1895, its convention delegates proclaimed their purpose as openly as their Mississippi counterparts and adopted similar exclusionary devices. The handful of black delegates at the South Carolina convention declined to follow Montgomery's lead: they saw their role as one of protest and witness to injustice.[76] Over the course of the ensuing decade, Louisiana (1898), Alabama (1901), and Virginia (1902) also enacted new disfranchising constitutions, while North Carolina (1901) added disfranchising provisions to its existing constitution. Like South Carolina, each borrowed from the set of disfranchising devices that Mississippi had created.[77]

The 1890 constitution marked the end of the Bourbon era and the beginning of the "straight out" era in Mississippi, one in which Southern whites shed all remaining defensiveness over the new order in favor of a straight-out affirmation of white supremacy and focused on resolving political disputes among themselves.[78] Mississippi's new suffrage restrictions were challenged, but the challenges received short shrift despite the openness with which the 1890 convention had expressed its intention to disfranchise black voters. In *Ratliff v. Beale* (1896), Mississippi's supreme court was asked to determine whether the constitutional poll tax was compulsory. The justices held that it was not and Chief Justice Tim Cooper, speaking for his colleagues, provided one of the most vivid insights into the straight-out mind:

> [T]he convention swept the circle of expedients to obstruct the exercise of the franchise by the negro race. By reason of its previous condition of servitude and dependence, this race had acquired or accentuated certain peculiarities of habit, of temperament, and of character, which clearly distinguished it as a race from that of the whites,—a patient, docile people, but careless, landless, and migratory within narrow limits, without forethought, and its criminal members given rather to furtive offenses than to the robust crimes of the whites. Restrained by the federal constitution from discriminating against the negro race, the convention discriminated against its characteristics and the offenses to which its weaker members were prone.[79]

Two years later, the US Supreme Court summarily rejected another challenge to Mississippi's suffrage provisions. In *Williams v. Mississippi* (1898), a black defendant indicted by an all-white jury for murder argued that because only electors could serve as jurors under Mississippi law, the 1890 suffrage provisions violated black Mississippians' right under the federal Fourteenth Amendment not to be excluded from jury service and, thus, denied him his due-process right to a fair trial. Mississippi's supreme court rejected the challenge, as did the federal high court, relying on the fact that Mississippi's suffrage restrictions did not discriminate against blacks on their face. "[I]t has not been shown that their actual administration was evil; only that evil was possible under them," said Justice Joseph McKenna, and that was not enough to invalidate them.[80]

The rise of Jim Crow. In addition to disfranchising constitutions, the straight-out era witnessed the rise of Jim Crow laws formally codifying segregation in nearly every area of public life. During Reconstruction, social equality had remained the most elusive goal of all: even the most dedicated racial reformers recognized the depth of white resistance to social mixing. Most reformers doubted that laws could effectively reduce that resistance, and with some exceptions such as Mississippi's 1873 accommodations law, few tried.[81]

Mississippi began building its Jim Crow system shortly after the end of Reconstruction. The Bourbons stared with schools: in 1878, the legislature formally mandated school segregation.[82] In 1903, Governor James Vardaman, a champion of white-belt farmers and one of the leading straight-out voices in Mississippi, urged that the state's school fund be divided between the races in proportion to taxes paid rather than based on population, a change that would have decimated the already minimal funds provided for black education. Legislators concluded that Vardaman's proposal went too far, and from a constitutional perspective they were right: several Southern state courts had already concluded that segregation of school funds would violate state constitutional common-school provisions and, perhaps more importantly, the Fourteenth Amendment's guarantee of equal protection of the laws.[83] In *McFarland v. Goins* (1909), Mississippi's supreme court agreed and struck down a law authorizing counties to tax all citizens in order to construct whites-only high schools. "Civil rights do not mean social rights," said Justice Robert Mayes, but the Fourteenth Amendment prohibited "taxing the property of the two races for the benefit of one." Nor was Vardaman's proposal necessary to preservation of the racial order: Mississippi laws gave local school officials wide discretion to allocate funds among black and white students as they saw fit, which meant that as a practical matter most resources would go to white students. The US Supreme Court held in 1899 that local administrators had broad leeway to allocate funds notwithstanding the Fourteenth Amendment, and after the *McFarland* decision, legislators apparently concluded that was sufficient to protect the racial order in the schools. The Mississippi court subsequently confirmed that conclusion, holding that administrators could create separate school districts with separate tax bases for black and white residential areas.[84]

Public transportation was next. In 1888, Mississippi became one of the first states to enact a law requiring segregation of railroad passengers.[85] When the railroad-segregation law was challenged, a legal complication presented itself. Most Mississippi railroads were part of interstate systems, and in *Hall v. DeCuir* (1878), the US Supreme Court had indicated that state civil rights laws did not apply to interstate commerce: under the federal Constitution, only Congress could regulate such commerce. In *DeCuir*, the high Court had struck down a Louisiana accommodations law prohibiting segregation on steamboats, but the principle appeared just as applicable to laws mandating segregation. In *Louisville, New Orleans & Texas Railroad Co. v. State* (1889), Mississippi's supreme court neatly skirted this issue and found a way to uphold its state's railroad-segregation law. It noted that the railroad in question had been charged with failing to provide separate cars for black and white passengers, not with forcing the races to ride separately, therefore it did not need to address the constitutionality of passenger segregation. The US Supreme Court accepted this distinction, holding that a requirement to provide separate cars did not deny black passengers equal rights under the Fourteenth Amendment.[86]

Seven years later, the high court held in *Plessy v. Ferguson* (1896) that segregation of public facilities would not violate the federal Constitution if equal facilities were provided to each race. *Plessy* put an end to legal challenges to most Jim Crow laws, but it did not put an end to protest, and practical problems of enforcement led to additional legal disputes. That proved true for Mississippi's streetcar-segregation law, enacted by the 1904 legislature at the urging of Governor Vardaman. Prior to 1904, blacks and whites had ridden streetcars together in Mississippi cities with little incident, and after the law was enacted, Vicksburg's black community, led by Willis Mollison, organized a boycott to protest the new law. The boycott failed, but the fact that it was even attempted, in an age where any show of black assertiveness created a risk of violent retaliation by whites, suggests that white support for Jim Crow was not monolithic. In addition, streetcar companies often separated black and white passengers within a single car because they could not afford to provide multiple cars, and in 1905, a white Natchez streetcar passenger complained that she was forced to change seats repeatedly as her car filled with black passengers and the partition between the races was moved. Mississippi's supreme court agreed: it criticized the streetcar law's vague wording, which would lead to "nothing but constant friction," and it urged that fixed partitions be installed in streetcars.[87]

In *Alabama & Vicksburg Railroad Co. v. Morris* (1912), the court again addressed the issue of whether Jim Crow laws applied to interstate railways when a white passenger traveling from Vicksburg to New York complained about the lack of a whites-only sleeping car. On this occasion, the court did not try to avoid the issue of whether Jim Crow laws applied to interstate commerce. Justice Sam Cook, speaking for the court, held that the state's railroad law applied to interstate trains, at least while they were in Mississippi. Cook recognized that his holding went against the prevailing interpretation of *DeCuir*, but he argued that the railroad-car law was "a wise and necessary exercise of the police power of the state for the protection of both races." Cook expressed frustration at the practical difficulties the interstate-intrastate commerce distinction caused: "A riot upon an interstate train growing out of the refusal . . . to recognize a situation known to every Mississippian—black and white—would endanger the lives and disturb the peace of all." The railroad did not ask the US Supreme Court to review the Mississippi Supreme Court's decision, but most state courts viewed *Morris* as an anomaly and continued to hold that segregation laws did not apply to interstate commerce. Nevertheless, segregation became the practical rule for all travel in the South whether or not it involved the crossing of state lines.[88]

Peonage laws. A final controversy of the early Jim Crow era, one that descended from the vagrancy laws of the Restoration era, concerned peonage. Between 1880 and 1905, most Deep South states enacted labor laws designed to control black farm workers. Mississippi enacted three such laws: a 1900 peonage law making it a criminal offense for workers with one-year contracts (the typical length of a tenant-farmer contract) to leave before the end of the contract term for other employment; a companion anti-enticement law penalizing employers who tried to recruit workers already under contract to others; and a toughened 1904 vagrancy law that provided fines and imprisonment for those who led an "idle, immoral or profligate life" and those who had no visible means of support but were able to work.[89]

Critics charged that such statutes improperly injected criminal law into civil contract disputes, that they effectively restored imprisonment for debt—a practice that Mississippi had prohibited since statehood—and that they restored slavery in all but name. Southern courts rejected early legal challenges to such laws, although they agreed that criminal penalties could not be imposed unless a worker willfully or fraudulently breached his contract—for example, by knowing at the time he made it that he would leave before the crop was harvested.[90] A reaction came in 1903 when articles about the misery and abuses that accompanied peonage appeared in the national press, and Thomas Goode Jones, a federal judge and former Alabama governor, openly denounced his state's harsh peonage law in his instructions to a grand jury. In *Clyatt v. United States* (1905), the US Supreme Court, which during that era was generally deferential to Southern race laws, stated in strong terms that Alabama's law violated the Thirteenth Amendment.[91]

Clyatt left open the possibility that deceitful behavior could still be criminalized, and several Deep South states responded by amending their peonage laws to create a rebuttable presumption that workers who left before the end of their contract term did so deceitfully. In other words, the burden would be placed on workers to prove their innocence rather than on the state to prove their bad intent. Southern courts divided over whether the new laws violated workers' constitutional right to due process of law. In *Bailey v. Alabama* (1911), the Supreme Court held that they did, and it issued an unusually direct criticism of the laws as "an instrument of compulsion peculiarly effective as against the poor and the ignorant, its most likely victims."[92]

In 1913, Mississippi's 1900 peonage laws were challenged for the first time and Mississippi's supreme court, mindful of the *Bailey* case, struck them down. The court sympathized with the legislature's desire "to make more stable labor conditions on our Mississippi farms," but it concluded that "[t]o permit an abridgment [of workers' liberty rights] in this instance might lead to a more extended and serious interference" by federal authorities.[93] By contrast, the court made an effort to save the anti-enticement law from constitutional challenge by gradual limitation of its scope. In 1921, the court held that the law applied exclusively to employers who knew their tenants were under contract to another; mere suspicion was not enough to support a conviction. In 1928, the court reaffirmed its holding and warned that a looser interpretation of the law might run afoul of *Bailey*; the following year, it repeated the warning after the legislature tried to extend liability to employers who could have learned of their tenants' prior employment through reasonable inquiry.[94]

Mississippi's early Jim Crow era thus ended with a small victory for those at the bottom of Mississippi's racial and economic hierarchy. The state's straight-out edifice of segregation and racial control remained solid, but it was not legally impregnable. From the beginning of the postwar period, when Mississippi's Restoration leaders had tried to leave antebellum controls intact except for the elimination of slavery and the granting of a small core of rights essential to blacks' survival, Northern public opinion and Congress had made clear that was not enough. Full basic civil and political rights, including the right to vote and participate in government, were also required. Just as antebellum slave owners had permitted slaves certain liberties knowing that Mississippi's slave code, and its harsh controls, was always available for use if needed, so, after Reconstruction ended and the North turned to other matters, the Fourteenth and Fifteenth Amendments and related federal civil rights laws remained in place, always at the ready for use if the Southern racial order drifted too far backward.

The challenge for Mississippi Bourbons and straight-outs was to maximize racial control without running afoul of federal law and arousing Northern anger, and they applied considerable legal ingenuity to that task. The US Supreme Court signaled in *Williams* that the 1890 constitutional convention had succeeded in its effort to effectively eliminate black suffrage, and it signaled in *Plessy* that Jim Crow laws would also pass constitutional muster if equal facilities were provided to both races. But the court studiously avoided any hint of praise for the straight-out legal order in *Williams* and *Plessy.* Instead, it bowed, with a faint air of resignation, to what it saw as the racial realities of the times.

Thus, even in the depths of the Jim Crow era there were some seeds of legal hope for black Mississippians. Federal authorities also insisted, and Mississippi courts and lawmakers recognized, that at least a trace of genuine neutrality must accompany formal neutrality in race laws. The few blacks who could meet suffrage requirements must be allowed to vote; and if black citizens could be segregated from whites, still, the law said they could claim access to the same amenities of civilization that whites enjoyed. Mississippi's Reconstruction era had demonstrated, if only briefly, that law could be a powerful tool for fostering civil, political, and social equality, and the memory of that possibility lingered after Reconstruction's end. These seeds of hope, symbolized by Horatio Simrall's insistence on proper legal form notwithstanding his skepticism about civil rights, as well as by Isaiah Montgomery's example of black success within Mississippi's post-Reconstruction political and business world, would sprout many decades later during a second civil rights revolution.

CHAPTER FIVE

Thresholds of Change: Mississippi Law in the Progressive and New Deal Eras

Every intervention of any consequence by the state and national governments in the economic and social life of the citizens has been so branded [as socialism] . . . We must not permit ourselves to be subjected to the tyranny of symbols. . . . Growth is the life of the law, and when it ceases to grow and keep pace with social and economic needs it becomes a hindrance instead of an aid to the public welfare.
—Justice Sydney Smith (1938)[1]

In many ways, Justices William Anderson and Virgil Griffith exemplified the best of post-Reconstruction Mississippi. Anderson was born during the Civil War, at a time when his planter father was away fighting for the Confederacy; he came of age after Reconstruction but retained an interest in Mississippi history and tradition throughout his life. After his election to the state senate in 1907, he allied with planter and merchant interests in opposing James Vardaman's campaign for the US Senate. Anderson was uncomfortable both with Vardaman's open expressions of racism and with many of his proposed populist reforms, even though Vardaman commanded deep support from the white-belt farmers who made up much of Anderson's Tupelo-area constituency. Governor Edmund Noel, another traditionalist, gave Anderson a temporary appointment to the Mississsippi Supreme Court in 1911; in 1920, Anderson returned to the political field and was elected to a full term on the court, where he served until 1945.[2]

Griffith was younger than Anderson but came from a similar planter background. He was less interested in politics than Anderson, but he excelled at the law. He became a leader of the Biloxi and Gulfport bar, published several books including a treatise on Mississippi equity law that became the standard reference on the subject, and in 1930 he served on a commission tasked with revising the state's legal code. Griffith was appointed a chancery-court judge in 1920 in recognition of his talents and was elevated to the supreme court in 1929, where he served for the next twenty years.[3] Anderson and Griffith resembled Horatio Simrall in their reverence for law as a means of preserving social order and their distaste for the turbulence that attended that order in early twentieth-century Mississippi, although if anyone had compared them to Simrall during the Jim Crow era, it surely would have made them uncomfortable. In the mid-1930s, the tensions between legal ideals and social reality came to the fore when they dissented in two much-publicized and highly important cases, *Brown v. State* (1935) and *Albritton v. City of Winona* (1938).[4]

Brown began on March 30, 1934, when Raymond Stuart, a white planter in Kemper County, was found murdered. Suspicion centered on two of Stuart's black tenants, Ed Brown and Henry Shields, and their neighbor, Arthur "Yank" Ellington. Led by Deputy Sheriff Cliff Dial, a mob of angry whites seized Ellington and conducted a mock hanging in order to get him to confess. When Ellington refused, he was mock-hanged again and whipped before being released. Two days later, Dial arrested Ellington and continued the whipping, telling his victim that he would continue until he obtained a confession. Other deputies arrested Brown and Shields, forced them to strip naked, and whipped them until, in Griffith's words, "confessions had been obtained in the exact form and contents as desired by the mob." The defendants were moved to nearby Meridian for fear of further mob action and District Attorney John Stennis, then at the beginning of a career that would eventually take him to the US Senate, arranged for a quick trial. On April 2, Sheriff J. D. Adcock took formal confessions from the badly injured men; on April 3, they were indicted and had attorneys appointed for them; on April 4, their trial began; and at the end of the following day they were convicted and sentenced to death.[5]

Brown and his co-defendants appealed, arguing that their confessions had been coerced and therefore should not have been admitted at trial. Mississippi's supreme court initially upheld the convictions, reasoning that although the defense lawyers had attempted to prevent the confessions from being introduced at trial, they failed to renew their objection after the confessions were introduced. This was too much for Anderson: he argued that notwithstanding earlier decisions that supported the court's ruling, it was undisputed that the confessions were obtained by brutal means and that without the confessions there could have been no convictions. In such a situation, Anderson argued, an exception should be made to procedural rules in the interest of justice and due process.[6]

Anderson's dissent raised a specter. Two years earlier, black defendants accused of raping two white women near Scottsboro, Alabama, had been subjected to similar threats of violence and to summary trial; their convictions had attracted widespread national attention and criticism and had met reversal at the hands of the US Supreme Court. Anderson's dissent made clear that the *Brown* case could be another Scottsboro debacle, a result that respectable Mississippians dearly wished to avoid. Former governor Earl Brewer, a political ally of Anderson's who had shared his antipathy to Vardaman twenty years before, agreed to take over the defense. Brewer asked the supreme court to reconsider its decision, arguing that the coerced confessions violated federal as well as state law.[7] A majority of the justices adhered to their previous position, but an outraged Griffith now joined Anderson. The trial record, he said, "reads more like pages torn from some mediaeval account than a record . . . of a modern civilization which aspires to an enlightened constitutional government," and the trial "was never anything but a fictitious continuation of the mob which originally instituted and engaged in the admitted tortures."[8]

Griffith and Anderson concluded their dissent on a note of resignation, recognizing that in 1930s Mississippi the law was not yet strong enough to overcome the state's longstanding culture of honor and violence and of distrust of authority. "If mobs and mob methods must be," said Griffith, "it would be better . . . [to] let them finish; and that no court shall . . . cover by the frills and furbelows of a pretended legal trial the body of that which is in fact the product of the mob." Brewer appealed to the US Supreme Court on behalf of his clients, and in 1936, the high court reversed their convictions and condemned the Mississippi proceedings in an opinion that borrowed heavily from Griffith's and Anderson's dissents.[9] Brown, Shields, and Ellington were spared death, but District Attorney Stennis refused to dismiss the charges against them and insisted on new trials. Fearing summary execution at the hands of a mob even if they were acquitted, Brown and his colleagues accepted Stennis's offer of short prison terms and left Mississippi soon after their release. The use of violence and summary prosecutions in defense of the established racial order continued; lynching did not fully end in Mississippi until the late 1950s.[10]

Anderson's and Griffith's opinions in the *Albritton* case were less dramatic but no less important to Mississippi law. During the Depression, Mississippi, like other states and Franklin Roosevelt's administration, looked for new ways to prime its economy, and in 1929–30, Mayor Hugh White of Columbia came up with an idea. Mayor White created a "Balance Agriculture with Industry"

(BAWI) program, under which Columbia offered to construct business facilities free of charge and grant tax exemptions to businesses that would move to the city and guarantee a minimum number of jobs for a certain period of time. The program made Columbus a bright spot in Mississippi's otherwise dismal economic picture, and in 1936, White won the governorship by promising to expand BAWI statewide.[11]

But Governor White faced a problem. Mississippi's constitution explicitly forbade the state and its municipalities from providing financial support to private enterprises and many, including White himself, feared those provisions would doom BAWI. White's lawyers devised a creative solution: when the BAWI law was challenged, they argued that the program's primary purpose was not to subsidize private enterprise but to promote the public welfare. To the surprise of many, Mississippi's supreme court agreed and upheld the BAWI law, bluntly recognizing that in an economic depression practicality must sometimes trump legal niceties. "The due process of law provisions of our constitutions," said Justice Sydney Smith, "do not enact Adam Smith's concept of the negative state," a concept that "has long since been discarded . . . [T]here has been a growing appreciation of public needs and of the necessity of finding ground for a rational compromise between individual rights and public welfare." Law, he said, must be allowed to "adapt[ ] life to the continuous change in social and economic conditions."[12]

This went against Griffith's and Anderson's deep belief that law's primary purpose was to promote predictability and social order. Griffith reluctantly agreed that BAWI promoted the public welfare and thus was constitutional, but he criticized the majority for suggesting that the public-welfare concept opened the door to all forms of government promotion of enterprise. Anderson, who had previously opposed a mortgage moratorium enacted in the depth of the Depression for violating creditors' property rights, was more vehement about BAWI: the majority's rationale, he argued, would allow the state to "take over all property and business of every kind within its boundaries." Mississippi "would be safe not for democracy but for communism . . . This is not a case of stretching the Constitution to meet new conditions, but it is a case of breaking it." This time, however, Griffith and Anderson failed to stem the tide. BAWI became a model for economic development throughout the South and has remained so to this day.[13]

Albritton was the legal pinnacle of Mississippi's involvement in Progressive-era and New Deal reforms. In Mississippi and the South, unlike the rest of the nation, those reform movements and the law they generated were closely tied to the imperative of preserving the existing racial order and carried an agricultural flavor.[14] Northern Progressives focused first on improving government through reforms such as direct primaries, civil-service systems, and lawmaking by popular initiative and referendum; second, on moving from a property-based tax system to a more diversified system reflecting the many new types of property and revenue that the industrial revolution had created; third, on increased government regulation of public utilities; and lastly, on workplace laws including safety laws and minimum-wage and maximum-hours laws for women and children.[15] Good-government reform was also important to Southern states, and workplace laws attracted interest because textile manufacturing, the region's first key industry, was particularly in need of workplace reform. But the traditional property-tax-oriented system still suited Mississippi's agricultural economy, and that economy was not sufficiently advanced to generate a substantial need for regulation of utilities other than railroads. Tax and utility reform would not come until the emergency of the 1930s, which forced Mississippi to leap ahead economically and legally. Despite such reforms, at the end of the New Deal era in 1940 Mississippi's economy and culture remained much the same as they had been at the dawn of the Progressive era.[16]

Mississippi and Southern Progressivism

During the Progressive era, a period spanning the last years of the nineteenth century and the first two decades of the twentieth century, states throughout the nation enacted a broad variety of legal reforms in order to manage their transition to a modern industrial and commercial economy and smooth the rough edges of capitalism. The Progressive movement was both widespread and diffuse. It was at least as much a legal as a social movement: reformers had to design their new laws to withstand the constitutional challenges that seemed to arrive at every turn.

In the early 1870s, US Supreme Court Justices Joseph Bradley and Stephen Field introduced the idea that the federal Fourteenth Amendment, which provided that states could not deprive their citizens of liberty or property without due process of law, protected the right to acquire property without limit and to do business in one's own way, and extended to corporations as well as individuals.[17] Field and Bradley received support from state judges, including Michigan's Thomas Cooley and Iowa's John Dillon, both of whom wrote highly influential decisions and treatises advancing the idea that the core purpose of state and municipal police power—that is, the power to act for the public's safety and welfare—was to preserve citizens' liberty and property.[18] These concepts of due process and the police power were closely related to several other contemporary strands of legal and political thought, including the free-labor doctrine, which viewed industrial relations as a matter of free bargaining between individual workers and employers and viewed all collective action, whether of capital or labor, with suspicion;[19] and the delegation doctrine, which held that all policy decisions must be made by legislators directly and could not be delegated to administrative agencies.[20] Scholars have labeled these doctrines collectively as "substantive due process."

As the nineteenth century drew to a close, regulatory laws and challenges to those laws began to proliferate. Most of the laws survived challenge, but state and federal judges overturned a noticeable number of laws on substantive-due-process grounds. Reformers were increasingly alarmed by the judges' premise that government could only be a source of interference with liberty, not a source of liberty itself, and that judges should approach such laws skeptically rather than defer to legislative judgment.[21]

Both Northern and Southern Progressives made governmental reform a top priority out of desire to reduce the influence of political parties, which were increasingly regarded as obstacles to direct expression of the popular will. They implemented that goal by requiring that party nominations be made by the people through direct primaries rather than by party insiders at conventions. Southerners viewed direct primaries not only as a means of giving white-belt Democrats a larger voice in their party and ending Bourbon dominance but also as a supplement to the disfranchising constitutions of the straight-out era, a means of settling political differences between white factions and ensuring white control of the political process.[22]

Some direct-primary laws took nominations completely out of the hands of parties, providing that primaries would be run and paid for by the state. Mississippi's direct-primary law, championed by future governor Edmund Noel and enacted in 1902, was different: because the Democratic Party was Mississippi's chosen vehicle for preservation of white supremacy, its role as an autonomous organism was preserved. The state prescribed the division of party leadership positions between white-belt and black-belt counties and it supervised elections, but all other aspects of election conduct were left to party officials, who had greater freedom than the state to make regulations excluding blacks from participation. Mississippi's supreme court rejected a challenge to the law based on an argument that it discriminated by making it too difficult for white-belt dissidents to get on the ballot. The court held that aspirants to political office had no constitutional right to a particular nomination process and noted that it was not difficult for primary losers to have their names placed on the ballot as independent candidates.[23]

Mississippi was also an early supporter of two other Progressive direct-government measures: the initiative and the referendum, which allowed voters to enact and repeal statutes independently of the legislature. The initiative-and-referendum movement began in earnest about 1905; it was popular in the West, including Mississippi and the old southwestern states, but less so in the Midwest and Northeast.[24] Mississippi's legislature adopted the initiative and referendum for local measures in 1914. Two years later, voters ratified a constitutional amendment authorizing use of the initiative and referendum for state-wide measures, but in 1922 the supreme court struck down the amendment, holding that it effectively destroyed many of the powers that the constitution vested in Mississippi's governor and legislature. The amendment "gives to the people, and to a very small percent of the people, the right to suspend laws of every kind," said Justice George Ethridge, and that would not do.[25]

Curiously, Mississippi did not join in civil-service reform, the other important good-government movement of the Progressive era. This perhaps was because state and local governments had not yet become major sources of jobs in Mississippi as they were in other states, and because Mississippi society was sufficiently close-knit that a formal, impersonal personnel selection process was not felt to be necessary. Mississippi also returned to an elective judiciary in 1916. That change, like the open primary, was a fulfillment of the straight-outs' "implied pledge . . . that once the Negro was removed from political life the white men would be given more voice in the selection of their rulers."[26]

At the dawn of the Progressive era, Mississippi was one of the most rural, least industrialized American states and it would remain so for another forty years. This, too, affected Mississippi Progressivism. During the Progressive era, many of the more industrialized states supplemented property taxes with corporate, income, and inheritance taxes in recognition of the fact that an increasing portion of American wealth was to be found in wages, dividends, and accumulated corporate and personal assets.[27] Mississippi did not follow suit: tax reform would not come to the state until the financial crisis of the 1930s.[28] Likewise, Mississippi took few steps to increase public utility regulation: in 1900, it already had a relatively strong railroad-commission law, and the legislature extended the commission's powers only modestly during the Progressive era. Gas, electric, and telephone utilities hardly existed outside the larger cities, thus there was little pressure for comprehensive regulation of those utilities until the 1930s.[29]

Two reform areas in which Mississippi was more in the national mainstream were health laws and workplace reform. During the Progressive era, nearly all states enacted a broad variety of public-health laws including pure-food and drug laws, labeling laws requiring disclosure of product ingredients and hazards, licensing requirements for physicians and dentists, and vaccination laws.[30] Public-health laws were a matter of particular urgency in Mississippi: outbreaks of malaria, typhoid, and yellow fever afflicted the state throughout the late nineteenth and early twentieth centuries. Malnutrition and parasite-related diseases were also a serious problem: for example, beginning in 1909 the Rockefeller Foundation launched a major drive to eliminate hookworm disease in Mississippi and other Southern states. Mississippi's legislature created a state department of public health in 1897; initially the legislature provided no funding, but as the Progressive era advanced it gave the department increased power and funds to meet health emergencies as they arose.[31] The 1910 legislature also established purity standards for a wide variety of food products and gave the state chemist broad powers to inspect those products and enforce state standards. Mississippi's new health laws reflected genuine humanitarian concern for poor whites but also a desire to accelerate the state's industrialization process by creating conditions that would attract new business.[32]

Mississippi also participated in the workplace-reform movement despite its comparative lack of industry. Like many other Southern states, Mississippi had tried in the late nineteenth century to take advantage of its cotton production by fostering a local textile industry. By 1900, textile mills were notorious for their employment of large numbers of small children, their long hours and low pay, and their hazardous machinery.[33] Northern philanthropic foundations and unions began investigating conditions in Southern mills at the end of the nineteenth century, but they made little progress until the cause attracted the attention of Edgar Gardner Murphy, an Alabama minister, in 1901. After Murphy failed to persuade Alabama's legislature to enact a child-labor law, he embarked on a regional crusade, adding a Southern twist to arguments for regulating child labor. In addition to being a moral imperative, said Murphy, child-labor laws were needed to protect the rising generations that would be tasked with preserving the Southern social and racial order as the twentieth century progressed.[34]

The movement reached a turning point when the National Child Labor Committee was formed in 1904. Taking note of Murphy's work, the committee formed alliances with clergy in Mississippi and elsewhere. The alliances proved influential with Southern legislators. At the urging of Governor Noel, Mississippi's 1908 legislature enacted a law prohibiting children under age twelve from working in mills or factories and limiting children under sixteen to a ten-hour day. The 1912 and 1914 legislative sessions marked the high point of workplace reform in the state: they prohibited employment of girls younger than fourteen and limited young workers to an eight-hour day and a forty-eight-hour week. Lawmakers also enacted a ten-hour law for all factory work and later extended that law to women working in stores, theatres, clothing stores, and certain other businesses. In response to complaints about employers who withheld wages as a means of controlling their workers, the legislature also enacted a wage-payment law requiring that workers be paid at least twice per month.[35]

The new workplace laws had only limited value in practice. The hours laws did not apply to agriculture and other occupations that collectively accounted for the bulk of Mississippi's work force, and employers could require their employees to opt out of wage-payment laws as a condition of employment. In addition, Mississippi declined to join the workers' compensation movement. During the 1910s, many states abandoned use of tort lawsuits to decide whether workers should be compensated for workplace accidents, an inefficient and unpredictable arrangement for employers and workers alike, in favor of a system that paid predetermined compensation rates based on the severity of injury regardless of whether the employer or the worker was at fault. Mississippi continued to favor the traditional tort-based compensation system; it did not adopt a workers compensation system until 1948, becoming the last American state to do so.[36] Still, the laws of 1912 and 1914 represented an important philosophical advance if nothing else.

American state courts' attitudes toward reform laws and the use of substantive due process varied greatly. During the early Progressive era courts in several states, most notably New York, Ohio, and Illinois, became well known for their propensity to strike down reform laws.[37] Many reformers came to view the judiciary as an obstacle to reform, and in 1912 their anger boiled over; during that year's presidential campaign Theodore Roosevelt, seeking to reclaim the presidency as the Progressive Party's candidate, proposed legislation allowing voters to recall unpopular judges and decisions.[38] Most Americans still believed judicial independence was more important than judicial progressivism and Roosevelt's proposal went nowhere, but judicial attitudes began shifting in many states at about the same time, perhaps partly in response to Progressive complaints. After 1910, many courts deferred to legislative judgments more readily than they had before. In addition, voters in New York and Ohio enacted constitutional amendments designed to overturn some of their courts' most notorious anti-reform decisions, and thereafter their courts put up little resistance to the amendments.[39]

Once again the pattern was different in the South. Reform laws were challenged much less frequently than in other regions, and almost without exception Southern supreme courts gave reform laws a friendly reception and used substantive due process sparingly. In Mississippi the case of *State v. J. J. Newman*

Lumber Co. (1912), in which an employer challenged the state's ten-hour law, provided the leading example.[40] Workplace-hours laws had had a checkered history in other states. In *Ritchie v. People* (1895), the Illinois supreme court had struck down an eight-hour law for women on the ground that the law interfered with employers' and employees' freedom of contract and did not promote health. The US Supreme Court had applied similar reasoning in striking down a New York hours law for bakers in *Lochner v. New York* (1904), but it also upheld a Utah hours law for miners in *Holden v. Hardy* (1898) and an Oregon hours law for women, similar to the law struck down in Illinois, in *Muller v. Oregon* (1908).[41] The fate of Mississippi's hours law thus appeared uncertain, but the *Newman Lumber* court unanimously upheld the law, relying heavily on the *Holden* decision and downplaying *Lochner.* "[W]hen we consider the present manner of laboring . . . [and] the general present day manner of life, which tends to nervousness," said Justice Richard Reed, the hours law "seems to us quite reasonable." When the employer urged that the law violated employees' freedom of contract, Justice Sam Cook noted sarcastically that "it is rare for the seller of labor to appeal to the courts for the preservation of his inalienable rights to labor. This inestimable privilege is generally the object of the buyer's disinterested solicitude."[42]

Newman Lumber was the only substantive-due-process challenge of importance that reached Mississippi's supreme court during the Progressive era, even though decisions in other states cast real doubt on the constitutionality of other Mississippi reform laws. Between 1892 and 1904, several state supreme courts upheld laws requiring regular wage payment,[43] but others struck down such laws for interference with freedom of contract, sometimes using strong condemnatory language.[44] Nevertheless, no employer ever challenged Mississippi's 1912 wage-payment law. Similarly, compulsory vaccination laws attracted frequent challenges and were occasionally struck down as an interference with constitutional liberty rights until the Supreme Court approved such laws in *Jacobson v. Massachusetts* (1905), but Mississippi's law authorizing compulsory vaccination at the county level, enacted five years before *Jacobson*, never elicited a challenge.[45]

Three factors in particular account for the paucity of challenges in Mississippi to Progressive-era reform laws and the Mississippi court's readiness to accept such laws. First, Mississippi did not go as far down the Progressive reform path as did many states. Some of the most controversial measures of the era that ultimately failed the substantive-due-process test, including "yellow-dog" laws that prohibited employers from requiring workers to forego union membership as a condition of employment and laws prescribing minimum wages for women, were never enacted or even proposed in Mississippi.[46] Second, Mississippi's justices took their independence and their duties of statutory review seriously, but the court had a long tradition of deference to the legislature, and the justices were reluctant to strike down laws unless they violated federal or state constitutional provisions beyond doubt.[47] The court struck down only one important Progressive measure, the initiative-and-referendum amendment, and it did so only reluctantly and hesitantly, believing that the amendment threatened to tear down much of the state's constitutional structure. Lastly, the imperative of white racial unity played a real if unstated role in shaping judicial deference. White-belt and black-belt legislators often had different agendas but once reform laws were enacted they represented the collective will of white Mississippi, and judges knew that opposition could harm that expression of unity.

Defending Jim Crow

As the *Brown* case vividly illustrated, racial issues surfaced in their rawest form when Mississippi blacks were charged with crimes against whites. The Fourteenth Amendment guaranteed criminal defendants, including black defendants, the right to due process of law in pre-trial and trial proceedings, and in 1880, the US Supreme Court had held that the amendment barred states from enacting laws that formally excluded blacks from jury service. But the high court had also stated that there was no constitutional right to a racially mixed jury, even in jurisdictions with a majority-black population,[48] and soon afterwards it held that the long-term absence of blacks from juries was not enough to show a government practice of discriminatory exclusion. Defendants who wished to challenge all-white juries had to present direct proof of exclusionary intent, such as admissions by local officials.[49] In *Strauder v. West Virginia* (1880), the court had also indicated that states were free to limit jury eligibility based on illiteracy and other criteria that were racially neutral on their face but targeted blacks in practice. This was an early endorsement of the strategy later used in Mississippi's 1890 constitution to limit black voting, and several Southern states, including Mississippi, were content to confine jury service to eligible voters and let voting laws do the work of excluding blacks from juries.[50]

This tacit legal assurance of all-white juries was not enough to satisfy many white Mississippians that the criminal justice system would do its part in preserving the racial order. They regularly expressed their doubt in in the form of lynchings, an enduring manifestation of the old culture of honor and violence and of hostility to authority. Lynchings had occurred in all regions of America since colonial times, most commonly in frontier areas where court systems were in their infancy and local law enforcement was weak. They acquired an additional racial aspect in the antebellum South: slaves and free blacks accused of murder, rape, and other serious crimes were sometimes tortured and killed by mobs when local mechanisms of formal justice were perceived as working too slowly.[51]

Racial lynchings abated during the Civil War and the Reconstruction years but returned in force during the straight-out era. Mobs bent on reprisal would form suddenly and act swiftly, without heed to legal process; sometimes they would torture and kill their victims, sometimes they were content to whip and beat them. By 1900, lynching of whites and lynchings outside the South had largely come to an end, but in the South lynching remained an important, if not an officially sanctioned, means of vindicating white honor and enforcing racial control. Upper and middle-class Mississippi whites seldom participated in lynchings, but many tolerated and thus enabled them. "Race," said Senator John Sharp Williams, "is greater than law now and then, and protection of women transcends all law." Mississippi led the South and the nation in the number of lynchings between 1882, when the first effort was made to compile statistics, and the end of the pre-modern era in 1945. Lynchings in Mississippi were particularly common during the early years of the straight-out era (1890–1910) and immediately after World War I, when many whites feared that returning black veterans would refuse to settle back into the prevailing racial order.[52]

The culture of honor and violence also played other roles in Mississippi's justice system. For black defendants, arrest usually meant that the local white community had already decided they were guilty. When a defendant refused to accept this informal judgment—for example, by refusing to confess—violent response became acceptable. Deputy Dial's abuse of Brown and his fellow defendants in order to extract confessions was not untypical: instances of whipping and other forms of physical abuse including the "water cure," pouring water down a defendant's nostrils and throat until he nearly drowned, appear regularly in early twentieth-century Mississippi criminal case reports.[53] As Justice Griffith indicated at the close of his dissent in *Brown,* the courts themselves could not escape the effects of lynching. Too often, judges and lawyers overrode even basic considerations of due process in a rush to conviction, not because they believed that was necessary to serve the racial imperative but because they feared that delay would incite the public to push aside legal forms and go to lynching. A too-nice regard for due process would not alter the defendant's fate; it would only provoke further lawlessness and damage the justice system.[54]

But there were countervailing forces as well. For some Mississippians, respectability was as important as the racial imperative. Some prominent citizens and officials, even vocal white supremacists such as James Vardaman,

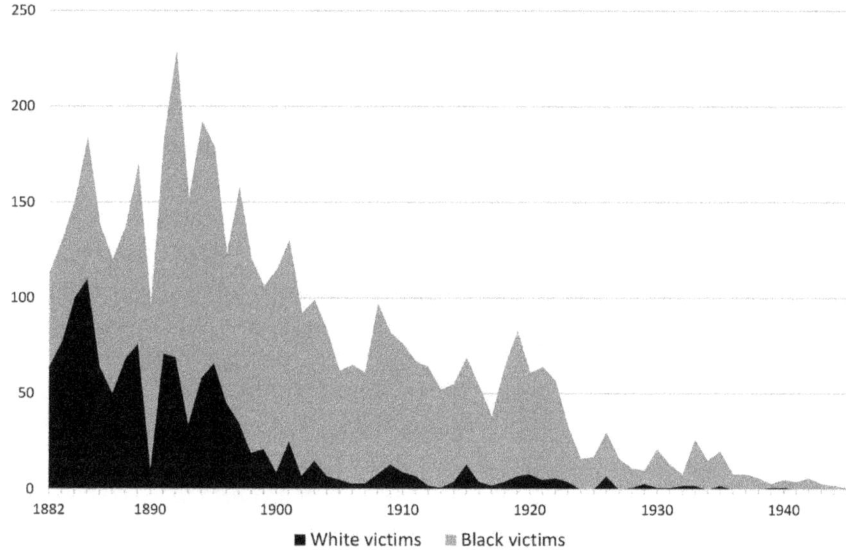

Figure 5.1. Lynchings in the United States, 1882–1945

publicly denounced lynching and did what they could to prevent it. They also wished to avoid Northern attention and criticism and they felt that maintaining legal order and the forms of legal process was the best way to achieve that goal, although, as will be seen, when outside criticism descended, Mississippians were quick to defend their legal system with all its faults rather than engage in self-examination.[55] Mississippi trial judges often required local lawyers to represent indigent black defendants. Some lawyers, fearing ostracism and retaliation by their neighbors and paying clients, did as little as possible, but others, such as Governor Brewer, were impelled by conscience or a sense of social obligation to seek real, not merely formal justice.[56]

Mississippi's supreme court made a genuine effort during the Jim Crow era to preserve a measure of due process for black defendants without defying prevailing white mores too openly. The court consistently overturned convictions in cases where prosecutors openly appealed to jurors' racial prejudices in urging conviction,[57] appealed to the common belief among whites that all black men lusted after white women,[58] or, in one case, introduced evidence that the defendant had a reputation as a "bad negro"—a deadly label in the eyes of most whites.[59] *Brown* was one of many cases in which defendants challenged their convictions based on coerced confessions, and the court had difficulty drawing a clear line between what constituted coercion and what did not. For example, in *Fisher v. State* (1926) it overturned a conviction obtained by use of the "water cure" and by taking the defendant to a tree where other blacks accused of the murder at issue had been lynched—circumstances not dissimilar to those in *Brown*, where a majority of the court refused to overturn the suspect confessions. But in *Perkins v. State* (1931), the court, including Justices Anderson and Griffith, concluded that a confession procured by pistol-whipping a defendant and falsely telling him the confession was needed only to help the victim's family recover on a life insurance policy, was voluntary and admissible.[60] The court went furthest in a black defendant's favor in *Byrd v. State* (1929), where it overturned a murder conviction because it disbelieved the prosecution's white witness and credited other witnesses that vouched for the defendant's good reputation.[61]

In the end, it is questionable whether these holdings made any real difference to black defendants. Often, reversal of a conviction led only to a second trial and a second conviction, with special efforts by police and court officials (now on notice of what had offended the supreme court) to avoid creating grounds for another reversal. Mississippi's supreme court also displayed stubbornness. Outside criticism of Southern legal process touched the justices' sense of honor, and they responded not with violence but with strict application of technical rules. For example, in *Byrd* the court had hinted that it might be willing to overlook formal rules of evidence and procedure, such as deadlines for challenges to coerced confessions, in order to overturn clearly unjust verdicts. But after witnessing Northern denunciation of Alabama's justice system in the Scottsboro cases, the court retreated from *Byrd* and returned to strict enforcement of formal procedural rules in an effort to insulate its decisions from federal review. That stubbornness accounted for its decision in *Brown*.[62]

But the *Brown* court's gambit did not work. The US Supreme Court's reversal of the Mississippi court's decision was one in a series of signals the high court sent Southern courts after 1900 as it grew increasingly impatient with Southern treatment of black criminal defendants. In *Carter v. Texas* (1900), the high court indicated for the first time that evidence of a past pattern of excluding blacks from juries could be used to show present unconstitutional discrimination in jury selection. Thirty years later, in *Norris v. Alabama* (1935), one of the Scottsboro cases, the court took a crucial further step: it created a legal presumption that a historical absence of black jurors proved present-day discrimination, and it placed the burden on Southern officials to show otherwise. After *Norris*, the court accepted an increasing number of jury-selection discrimination cases from Southern state courts and used them show that it was serious about enforcing the *Norris* rule.[63]

Mississippi's turn came in 1947 when Eddie Patton, a black defendant, challenged his murder conviction by an all-white jury in Lauderdale County on the ground that even though one-third of the county's population was black, no blacks had served on a county jury for more than thirty years and no blacks were presently on the jury panel. Mississippi's supreme court rejected Patton's challenge on the ground that only voters were eligible to serve and, thus, the lack of black jurors was due to the state's restrictive voting laws. That did not satisfy the federal high court: "When a jury selection plan, whatever it is, operates in such a way as always to result in the complete and long-continued exclusion of any representative at all from a large group of negroes," said Justice Hugo Black, indictments and convictions by all-white juries "cannot stand."

When the case went back to Mississippi, Patton was again convicted by an all-white jury and his conviction was again upheld, but the state's supreme court adopted a decidedly defensive tone. Speaking for the court, Justice Julian Alexander argued that local officials had "combed the meager roster of qualified Negroes who had since seen fit to register," having been "aroused from a lethargy which had theretofore brought the comfort of an absolution from civil duties." The US Supreme Court decided not to intervene in Patton's case further, and he was executed in early 1950.[64] Southern courts continued to skirmish with the Supreme Court over all-white juries into the 1960s, but Patton's case was the last jury skirmish that took place between the high court and Mississippi.[65]

One other Mississippi jury-selection case involving a black criminal defendant gained national attention. In 1945, Willie McGee of Laurel was charged with raping Willette Hawkins, a white woman. The Mississippi Supreme Court invalidated McGee's first conviction because the trial court had not granted McGee's request for a change of location, and in 1948 it invalidated his second conviction because the state had not shown that the jury-selection process complied with the new *Patton* standard. After McGee was convicted a third time, the Civil Rights Congress, a national civil rights organization, took up his cause, but the supreme court upheld the third conviction. It concluded that serious efforts had now been made to follow the *Patton* standard in the final trial: both the grand jury and petit jury panels had included blacks, although the one black petit-jury panel member was excused at his own request (the court did not address whether he did so because he believed a vote to acquit would have placed him in serious danger). The Congress also argued that McGee and Hawkins had had consensual sex, which the court rejected as a "revolting insinuation." On appeal to the US Supreme Court, the Congress elaborated by suggesting that McGee's conviction should be overturned because Mississippi, due to whites' antipathy to interracial sex, discriminated against blacks in imposing the death penalty in rape cases. But the high court, perhaps cautious because the Congress was perceived as being associated with Communist elements, refused to hear the appeal, and McGee was executed in 1951.[66]

Mississippi defense lawyers who could not obtain relief from the higher courts in controversial cases sometimes appealed for clemency and occasionally obtained it. In the early 1930s, Governor Martin S. Conner commuted death sentences for Tom Carraway of Gulfport and Ervin Pruitt of Meridian to life imprisonment. Carraway's and Pruitt's cases had much in common. Both were highly publicized and highly controversial: Carraway had been convicted of raping a white woman, and Pruitt had been convicted of poisoning a child rumored to be the product of a liaison between him and Luella Williamson, who was also white. The specter of mob violence and lynching hung over both trials, and the evidence against the two men was seriously flawed. Several judges found the women's testimony incredible, and Carraway's conviction was based largely on a deputy sheriff's trial testimony that Carraway had confessed to his crime. In post-trial proceedings, it became clear that the deputy had mischaracterized Carraway's remarks but that William Colmer, the district attorney, had failed to correct him for fear that doing so would incite the courthouse audience to violence and a lynching. Mississippi's supreme court upheld the convictions, but Justice Griffith dissented sharply in both cases, arguing that the women's testimony was too flawed to support conviction and that the majority's decision to uphold Carraway's conviction because he had not followed the proper procedure for making objections at trial was outweighed by the clear miscarriage of justice that had taken place. Both Pruitt and Carraway obtained substantial white support for clemency: in Pruitt's case the prosecuting attorneys, the trial judge, and hundreds of Meridian whites supported his petition to Conner.[67]

Although clemency was available as a tool to check racial injustice, it was seldom used. Black defendants who had been unjustly convicted of capital offenses faced long odds. Unless a defendant had a competent and committed attorney, and unless the injustice was stark enough to convince Mississippi's justices to go against the prevailing racial order and their own tradition of adherence to procedural rules and deference to juries, or to convince the US Supreme Court that the defendant's case was important enough to warrant the high court's time, his only real choice was to resign himself to death.

Minorities at the Bar: A Time of Emergence

Representation in the legal profession is an important tool for any group to have if it wishes to have a voice in shaping its state's legal system. During the early twentieth century, black and female Mississippians began to be heard through the bar, albeit in very different ways.

Reconstruction removed barriers to practicing law as well as many other barriers that black Mississippians had faced. Judges appointed by Governors Alcorn and Ames were receptive to admission of black applicants, and some established white lawyers were willing to instruct promising black candidates in the law. James Piles was the first black lawyer admitted to practice in Mississippi (1869); a handful of additional lawyers were admitted in the early 1870s. Judges became less receptive to black candidates after Reconstruction ended, but throughout the Bourbon era a surprising number of prominent white lawyers, most notably Governor Anselm McLaurin, continued to help black candidates through the admissions process. It is not clear whether they were motivated by a sense of decency and noblesse oblige, a desire to avoid the risk of congressional reaction if blacks were excluded from the Mississippi bar, or both.[68]

There were many limits. Black lawyers were found almost exclusively in the black-belt counties. The few who tried to practice in white-belt counties sometimes met with physical harassment by courtroom crowds, such as having a mix of cayenne pepper and horsehair poured on them that resulted in severe burning and itching. Although some white judges and lawyers treated black lawyers courteously, others flatly refused to allow them to appear in court or resorted to subterfuges, such as rescheduling cases without notice and trying the cases before the black lawyers involved were due to appear. As the straight-out era unfolded, there was a reaction against black lawyers. The general feeling that the 1890 constitution had fixed the permanency of the existing racial order and that federal pressure for equal rights was receding sent a signal to white judges and lawyers that a show of equality was no longer necessary, and most black Mississippians in need of legal services came to believe they would be better off with white lawyers.

Consequently, the number of black lawyers in Mississippi declined during the early twentieth century, but a handful persevered and even thrived, most notably Willis Mollison and Sidney D. Redmond. Mollison specialized in personal-injury cases against the Illinois Central Railroad: he took advantage of white jurors' resentment of the railroad's discriminatory rate practices and other abuses, a resentment which sometimes outweighed racial antipathy toward black plaintiffs, to build a lucrative practice. Like most black lawyers, Mollison felt a deep sense of obligation to the larger black community. He helped lead the 1904 boycott against streetcar segregation in Vicksburg and he occasionally won small victories in the ongoing battle for procedural fairness for black criminal defendants. Mollison eventually moved to Chicago where he built a second and equally successful legal career; but Redmond remained.[69]

Redmond was an extraordinary man whose contributions to black progress have received less attention than they deserve. Born into poverty in Holmes County, he obtained an education and became first a college mathematics instructor, then a physician, and then was admitted to the Mississippi bar about 1910. Redmond was also a canny investor and politician: he became one of the wealthiest Mississippians of either race, and he used his service as a national Republican committeeman for Mississippi to establish a network of powerful connections in Jackson and Washington. Redmond's love of money brought him repeated trouble at the hands of legal authorities: he was disbarred in 1915 for generating litigation in a manner deemed improper by bar officials, was reinstated in 1920, was charged in 1929 with offering to sell federal offices but was acquitted, and was again disbarred in 1930, when it was alleged that he had falsely told a client in an estate proceeding that the chancellor would allow him a $1,000 fee. Mississippi's supreme court reversed the 1930 disbarment proceedings, holding that $1,000 would be a reasonable fee and that there was no conclusive evidence of what Redmond said to his client.

More important, at a time when the NAACP was looking for local lawyers to handle challenges to Southern jury-selection practices and denial of due process to criminal defendants, Redmond was the only lawyer in Mississippi willing to assist the organization. Redmond represented Ervin Pruitt, and his skill in framing Pruitt's case to appeal to the sensibilities of judicial moderates such as Griffith and Anderson and in recruiting white support for Pruitt's clemency petition saved Pruitt's life. Redmond's son, Sidney Revels Redmond, became a prominent St. Louis lawyer; he was one of the lead attorneys in *Missouri ex rel. Gaines v. Canada* (1938), the first case in which the US Supreme Court endorsed the NAACP's position that black facilities must be truly equal to those provided by whites in order to pass constitutional muster. In 1941, while serving as president of the National Bar Association for black lawyers, the younger Redmond urged more black lawyers to take on civil rights cases: "The tide has turned," he urged, and "those who suffer the wrong must surely bring the action and prosecute it vigorously."[70]

Women joined the Mississippi bar for the first time during the Progressive era. Women's struggle to gain the right to practice law had begun in the North half a century earlier, largely as an outgrowth of the civil rights movement that had brought Reconstruction to Mississippi. At the end of the Civil War, women's rights advocates urged Congress to extend full civil rights to women as well as blacks through legislation and the Fourteenth and Fifteenth Amendments, but Congress was not prepared to go that far. Advocates then took the battle to the states, concentrating on voting rights and the right to practice law. Several, most notably Myra Bradwell of Illinois, argued that the

Fourteenth Amendment's guarantee of protection for "privileges or immunities of citizens of the United States" should be interpreted to include women as citizens and to include the right to practice law. The US Supreme Court rejected Bradwell's argument (1873), as did some state courts. But legislatures in several states, including Bradwell's Illinois, responded by enacting statutes authorizing women to practice law, and judicial attitudes gradually softened. Early state court decisions denying women admission to the bar were based largely on traditional cultural views that women's proper role was confined to household management and motherhood and that women were too trusting and delicate to be exposed to the sordid fields of politics and commerce. The traditional stereotype never matched reality, and after 1880 judges steadily abandoned it: most later decisions rejected efforts to exclude women based on their common-law disabilities and on narrow interpretation of state statutes setting bar qualifications, and judges who accepted those arguments were soon overruled by statute.[71]

The historical arc was different for Mississippi women. None applied for admission to the bar in the nineteenth century. Lucy Harrison Greaves, the first to apply, was admitted at Gulfport in 1914, apparently without opposition. The reasons for the late entry of women into the Mississippi bar are obscure. Mississippi's legislature had passed a law in 1898 allowing all "qualified persons" to become lawyers, without mention of sex. In 1904, a bill that would have formally confirmed women's right to practice law had attracted substantial support, and there is no evidence that Mississippi judges would have rejected applications from women if any had been made before 1914. Perhaps the conservative elements in the early Mississippi women's rights movement provide an explanation. Nellie Nugent Somerville and Belle Kearney, the movement's leaders in Mississippi, were part of the second generation of women's suffrage leaders who believed the best path to suffrage was to focus on women's clubs dedicated to civic improvement rather than on direct political action as their predecessors had done; they hoped to persuade men to grant them suffrage through virtuous civic example. Somerville was born into an aristocratic Delta family and was quite comfortable with Mississippi's racial and economic hierarchy; Kearney's primary commitment was to temperance, and she spent much of her time lecturing outside Mississippi. Neither appears to have viewed the establishment of a beachhead in the bar as a matter of importance, and their example perhaps reflected and promoted a more general indifference among Mississippi women.[72]

Once Greaves established a beachhead, other women promptly followed. By 1920, ten women had been admitted to practice in Mississippi. Several came from prominent legal families and may have been motivated by family tradition and upbringing as well as personal desire; some practiced with their husbands, and some did not practice at all. A few took independent paths. Sara Buchanan and Burnita Shelton Matthews moved to Washington as young women and joined, respectively, the US Department of Labor and the National Woman's Party's legal department. Buchanan prepared legal surveys of women's property laws that provided an important catalyst for cleanup of outmoded laws in several states; Matthews prepared and lobbied for laws extending a broad variety of rights to women, and in 1948 she became one of the first female federal judges.

Depression and Mississippi's Little New Deal

Some historians have suggested that the 1930s were a transformative time in Mississippi, that the Depression and the New Deal marked the end of a predominantly agricultural Mississippi led by planters and small-town merchants and the start of a transition to a more economically diversified, more urbanized state that would become part of the Sunbelt South. Others have argued that World War II was the true progenitor of modern Mississippi, and on the whole their case is more persuasive.[73] In 1938, the Roosevelt administration published a *Report on the Economic Conditions of the South* that depicted Mississippi as a poverty-stricken backwater whose culture and economy had changed little since the late nineteenth century, and statistics show that urbanization and economic diversification did not begin in earnest in Mississippi until the 1940s.[74] Nevertheless, the Depression era had a deep and lasting impact. It caused many Americans to accept for the first time the idea that government should have a permanent role in guiding national and state economies, and this was particularly true in Mississippi.

Government achieved its new role in American life during the Depression almost entirely through enactment of laws. Federal laws dominated the process. That was not surprising: individual states lacked sufficient resources to deal with the most severe economic crisis in American history, but the states also played an important role in reform. Farm states, including Mississippi, had suffered through an agricultural slump that began nearly a decade before the stock-market crash of 1929.[75] Most states experimented with emergency relief measures before and just after Franklin Roosevelt took office in 1933, and many enacted state versions of the sweeping economic-relief and social-welfare laws that were the centerpieces of the federal New Deal. As in the Progressive era, many of the new reform laws elicited constitutional challenges, and as a result state judges played an important role in shaping New Deal-era reform just as their predecessors had done during the Progressive era. Mississippi was no exception to this pattern.

One of the earliest symptoms of the Depression was a nationwide wave of bank failures that began in 1930. Bank failures were not a new phenomenon in Mississippi: in the 1840s, the state had endured a wave of failures, repudiation of state banking bonds, and consequent long-term loss of credit following its disastrous early experiments with state support of the Union Bank and Planters Bank. Following a new national wave of bank failures at the turn of the twentieth century, the 1914 legislature created a supervisory banking commission and a modest safety fund to protect customers of insolvent Mississippi banks, but the agricultural slump of the 1920s undermined the effectiveness of the new controls.[76]

By 1932, more than one hundred banks in the state had failed and in response the legislature adopted a reorganization law, known as the "75 Percent Law," similar to those enacted in many other states. The law provided that if three-quarters of all depositors in an insolvent bank agreed to a plan for gradual repayment of their deposits, the bank could reorganize and reopen under close state supervision. The law was challenged as an unconstitutional impairment of depositors' rights to their money, but in 1934 Mississippi's supreme court rejected the challenge, bluntly recognizing that the times called for emergency measures. "[I]n the effort to salvage something in the general wreck of things," said Justice Griffith, "we must not permit ourselves to be maneuvered into positions which would view the federal and state constitutions as sculptured idols, frowning with changeless features upon a changing world."[77]

Mississippi also joined many other states in enacting mortgage-moratorium laws. The agricultural slump of the 1920s had severely weakened farmers' and other landowners' ability to pay off their mortgages, and as the Depression settled in the number of foreclosure proceedings skyrocketed. The low point was reached in 1932, when nearly one-fourth of Mississippi's land area was put up for foreclosure sale in a single day.[78] Far to the north, William Prosser, a University of Minnesota law professor who would later gain fame by reshaping American tort law, devised a strategy that he believed would withstand a substantive-due-process challenge and would give hard-pressed farmers and homeowners time to recover and resume regular mortgage payments. Prosser argued that if a moratorium law recited that the foreclosure crisis was a threat to public safety and welfare, specified that the foreclosure moratorium would terminate at a definite time, and required that the owner pay the bank a reasonable amount during the moratorium period, it should survive court scrutiny. Prosser's strategy worked: Minnesota's moratorium law, which incorporated his suggestions, was upheld by the US Supreme Court in *Blaisdell v. Home*

Building & Loan Association (1933). The high court warned that it would never allow impairment of a creditor's right to be repaid, even in an emergency, but it held that such right could be balanced against the need to "safeguard the economic structure upon which the good of all depends" and it concluded that the Minnesota law's creditor protections satisfied that balance.[79]

Following the *Blaisdell* decision, Mississippi copied Minnesota's example and enacted a moratorium law in 1934. Mississippi's law provided that foreclosures would be suspended for two years, but it required owners to attempt to obtain federal mortgage relief before they could invoke the law's protections and to pay the creditor a reasonable amount during the suspension period. The law also provided that it would expire in May 1936.[80] State moratorium laws were regularly challenged even after *Blaisdell*; some state courts were closely divided over the laws' constitutionality[81] and others struck down laws that provided insufficient creditor protection.[82] Mississippi's court was more deferential: in *Wilson Banking Co. Liquidating Corp. v. Colvard* (1934), it upheld the state's moratorium law even though it conceded that "the act, in some measure, temporarily impairs the obligations of the mortgage contract." *Colvard* pricked Justice Anderson's conservative instincts, and he issued a blistering and somewhat eccentric dissent. Anderson argued that there was no true emergency: Mississippi had weathered economic crises before, and the Depression was as nothing compared to the hardships and iniquities of Reconstruction. That era, said Anderson, had produced "a strong, independent, self-reliant citizenship" and as with slavery, "[t]he people [now] have to pay the penalty for their economic wrongs; there is no help for it." There was a consolation, however: "[t]he South paid the penalty [for slavery], but . . . the people in the long run were benefitted instead of harmed."[83]

Anderson's denunciation notwithstanding, the moratorium law proved popular in Mississippi, and the legislature extended it in 1936 and again in 1938. Creditors challenged the 1938 extension, arguing that even though Mississippi had not regained its pre-Depression level of well-being, the emergency conditions of 1933–34 were now gone. Mississippi's supreme court agreed with their view and struck down the extension.[84] Reaction to moratorium extensions was mixed in other state courts: several agreed with the Mississippi court, but others upheld extensions that lasted into the World War II period.[85]

One of the most fashionable economic doctrines that grew out of the Depression held that overproduction of crops and goods was the main cause of the nation's economic problems. Many federal and state lawmakers believed that centralized management and restriction of competition and production would stabilize prices and would provide greater economic security to farmers and other producers.[86] Mississippi legislators agreed, and in 1931, they joined a movement for a collective Southern agreement to reduce cotton production. Mississippi's 1931 cotton law required the state's farmers to reduce their 1931 cotton acreage by at least 70 percent in subsequent years, to rotate their crops and to plant cover crops in fallow fields. However, the plan was contingent on other states representing 75 percent of all American cotton production agreeing to similar restrictive plans by 1932. That did not come to pass, and Mississippi's cotton law never went into effect.

The 1931 legislature also created an agricultural loan fund, and the 1932 legislature made clear that Mississippi was not ready to give up its cotton economy. Lawmakers proclaimed that cotton "remains [the] only one dependable source of income for Southern farmers" and asked the federal government to promote cotton consumption.[87] In the end, the federal Agricultural Adjustment Act, which paid farmers to take a portion of their land out of production in order to stabilize agricultural markets, proved to be the key to agricultural stabilization in Mississippi until the Act's demise at the hands of the US Supreme Court in 1936. The act benefited primarily large landowners. Very little federal money flowed to small farmers and virtually none to the state's many tenant farmers, an increasing number of whom sought relief by migrating to Northern industrial centers and to the West.[88]

Mississippi was much less engaged with the second major phase of the managed-production movement, namely, the creation of industrial codes restricting competition and unfair trade practices. In 1933, Congress enacted the National Industrial Recovery Act (NIRA), which allowed industries to create their own codes of production and competition under federal supervision. Some states enacted their own versions of the NIRA, but Mississippi did not.[89] Challenges to the NIRA and its state equivalents came quickly. Opponents argued that Congress and state legislatures could not constitutionally delegate regulatory power to the industries being regulated, and that the codes deprived businesses of their property and liberty right to conduct their affairs as they saw fit. In *A. L. A. Schechter Poultry Corp. v. United States* (1935), the US Supreme Court effectively ended NIRA codes when it struck down New York's poultry-industry code and warned that Congress could not delegate code-making to regulated industries.[90] The NIRA's demise made little difference to Mississippi. Industry still accounted for only a small part of the state's economy, and few NIRA codes were enacted in the state.[91]

After the Roosevelt administration completed its enactment of relief laws designed to meet the immediate emergency, it turned to a more ambitious project: putting in place a long-term social support system that would provide citizens with a measure of security in future economic crises. A two-year planning effort resulted in the Social Security Act of 1935, which created the retirement-security system well known to nearly all Americans, and several other important programs: a federal unemployment-compensation program, aid programs for disabled persons and needy children, and support for vocational and family-life education. The act placated fiscal conservatives by providing that the programs would be funded primarily from employer and worker contributions rather than general federal tax revenues. In response to objections that such programs would allow massive federal displacement of state authority over public welfare, the act gave each state an opportunity to take a measure of control over the program. If a state set up its own aid programs that complied with federal guidelines, employers could offset their tax payments to those programs against their federal Social Security tax obligations.[92] Mississippi Governor Martin Conner immediately called a special session of the legislature to take advantage of the Social Security Act, and the legislature promptly created a department of emergency relief tasked with preparing a state social security system and setting up a provisional old-age assistance program.[93]

Mississippi's state program proved to be longer on good intent than on results. It required payment to all citizens sixty-five or older of an amount "sufficient . . . to provide a reasonable subsistence compatible with decency and health," but the program was limited to amounts appropriated by the legislature, which provided no immediate funding. The 1936 legislature revised Mississippi's old-age assistance program to make it more compatible with the Social Security Act and created the state's first unemployment compensation law. It provided, however, that funding for both programs must come from the federal tax-offset system rather than a direct appropriation of state funds.[94]

For good measure, the 1935 and 1936 legislatures authorized Mississippi counties and cities to contribute funds and property where that was necessary to qualify for federally funded relief projects. They also joined the wave of national enthusiasm for public-power projects that was another hallmark of the New Deal: lawmakers authorized municipalities to build and operate power plants and authorized private groups to form electric-power associations. The 1936 legislature also authorized municipalities to form flood control districts in order to take advantage of federal assistance available under a law passed in response to the 1927 Mississippi River flood that had devastated the Delta and other areas along the river.[95]

Like other key New Deal measures, the Social Security Act promptly faced constitutional challenge. Opponents resurrected one of the primary concerns voiced during the act's formulation, arguing that it violated state sovereignty by effectively forcing states to enact their own old-age and unemployment compensation programs under penalty of losing federal tax credits if they did not. The US Supreme Court narrowly rejected this argument by a 5–4 vote in *Steward Machine Co. v. Davis* (1937), and it rejected other constitutional challenges to the act by a wider margin in the companion case of *Carmichael v. Southern Coal & Coke Co.* (1937).[96] Both cases originated in Alabama, whose enthusiasm for federally supported benefit programs mirrored that of Mississippi. Unlike the federal high court, Alabama's supreme court had endorsed the Social Security Act unanimously and without hesitation. When a state-rights challenge to the act's unemployment-compensation program came before Mississippi's supreme court a year later, that court followed suit and summarily rejected the challenge. The court noted that the *Steward* and *Carmichael* cases had effectively decided the matter, but it went further: Justice Ethridge stated bluntly that "the role between the federal and state government is a co-operative plan for dealing with unemployment," a problem "that concerns each government; and . . . one with which neither government alone can deal effectively."[97]

The BAWI program was the capstone of Mississippi's legal response to the Depression, and it remains one of the state's most important and enduring contributions to American law. Although BAWI was genuinely innovative, it had historical antecedents: it represented a new chapter in the state's long and complex relationship with governmental support of private enterprise. In response to the problems created by state support of the Union Bank and the Planters Bank in the 1830s and by state and municipal support of railroad construction after the Civil War, the 1890 convention had inserted sections 183 and 258 in the state's new constitution, explicitly prohibiting the state and its municipalities from supporting or lending their credit to private enterprise.[98] But many local leaders wanted to attract industry to their communities and move Mississippi away from its attachment to cotton. Between 1890 and 1930, they regularly ignored sections 183 and 258 and offered financial inducements to enterprises that showed interest in relocating or starting new plants in their communities.[99] In the 1930s, the tension between desire for economic expansion and fear that government subsidy of expansion efforts would result in disaster remained as strong in Mississippi as it had been a century before.

Mississippi's supreme court had recently given notice that it would enforce section 183 even in the depths of the Depression,[100] and this gave Governor White cause for concern whether the BAWI law would survive in the court's hands. White wanted to frame the issue before the court in terms of the dichotomy between traditional notions of substantive due process, including dissident taxpayers' right not to have to pay for projects of which they did not approve, and the broadened concept of states' police powers which had developed during the Progressive and New Deal eras. He hoped to persuade the court that

Figure 5.2. Advertisement for Balance Agriculture with Industry program, 1936–37. Courtesy of the Archives and Records Services Division, Mississippi Department of Archives and History.

the modern view of police powers, combined with the economic emergency the Depression had brought (which the US Supreme Court had suggested in *Blaisdell* was a factor to be considered in constitutional cases), trumped the restrictions of sections 183 and 258. White also relied heavily on the federal high court's decision in *Green v. Frazier* (1920) upholding as a proper exercise of the police power a North Dakota law authorizing the state to create its own banks and grain elevators, but as things turned out he did not need *Frazier.* In *Albritton*, the court's majority accepted without hesitation his argument that broad police power, coupled with economic emergency, overrode sections 183 and 258. The majority's sweeping pronouncements that individual rights could sometimes be "rational[ly] compromise[d]" in the interest of public welfare, and that law must, above all, keep up with changing social needs, exceeded White's fondest hopes.[101]

Albritton marked a dramatic expansion of the Mississippi court's tradition of legislative deference, and that likely explains the vehemence with which Justice Anderson dissented. Anderson must have felt that his colleagues were departing from the values of Bourbon legal conservatism in which he had been raised, and were opening a new path of legal permissiveness that was uncharted, unchecked, and perilous. But the new path prevailed in Mississippi, at least in the economic-development sector. Twenty-one communities used BAWI to attract new businesses; by far the most notable success was Pascagoula's recruitment of the Ingalls Shipyard Company, which prospered during and after World War II and eventually became the state's largest employer.[102] In 1940, the legislature let BAWI expire, not due to dissatisfaction with the program but based on lawmakers' belief that the shift to a wartime economy made the program unnecessary. But Mississippi did not receive as large a share of federal defense funds during the war years as it had hoped, and in 1944, the legislature reinstated BAWI, which became a permanent centerpiece of the state's economic-development efforts. The BAWI model spread throughout the South and into other states, some of which ignored or overrode existing anti-subsidy laws as had Mississippi.[103]

BAWI has remained controversial. Some critics, most notably W. J. Cash, have contended that BAWI did little to improve the lot of ordinary workers. Mississippi's primary attraction to outside businesses has always been its ability to offer low-wage labor, and communities that used BAWI focused on obtaining job guarantees without addressing minimum wages and working conditions. Other critics have argued that BAWI's expansion throughout the South simply created a situation in which state competition for new businesses led to unduly generous subsidies and concessions which, over the long run, have not been repaid by the benefits those businesses have generated.[104]

Regardless of its ultimate economic value, BAWI in the 1930s was a vivid symbol of larger forces that were starting to take Mississippi in fundamentally new directions. A state long dependent on agriculture and on a single crop, cotton, had supported in a modest way Progressive efforts to shape law to meet the needs of an industrializing society. In New Deal-era Mississippi, lawmakers redoubled their efforts at economic reform and firmly supported the effort to create a structure of laws that would insulate their constituents from distress and want in future. Like other Americans, Mississippians began to accept, with varying degrees of resistance, their new lives under an increasingly national-ized legal system, one that would give government a greater role in those lives than it had ever had before.[105] The old legal world in which Justices Anderson and Griffith had lived was fading, but it was an open question of whether the old world's emphasis on individual rights as a guaranty of order and security would also fade away. That question would shape Mississippi history and law after World War II, and it continues to shape the state's life today.

CHAPTER SIX

Moving Past the Crossroads: Law and Mississippi's Modern Age

We don't need to go back to the old days about voting.
—US Senator John Stennis (1982)

Few Mississippians played a more important role in the changes that swept the state after 1945, and none better exemplified the complexity of those changes, than James P. Coleman. Born in 1914 to a prosperous farm family in Ackerman, Coleman was a member of the rising generation who, Progressive-era reformers like Edgar Gardner Murphy hoped, would improve the lot of white Mississippians while preserving the Jim Crow racial order. Coleman began his career in Washington, where he served as an intern to a Mississippi congressman and became a friendly rival of another ambitious young intern, Lyndon Johnson of Texas. After returning to his home state in 1940, Coleman rose rapidly, serving as a district attorney and circuit judge and briefly as a Mississippi Supreme Court justice before being elected attorney general in 1951.[1]

Tensions were rising in Mississippi when Coleman took office. For fifteen years, the US Supreme Court had enforced its rule requiring that black citizens be given equal accommodations as a condition of segregation with a strictness not previously seen, and now there were signs that federal courts were moving toward outlawing segregation altogether.[2] Some white Mississippians believed their state could best cabin national civil rights sentiment by adopting a new system of "practical segregation" that relaxed the rigidities of the Jim Crow era and accommodated the federal high court's "equal means equal" policy. Others, influenced by the state's culture of honor and violence, chose open defiance and accepted the risks that accompanied that choice.[3]

Coleman began his journey by loyally enforcing the state's segregation laws as its attorney general and resisting the NAACP's call for integration of state colleges. But in May 1954, when the Supreme Court issued its decision in *Brown v. Board of Education* that school segregation was now unconstitutional, Coleman, like other Mississippians, was forced to choose between defiance and accommodation, and he slowly moved toward the latter. When he ran for governor in 1955, he pledged fealty to segregation, but unlike his rivals he refrained from incendiary language, stating that he would "stay[ ] on the job" and would "not keep our schools in a constant uproar while winning this fight." Anti-*Brown* sentiment had not yet reached high tide in Mississippi; Coleman tried to reassure voters that desegregation could be delayed indefinitely, and that was enough to elect him. [4]

Coleman believed in the rule of law but he also continued to believe in the rightness of segregation, and he spent much of his time as governor trying to implement "practical segregation" in his state. In 1956, he signed into law a bill requiring Mississippi officials to "prohibit . . . the implementation of or the compliance with [*Brown*]" and any "mixing or integration of the white and Negro races" by federal officials, but he did so only after the legislature agreed to limit resistance to "constitutional means." When the legislature created a state Sovereignty Commission charged with preserving segregation and investigating its opponents, Coleman approved the law, reasoning that it had passed by a veto-proof majority and that he could control the commission by appointing "sound, stable citizens, and no fire-eaters."[5] In 1958, Coleman approved laws authorizing state investigation of the NAACP and requiring the organization to provide a list of its members to state government, but he vetoed a companion law that required the NAACP to disclose its finances to state officials, and despite substantial white protest he authorized donation of state land to the federal government for construction of an integrated Veterans Administration hospital. Advocates of defiance denounced Coleman as a moderate, and his bid in 1963 for a second term as governor failed in large part because of that label.[6]

In 1964, Judge Ben Cameron, Mississippi's representative on the federal Fifth Circuit Court of Appeals, died and Coleman's old friend and rival Lyndon Johnson, now the president, considered Coleman as a possible replacement. Coleman now had to win over a very different audience than he had as governor. Cameron and Mississippi's federal district judges had been openly critical of *Brown* and had done what they could to slow desegregation. Coleman did not disavow his identity as a Mississippian, but he convinced a skeptical Johnson that he would faithfully enforce the law, including *Brown*'s desegregation mandate, and that his acceptance of the end of the old racial order was genuine.[7]

After Coleman joined the Fifth Circuit, he argued that no lasting racial change could occur unless reformers made an effort to understand white as well as black sensibilities and to address how those might be changed. In the late 1960s, his concerns began to look prescient. When federal courts began to order large-scale student transfers and busing to achieve racial balance more quickly, they tapped new wellsprings of resistance in both North and South. White flight from school districts subject to such orders increased, and beginning in 1974, the Supreme Court slowly retreated from its push for desegregation by any means necessary.[8] Coleman articulated the dilemma when he served on a judicial panel overseeing desegregation of the Jackson public schools. The panel had instructed Jackson's school board to devise a desegregation plan, but by 1969, no plan was imminent. A frustrated Fifth Circuit ordered the board to complete desegregation by the fall of 1970, and an even more frustrated Supreme Court ordered immediate desegregation. Coleman complied: he agreed that segregation "has to be buried," but he warned against "burying the public schools in the same grave through the use of unreasonable and educationally unsound requirements for both black and white."[9]

Coleman's sympathy for tradition also surfaced in legislative reapportionment cases. Mississippi had not reapportioned its legislature since 1890, and by 1965, the state's larger cities and the Gulf Coast region, both of which had grown substantially since World War II, were complaining loudly about underrepresentation. In addition, the US Supreme Court had recently held that the federal Constitution required absolute population equality among legislative districts, and new federal voting-rights laws made black Mississippians a force in the state's electorate for the first time in nearly a century. When the legislature deadlocked over redistricting, the task fell to Coleman and his colleagues; it would occupy them for more than a decade.[10]

Coleman, familiar with the strong role of counties in Mississippi government, wanted to maintain the state's tradition of preserving county lines when drawing district boundaries, but the Supreme Court did not: it insisted on equalized single-member districts, which would allow election of more black legislators. In 1976, Coleman attempted to comply, grumbling that the high court was "revolutionizing" Mississippi government and that a "shift of a few dangling precincts" to achieve a smaller population variation would not affect election outcomes.[11] But the Supreme Court rejected Coleman's new plan. Justice Thurgood Marshall, one of the architects of the NAACP's thirty-year desegregation campaign that had culminated in the *Brown* decision, sharply criticized Coleman and his colleagues for delays which Marshall analogized to the earlier delaying tactics of Coleman's predecessors. In 1978, Mississippi's legislature finally devised an apportionment plan that passed muster under the federal Voting Rights Act, and the Supreme Court, perhaps exhausted after many years of litigation, left the plan in place.[12]

Coleman's personal journey was in many ways emblematic of Mississippi's larger journey through the nation's mid-twentieth-century civil rights revolution and its journey toward the American mainstream in other areas of law. Of course, the journey of black Mississippians was quite different from Coleman's: as Justice Marshall's remarks underscored, they had no doubts about ending the Jim Crow order, even though their efforts subjected them to economic and physical threats that the most ardent white supremacists would never have dreamed of visiting on Coleman. Still, their legal journey matched Coleman's journey in complexity.

Mississippians of both races have also grappled with a host of postwar issues generated by the rise since 1960 of expressive individualism—a new view of liberty as freedom to express one's personality in whatever way one wishes, a view which has competed with more traditional conceptions of liberty as freedom of choice within a finite universe of values deemed tolerable by society at large. Expressive individualism has manifested itself in many forms, most notably efforts to expand the civil rights of women and gay Americans and to subsidize parents who choose private rather than public schools for their children. Other changes driven by expressive individualism, including increased tolerance for gambling, increasing division and dissent within state courts, and a renewed interest in state courts as defenders of rights not adequately protected by federal courts, have been less dramatic but no less important. Mississippians have embraced some of these changes and have rejected others. Their choices have brought Mississippi into the national legal mainstream in many ways, but the state continues to retain many distinctive legal characteristics.

In the Wake of War

World War II was a transformative experience for Mississippi that laid the foundation for many changes to come. The massive industrial expansion required to fill military needs ended the national Depression and, in Mississippi, marked a permanent move toward a more industrial and urban society. Existing industries, most notably Ingalls Shipbuilding, prospered; new industries were quickly built, and Mississippi's per capita income more than doubled during the war years. Mississippians who served in the armed forces were exposed to people, places, and experiences that profoundly changed their views of life; the same was true of those who stayed home and worked in war plants. "Mississippians were introduced to the country and the country discovered Mississippi," historian John Ray Skates observed, "and psychologically things could never be the same."[13]

Longstanding concerns about Mississippi's educational system surfaced at war's end, partly because of an increasing awareness that the state could not prosper without significant educational improvement and partly as a prelude to the racial struggle to come. Efforts to consolidate the state's thousands of rural school districts and to equalize district funding had begun in the Progressive era, but supporters had encountered constitutional obstacles and many parents feared that change would threaten the existing racial and social order.[14] That fear had been reinforced in the 1920s when the NAACP began its sustained attack on segregation. The Supreme Court had held in *Plessy v. Ferguson* (1896) that segregation was constitutional only if black citizens had access to opportunities and facilities equal to those of whites. The NAACP now pressed for true equality, which in the 1920s existed nowhere in the South, as a first step on the road to desegregation. The organization achieved its first major success in 1936 when Maryland's highest court indicated that under *Plessy*, separate-but-equal meant truly equal: states wishing to segregate their universities must provide fully equivalent schools for black students. The US Supreme Court agreed and applied the equal-means-equal doctrine in a series of decisions between 1938 and 1950 involving schools in other Southern states.[15] When the high court agreed to consider a direct challenge to public-school segregation in Kansas and several other states in 1952, many observers believed the *Plessy* era was about to end.[16]

Driven by a desire to make Mississippi educationally competitive and by a hope that the state could forestall desegregation by accepting the equal-means-equal doctrine, the 1952 legislature created a Citizens' Council on Education to devise a reform plan. The council endorsed equal-means-equal in startlingly strong terms and urged increased funding for all schools regardless of race, stating that many rural black schools were in "pathetic and in some cases . . . inexcusable" condition, "not fit for human habitation," and warning that failure to improve them might well tip the judicial balance in favor of desegregation. Hugh White, once again in the governor's office, convened a special session of the legislature in 1953 which adopted nearly all of the council's recommendations and launched a school construction program that continued into the 1960s.[17] In July 1954, White invited black leaders from around the state to a meeting in Jackson, expecting that they would endorse the new program and accept practical segregation. But it was too late: the Supreme Court had decided *Brown* two months before the meeting.[18] A new war (eight years later,

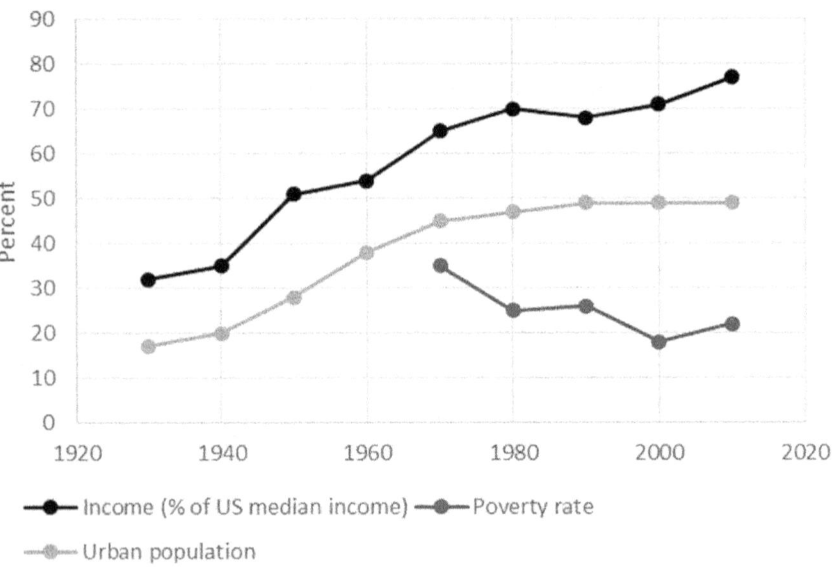

Figure 6.1. Mississippi: Demographic Trends, 1930–2010

the battle over James Meredith's admission to Ole Miss would confirm the accuracy of that term) was about to begin between white southerners and the federal government.

In the Wake of *Brown*

Most white Mississippians viewed *Brown* as an existential threat to their way of life. The legislature expressed its view in 1956 when, like several other Southern states, it enacted an interposition resolution, proclaiming that *Brown* constituted "a deliberate, palpable, and dangerous attempt by the court to usurp the exercise of powers not granted to it." Mississippi, the legislature said, "object[s] to the aforesaid invasion of its rights and does hereby interpose its sovereignty to protect those rights." [19] The Civil War had forever ended secession as a resistance option, but the option of resort to the state's culture of honor and violence and to extralegal self-help remained open. Mississippi lawmakers were not willing to endorse violence, but for the next ten years, Mississippi would be a laboratory for devising legal means to meet the federal threat.

Experimentation began almost immediately after *Brown* was decided. Many whites were prepared to close Mississippi's public schools rather than desegregate them, but jurists objected that that would violate the state constitution, which required maintenance of a public-school system, and courts in other states with similar constitutional provisions agreed.[20] Mississippi voters responded in late 1954 by approving a constitutional amendment that authorized lawmakers to shut down the school system if desegregation appeared imminent. For good measure, the legislature outlawed conspiracies to interfere with segregation laws, and voters who in 1952 had rejected a proposal to toughen voting requirements by adding a clause to the state constitution requiring voters to demonstrate "a reasonable understanding of the duties and obligations of citizenship under a constitutional form of government," now reconsidered and ratified the clause.[21]

Coleman's 1955 election as governor was a temporary victory for moderates, but in the end his record was a checkered one, particularly his acceptance of the Sovereignty Commission and of legislative efforts to intimidate the NAACP. Coleman felt that in light of the times he could do no more than he did to stem the anti-*Brown* tide; still, it is difficult to reconcile that explanation with his treatment of Clennon King. When King sought to enter the University of Mississippi in 1958, Coleman carefully planned King's meeting with registrars to ensure that King would be presented with a set of administrative requirements he could not fulfill, and that his rejection would be handled with a minimum of fuss and publicity. When King objected loudly to his treatment, he was escorted from campus and shortly afterwards was arrested and given a lunacy hearing, likely at Coleman's direction. King was then briefly committed to an asylum and soon left the state. Coleman later said that he offered to let King register but that King had tried to create a scene for publicity purposes. But other accounts suggest that in 1958 Coleman's moderation was far from fully evolved; he was determined to forestall any serious challenge to segregation and a part of him believed that any such challenge by a black Mississippian demonstrated lunacy.[22] In Mississippi, moderation ruled out violence and murder but it did not rule out judicious use of force. That fact was underscored a year later when, after Clyde Kennard attempted to register at Mississippi Southern College and refused to withdraw his application, he was convicted of trumped-up speeding and theft charges which even former segregationists later admitted were "a blemish on Mississippi justice."[23]

Desegregation efforts began in some states shortly after *Brown* was decided but did not begin in Mississippi until 1960 due to the fierceness of white resistance, exemplified by King's and Clennon's fates and constantly demonstrated by white officials, employers, and citizens in everyday life. Obstacles existed even at the judicial level. Reformers expected no help from state courts: they relied on federal law as the basis for their civil rights claims and looked to federal judges for help, but Mississippi's federal judges—including district judges Sidney Mize of Gulfport, William Harold Cox of Jackson and Claude Clayton of Tupelo, as well as Fifth Circuit judge Cameron—had lived their lives in a Jim Crow world and shared their white constituents' aversion to change.[24]

Cameron provided one of the best examples of the depth of Jim Crow sentiment in Mississippi. He was a quiet and studious man, a Republican who had spent his life on the state's political sidelines, but he believed in Mississippi's right to conduct its affairs as it saw fit and he stoutly defended that view after securing appointment to the Fifth Circuit from President Dwight Eisenhower in 1955.[25] Cameron believed that the Jim Crow system benefited both races. In his view, it reduced violence against blacks and fostered "a patient and tolerant attitude toward [racial] differences, and a determination to live and work side by side in the best manner the circumstances would permit." Cameron openly criticized *Brown* and persuaded himself that Mississippi's blacks "resent[ed] the efforts of the agitators who do not understand, to confer a status upon them which is achieved and can be maintained only under the force of the heavy hand of the law."[26] Other Republican judges who secured appointment to the Fifth Circuit under Eisenhower, including Elbert Tuttle and John Minor Wisdom of Georgia and John Brown of Texas, were shaped quite differently by their life experiences and their place in the South's political minority.[27] The duel between Tuttle and his allies and Mississippi's federal judges would shape the course of the civil rights movement in Mississippi and would permanently change the state.

As the modern civil rights struggle began in Mississippi, it moved simultaneously on three fronts: desegregation of public accommodations, public-school desegregation, and voting rights. Activists, led by black Biloxi physician Gilbert Mason, unsuccessfully attempted to desegregate Gulf Coast beaches in 1960. When the federal Department of Justice filed a supporting lawsuit, Judge Mize created an innovative albeit discreditable pattern of delay by setting a very leisurely schedule of hearings and trials and liberally granting postponements at the state's request, a pattern which he and his fellow district judges would repeat in cases to come. State attorneys argued that civil rights laws did not apply because the beaches were private property; in a collateral lawsuit filed by beachfront property owners, Mississippi's supreme court agreed, and after further delays Judge Cox issued a ruling agreeing with the state court. In 1968, the Fifth Circuit overturned Cox's decision, holding that private ownership did not exclude the public from recreational uses. Longstanding use of the beaches before 1960 by whites had created an easement for use available to beachgoers of all races.[28]

Mississippi activists also employed sit-ins, which in other states had proven to be an effective way of gaining publicity and rousing Northern indignation.

Sit-ins were used in a 1961 effort to desegregate Jackson's public library, and Medgar Evers and James Salter used them more extensively as part of a broader effort to desegregate public places in Jackson in 1962–63.[29] Sit-ins followed a fairly uniform pattern: protesters were asked to leave, they refused, the police were called, and the protesters were arrested when they again refused to leave. Many protesters challenged the segregation and breach-of-the-peace laws under which they were arrested as discriminatory, and sit-in litigation eventually proved to be a useful tool in overcoming segregation laws. Several sit-in arrests were upheld by Southern state supreme courts but overturned by the US Supreme Court, which affirmed that segregated-accommodations laws, like school-segregation laws, were unconstitutional. The high court also struck down arrests made under breach-of-the-peace laws in cases where protesters acted peacefully, but it preserved a narrow window of legality for arrests in cases where protesters actively resisted police or created a genuine danger of riot and injury.[30]

The Mississippi sit-ins generated little new law, perhaps because they came into common use only after sit-in litigation was well advanced in other states. Instead, it was the Freedom Rides that led to the demise of Mississippi's segregated-accommodations laws. In the summer of 1961, an integrated group of activists sponsored by the Congress of Racial Equality set off on a bus trip from Washington, DC, to New Orleans to promote desegregation and remind southerners that the Supreme Court had outlawed segregation in interstate transportation well before *Brown*. In Alabama, mobs confronted the riders, inflicted injuries, and burned their bus, eliciting much unfavorable attention in the North and prompting the first important federal military intervention in civil rights affairs since the desegregation of the Little Rock, Arkansas, public schools in 1958. Federal and Mississippi officials then negotiated an arrangement under which the riders would be allowed to travel in peace to Jackson, albeit with the expectation of arrest under state segregation laws when they arrived. Federal authorities would not interfere with the arrests and subsequent legal challenges would then take their course.[31]

The riders' challenge to Mississippi's laws mandating segregated public transportation was heard by a three-judge panel consisting of Judges Mize and Clayton and Fifth Circuit Judge Richard Rives, a Tuttle ally. Mize and Clayton tried a new delaying tactic, voting to postpone any federal decision until Mississippi's supreme court had given an opinion on the segregation law's constitutionality and on whether the arrests were justified as a necessary measure to preserve the peace. Rives denounced their tactic, and the US Supreme Court agreed, stating that Mize's and Clayton's decision was frivolous in light of the riders' well-established constitutional right to integrated travel, and it instructed Mize to grant the riders prompt relief. But Mize held out: when the case was sent back to him, he declared the segregation statute unconstitutional but made clear that he did so only under compulsion by the Fifth Circuit, and he refused to grant an injunction against further discrimination. The Fifth Circuit again overturned his decision and explicitly enjoined any further official action in Mississippi supporting segregation.[32]

Mize also remained obdurate in a companion case. He refused to credit black witnesses' testimony that state officials were continuing to enforce segregation in public transportation; he reasoned that "white" and "colored" signs at the Jackson bus station merely "assist[ed] members of both races who desire to use separate facilities," and insisted that the federal Constitution "does not prohibit a State from permitting, authorizing or encouraging voluntary segregation." The myth that black and white Mississippians alike subscribed to segregation and did not want change remained as strong in Mize's mind as in Cameron's. The Fifth Circuit responded with an extraordinary opinion warning Mississippi judges that its tolerance of delay was at an end. "We again take judicial notice," said Judge Wisdom, "that the State of Mississippi has a steel-hard, inflexible, undeviating official policy of segregation." He dismissed Mize's reasoning as a "disingenuous quibble" and as a "sophisticated circumvention" of the law.[33] Wisdom's opinion ended the legal battle over segregation of public accommodations in Mississippi, but the broader legal battle over segregation was far from over and the battle to change white Mississippians' hearts even less so.

The battle reached a climax when James Meredith, following in Clennon King's footsteps, sought admission to the University of Mississippi in January 1961. State officials responded with a masterwork of delay and evasion, first rejecting Meredith because he had not obtained recommendation letters from Ole Miss alumni and then adopting new rules for transfer students that Meredith could not meet. After his official rejection in May 1961, Meredith filed suit charging that race was the true reason for his rejection. Judge Mize repeatedly delayed proceedings and blocked Meredith's lawyers from questioning university officials before trial about their practices and motives.[34] When an initial hearing finally took place in August 1961, Mize refused to look past the university's stated reasons for Meredith's rejection and questioned without any real basis Meredith's motives and whether he had lied about his place of residence.

On appeal, the Fifth Circuit again gave Mize a dressing-down. It directed him to give Meredith full procedural fairness at trial and it struck down the university's alumni-letter rule, which would have required Meredith to perform the near-impossible task of persuading members of the university's then-all-white alumni body to support his cause in a very public way.[35] Mize delayed the final hearing on Meredith's application until January 1962. He then issued a decision in which he again accepted the university's denial that race played a role in Meredith's rejection, questioned Meredith's honesty, and added for good measure that Meredith was an "unstable," "depressed," and "nervous" person." Mize also took pains to defend the legislature's 1956 interposition resolution, arguing that it was not a gesture of defiance but merely reflected a desire to induce the Supreme Court "by all lawful means" to return to the gold old doctrine of *Plessy*.[36]

In June 1962, the Fifth Circuit again reversed Mize. Judge Wisdom excoriated Mize and university officials, concluding that the trial record revealed "a carefully calculated campaign of delay, harassment, and masterly inactivity," and the circuit ordered that Meredith be admitted to Ole Miss. Wisdom derided Mize's conclusion that despite the university's long history as an all-white institution, it had no segregation policy: "This about-face" in policy, he said, "could have been accomplished only by telepathic communication" among university officials. Wisdom also took offense at Mize's criticism of Meredith: far from being depressed and unstable, said Wisdom, Meredith was "just about the type of Negro who might be expected to crack the racial barrier at the University of Mississippi: a man with a mission and a nervous stomach." Dozier DeVane, a Florida district judge assigned to the appeals panel, took a Colemanesque middle position, affirming that Wisdom's decision was binding but warning that it would likely lead to violence. "Integration," said DeVane, "is not a question that can ever be settled by federal judges. It is an economic, social and religious question and in the end will be amicably settled on this basis."[37]

DeVane's prediction of violence proved accurate. Governor Ross Barnett denounced Wisdom's decision and the Kennedy administration's subsequent announcement that if necessary, it would use troops to enforce the Fifth Circuit's order. Barnett portrayed those acts as the moral equivalent of an invasion; he vowed to resist infringement of Mississippi's sovereignty at all costs, and the legislature promptly passed a resolution endorsing his position. Realizing that he would lose if a confrontation with federal authorities came down to use of force, Barnett quietly discussed with US Attorney General Robert Kennedy a deal that would allow Barnett to make a symbolic show of resistance and then step aside while federal officials enforced Meredith's admission. But at the last minute Barnett, influenced by the adulation he was receiving for his public displays of defiance, backed out. Federal troops then moved in, and in September 1962, Meredith was enrolled at Ole Miss following two days of fighting which resulted in the deaths of two rioters, the wounding of more than one hundred federal troops, and heavy physical damage to the campus.[38]

Meredith's enrollment marked the beginning of a period of recurring racial violence in the Deep South, most dramatically police use of clubs and firehoses on peaceful demonstrators in Birmingham, Alabama, during the summer of 1963 and the subsequent bombing of a black Birmingham church that killed four little girls. Those events, televised to a horrified national audience, led many northerners and some southerners who had formerly been indifferent to segregation to conclude that the time for change had come. Congress then enacted two landmark civil rights laws: the 1964 Civil Rights Act, which outlawed racial discrimination in public accommodations, employment discrimination, and discrimination by institutions receiving federal funding, and the 1965 Voting Rights Act.[39]

The Shaping of Modern Mississippi: Public-School Integration and Voting Rights

Public-school integration. Ten years of white resistance and lack of support for desegregation among Mississippi's federal judges had effectively prevented implementation of *Brown* in the state's public schools, but by 1965, national opinion and the Fifth Circuit would tolerate no further delay. "The time has come for foot-dragging public school boards to move with celerity," said Judge Wisdom. He and his colleagues were willing to allow Mississippi school boards to devise plans that addressed local sensitivities within the bounds of the law, but he warned that if they did not act quickly, the courts would impose their own plans.[40]

Even so, resistance ebbed only slowly. Thousands of white families abandoned public schools in favor of segregated private schools, which by the end of the twentieth century enrolled more than 10 percent of Mississippi pupils, and in 1964, the legislature encouraged them by providing subsidies for private-school students.[41] Many school districts adopted freedom-of-choice plans, a strategy that other Southern states had tried in the late 1950s in the hope of surviving court scrutiny while using tradition and custom to pressure black families to place their children in all-black schools. In 1968, federal district judge William Keady of Greenville upheld one such plan, but the Fifth Circuit, following a policy recently announced by the US Supreme Court in *Green v. County Board of New Kent County* (1968), reversed Keady's decision. Under *Green*, plans that merely permitted desegregation were not sufficient: boards must take positive steps to achieve significant integration.[42]

In *Swann v. Charlotte-Mecklenburg Board of Education* (1971), the high court went further and approved use of several blunt instruments to achieve integration. School boards could bus black and white students to out-of-neighborhood schools to achieve racial balance and they could also design student-assignment policies and gerrymander school-attendance areas to achieve that goal.[43] But busing and erosion of neighborhood schools proved deeply unpopular, and when busing was used to address segregation in Northern cities such as Boston and Denver in the early 1970s, the national political tide began to shift in favor of less drastic remedies. Critics also began to question whether integration was really producing better education for black students. In *Milliken v. Bradley* (1974), the court for the first time slowed the march toward integration, holding that lower courts could not join heavily white suburban districts with heavily black urban districts to achieve racial balance unless the suburban districts had impermissibly discriminated against their own black students.[44]

School desegregation cases in Mississippi followed a similar arc as a new generation of Fifth Circuit judges grappled with the practical difficulties of desegregation. Keady granted the Jackson school board several lengthy extensions of time to develop a workable plan, notwithstanding the Fifth Circuit's warnings that desegregation must proceed promptly. In 1969, Cox approved freedom-of-choice plans for several rural school districts. The Fifth Circuit overturned his decisions and asked the federal Department of Health, Education, and Welfare to develop desegregation plans, but when the department asked the court for additional time to develop plans, the circuit uncharacteristically agreed. The Supreme Court, then at the height of its commitment to compulsory integration, did not agree: in *Alexander v. Holmes County Board of Education* (1970), it instructed the Fifth Circuit to implement full integration without further delay. The circuit then instructed Jackson school officials to complete desegregation in time for the fall 1970 school semester, believing that was the minimum amount of time required to develop a workable plan. The Supreme Court again reversed, making clear that desegregation must be immediate. The circuit complied, but Coleman and his new Mississippi colleague Charles Clark argued that the high court's insistence on immediate action would make a difficult problem worse.[45]

Coleman and Clark's dissents in *Alexander* provided a valuable picture not only of shifting views within the Fifth Circuit but of the new generation of judges who would steer Mississippi through the final phases of its integration process.[46] Coleman and Clark both distanced themselves from the previous judicial generation. They took pains to emphasize that *Brown* was the law of the land and would be faithfully followed, and that they viewed delay not as a means of resisting desegregation but as necessary in order find a way to achieve enduring integration. This was a shift from advocacy of "practical segregation" to a view that might be termed "practical integration," a shift that was crucial if undramatic. Coleman pronounced that segregation "has been legally a corpse for fifteen years [and] . . . has to be buried," but that there were "many ways by which this can be accomplished without burying public schools in the same grave." Clark agreed: he chided the Supreme Court for failing to give more detailed guidance and for failing to recognize that it "need[ed] the willing cooperation of people to make its relief effective." The Supreme Court perhaps began to heed that admonition in *Milliken*, and from the mid-1970s onward, the history of desegregation litigation consisted mainly of incremental court orders carefully tailored to meet local conditions.[47]

Mississippi judges also applied practical-integration principles in other contexts. For example, after white violence broke out in McComb in 1964 in response to a campaign to integrate stores and schools, state and federal officials prosecuted the worst offenders, but nearly all prosecutions resulted in probationary sentences and small fines rather than prison sentences. This echoed the practice that Judge Robert Hill had followed a century before in Reconstruction-era north Mississippi, and to some extent it sprang from the same realities. Convictions were necessary to send a message that integration must be accepted, but imposition of harsh penalties would be too much for local opinion and would result in acquittals and in setbacks for the civil rights cause. Whether practical integrationists were right on this point remains a subject of controversy, as do Judge Hill's actions during Reconstruction.[48]

Voting rights. The 1965 federal Voting Rights Act addressed the South's long history of using the law to suppress black voting. The act prohibited use of educational requirements, literacy tests, "understanding" clauses, and a variety of other restrictive devices enacted by Mississippi and other Southern states during the Jim Crow era. It also prohibited use of racial gerrymandering to reduce the number of black legislators and provided that changes in state voting laws must receive preclearance, that is, advance approval, from the federal Justice Department before they could go into effect.[49] The act took effect soon after the US Supreme Court held in a series of decisions, beginning with *Baker v. Carr* (1962), that the Fourteenth Amendment's equal-protection clause required state and local electoral districts to be equal in population. The *Baker* line of cases overturned a long American tradition of drawing legislative districts to achieve balance between different factions and to ratify the outcomes of battles for power between those factions.[50] Mississippi's 1890 constitutional convention had forged an elaborate representational balance between black-belt and white-belt Mississippians, one in which black Mississippians were not allowed a voice. The 1890 apportionment had never been changed, but *Baker* and the 1965 act spelled its end.

Voting rights became an important part of the civil rights movement in Mississippi, and white resistance to change was fierce. In 1961, a Walthall County registration clerk attacked activist John Hardy as he attempted to register local black voters; Hardy was then arrested for breach of the peace. The Department of Justice tried to halt his prosecution on the ground that its only purpose was to dissuade blacks from voting. Judge Mize denied the department a temporary injunction but the Fifth Circuit once again reversed his decision, eliciting a sharp exchange between Judges Wisdom and Cameron. Wisdom described recalcitrant local officials as "political termite[s]" who would destroy the basic foundations of democratic government if not stopped; Cameron denounced federal interference with Mississippi's affairs and criticized Hardy as "a person of palpable irresponsibility who had come from a distant point . . . to stir up mistrust between the races."[51]

White Mississippians, then in the throes of resistance to the Fifth Circuit's orders to admit James Meredith to the University of Mississippi, were equally resistant to the circuit's voting-rights admonition. In 1960, they approved an amendment to the state constitution requiring that voters be "of good moral character," and in 1962, the legislature gave voting officials authority to enforce that provision and prohibited voters from receiving help in casting their ballots.[52] In 1964, Cameron and Cox[53] rejected a challenge to Mississippi's literacy and "good character" requirements for suffrage, but the Supreme Court summarily reversed their decision.[54] After the 1965 act went into effect, state officials recognized that further resistance to voting-rights reform was futile. Governor Paul Johnson, Barnett's successor, adopted a conciliatory tone and called the legislature into special session to approve removal of provisions in the 1890 constitution that violated the 1965 act. Voters reluctantly went along and by the end of 1965, Mississippi required only that voters be literate and that they fill out a basic informational questionnaire and take a simple oath of allegiance. By 1967, 60 percent of adult blacks were registered to vote in Mississippi. Black Mississippians had re-emerged as a political force after nearly a century in the depths.[55]

Devising a new legislative apportionment that would simultaneously meet the demands of federal law, of underrepresented urban and Gulf Coast voters and of newly empowered black voters posed a difficult and perplexing challenge.[56] Apportionment became a continuing struggle for the legislature and the federal courts, one which made Mississippi "a crucible in which modern federal voting rights law was largely forged."[57] In late 1965, Peggy Connor, one of the leaders of the new Mississippi Freedom Democratic Party, filed a lawsuit seeking an apportionment that would give black Mississippians a chance to elect legislators proportional to their numbers. Connor's lawsuit would unfold over fourteen years, underscoring the difficulty of the apportionment problem. After much prodding by a Coleman-led federal judicial panel, the 1967 legislature enacted an apportionment plan, but it failed judicial inspection because the population variation between districts was too great. Coleman and his colleagues then devised their own plan but frankly admitted that achieving both population equality and racial equity was difficult. Ever solicitous of local sensibilities, Coleman invited the legislature to try again; he and his colleagues disclaimed any desire to become state's arbiter of apportionment, but in the end that is exactly what happened.[58]

After the 1970 census indicated that a new apportionment was necessary, the legislature proposed a plan that did not meet the equal-population requirement, and Coleman's panel again was forced to step into the breach. The panel's plan featured multi-county, multi-member districts based on Coleman's desire to preserve Mississippi's tradition of districting by counties. Connor complained that the multi-member plan impermissibly diluted black voting strength, and the US Supreme Court agreed. A judicial duel ensued: the high court continued to insist on single-member districts and the Coleman panel gradually reduced the number of multi-member districts while continuing to maintain that a perfect single-member plan was impossible. In 1977, the high court rejected the panel's final plan and curtly told the panel that a fully compliant plan must be put in place immediately. Coleman threw up his hands and put pressure on the legislature, which finally produced a plan that gained federal approval and resulted in the election of seventeen black legislators in 1978.[59]

Coleman and Clark disliked not only the high court's insistence on single-member districts but also the 1965 act's federal preclearance requirement. At one point, the normally urbane Clark denounced preclearance as an unconstitutional interference with state sovereignty, even though the Supreme Court had upheld the requirement five years earlier. Clark charged that the requirement hearkened back to the "vicious" days of Reconstruction; he complained about "Mississippi's humiliation in bringing its laws to Washington for bureaucratic approval," and added that if that were not enough, the Justice Department's delays in granting preclearance were heaping "additional coals of discord . . . upon the head of an already strained federalism."[60]

Apportionment was particularly sensitive because it involved a crucial point of tension between white and black Democrats. During the late 1960s and the 1970s, Mississippi's Democratic Party transformed itself from a chosen vehicle of white supremacy into a biracial coalition, but at the same time white conservatives started to migrate to the Republican Party. White Democrats believed that their party's best chance of holding on to power was through "impact" districts containing blacks in numbers less than a majority but large enough to tip the districts' balance in favor of Democrats. They viewed the impact-district model as the most important product of a golden age of racial harmony and moderate social progressivism. But impact districts produced few black officeholders, and as Peggy Connor's lawsuit illustrated, many of the coalition's black members came to see the model as an obstacle to black empowerment and self-determination.[61]

The wave of black legislators elected in 1978 represented an important turning point; another came when Mississippi's five congressional districts were reapportioned after the 1980 census. Previously the districts had been drawn east-to-west on the "impact" plan, but now many black voters, supported by Republicans, pushed for a majority-black district that would virtually guarantee election of a black congressman but would imperil white Democratic incumbents in other districts. The legislature deadlocked and the issue went to a new federal panel headed by Judge Clark, which concluded that the 1965 act's goals could best be achieved through creation of a majority-black Delta district. In 1986, the new district elected Mike Espy, Mississippi's first black congressman since Reconstruction, amid a steady decline in the overall number of Democratic officeholders.[62] Republicans won the governorship for the first time since Reconstruction in 1991, gained a majority of the state's congressional delegation for the first time in 1994, and gained full control of the state legislature in 2012. The biracial Democratic coalition survives, but in a weakened condition, and it is not clear when, or if, it will regain power.[63]

Mississippi has continued to struggle with apportionment. The legislature was able to reapportion itself and the state's congressional districts after the 1990 census without court intervention, but it deadlocked after the 2000 and 2010 censuses and new apportionments were made by new federal judicial panels. A state district court attempted to take control of redistricting in 2002 but was rebuffed by Mississippi's supreme court, which held that only the legislature or federal courts could perform that task. "Mississippi too often defaults in meeting its responsibilities as a state," lamented Justice William Waller. "We wait for the federal government and the federal courts to intervene for us and then we complain about the loss of our state's rights." But Waller recognized that unless the legislature could free itself from deadlock, federal officials would continue to dictate apportionment in Mississippi.[64]

Mississippi in the Age of Expressive Individualism

Expressive individualism is one of the central threads of modern American law, a notion of liberty as encompassing the right to express one's beliefs and personality virtually without limit. It was an important force behind the mid-twentieth-century civil rights movement and it has played a part in many American social movements that have taken place since that time. But it has also had a more somber side, contributing to the increasing economic and social polarity that has marked American society since the early 1980s. Many Americans have turned away from communal forms of activity and have spent increasing amounts of time alone or interacting with small groups of like-minded people. Factors contributing to expressive individualism and polarization include rising distrust of government, the transition from an economy dominated by large corporations and unions to one that is more flexible but less secure, and a technological revolution that has encouraged Americans to communicate remotely.[65]

Expressive individualism has also provoked a powerful backlash fueled by a desire for clear, universal codes of morality and by a deep skepticism about the value of recent social changes. The clash between these forces has deeply influenced American law's evolution during the past half century and continues to do so today.[66] Mississippi has traveled a long path from near-complete denial to near-full acceptance of its black citizens' rights of expression and fulfillment, and in that sense it might be considered an exemplar of expressive individualism. But Mississippians of both races remain culturally conservative in many respects and have resisted the advance of expressive individualism on other legal fronts.

The decline of assimilationist values in education. White Mississippians' use of private schools to avoid desegregation was a setback for the tradition of using public schools as a vehicle for cultural assimilation, for instilling in children of all backgrounds a common set of American ideals and values. That tradition, long supported by old-stock Americans, had been challenged intermittently since the mid-nineteenth century by Catholic parents and others who wanted separate schools in which they could pass their own religious and cultural values to their children, but the Southern reaction to *Brown*'s desegregation mandate added a new aspect to the conflict.[67]

The federal courts overturned the 1964 legislature's effort to provide private-school funding as a means of resisting desegregation, and that failure permanently dampened enthusiasm for large-scale state funding of private schools.[68] Private schools never seriously threatened to displace Mississippi's public-school system; most parents kept their children in public schools, usually because they could not afford private-school fees. By the end of the 1970s, Mississippians were more concerned with the low overall quality of their schools than with the comparative merits of public and private schools. In 1980, Governor William Winter launched a campaign to toughen the state's school attendance laws and to create a universal kindergarten system: at that time, Mississippi was the only state that did not require its children to attend kindergarten. After much infighting, the legislature enacted most features of Winter's reform package in a 1982 special session and increased educational funding significantly.[69]

At the same time, as the practical difficulties of desegregating public schools became apparent and support for compulsory school integration eroded throughout the United States, the idea of voucher programs—state grants that parents of schoolchildren could use to pay for private schools—gained popularity. Wisconsin (1990) and Ohio (1995) enacted the first voucher laws, applying to troubled school districts in Milwaukee and Cleveland, respectively.[70] Assimilationists challenged the laws on numerous state and federal constitutional grounds, primarily that voucher systems violated constitutional clauses requiring states to maintain common-school systems and prohibiting support of sectarian schools. Early challenges failed, and after the US Supreme Court upheld Ohio's voucher law in 2002, a steady stream of states enacted voucher laws.[71] The clash over vouchers has largely bypassed Mississippi, likely because the state conducted its debate over government's role in supporting private schools before the voucher movement began to gain support. Between 2012 and 2015, Mississippi's legislature approved several small voucher programs for students with disabilities who wished to attend private schools with treatment programs, but it made no effort to enact a more general voucher program.[72] The state's focus continues to be on its public schools, not the creation of an alternative to the public schools.

Gambling. During the late 1980s and early 1990s, many states, including Mississippi, greatly expanded legalized gambling, That movement was made possible in part because expressive individualism had removed much of the stigma from gambling, treating it as a lifestyle choice rather than a moral issue. During the nation's early years, Mississippians and other southerners had viewed gambling as a threat to individual and societal salvation. Mississippi attempted to regulate gambling from its earliest days: Sargent's Code prohibited tavern keepers from "suffer[ing] . . . any unlawful games whatever," and the state's 1822 legal code contained extensive limitations on gambling. But human desire to take risk in the hope of gain was strong, and it fit snugly into the Southern culture of honor. Mississippi officials, like their counterparts in most other states, turned a blind eye to violations of the laws if the violators were discreet, but anti-gambling laws remained on the books.[73]

By the late 1980s, Mississippi, like many states, was looking for new sources of revenue in the wake of rising anti-tax sentiment, and it turned to legalized gambling as a solution. In 1985, the Gulf Coast business community experimented with "cruises to nowhere," excursions by casino boats into off-shore waters where it was thought Mississippi's anti-gambling laws did not apply. In 1989, the legislature legalized the cruises over objections by religious-minded lawmakers, and during the 1990s, it also legalized dockside gambling and riverboat casinos. Mississippi was in good company: between 1980 and 1995, nearly every state adjoining the Mississippi River legalized riverboat gambling, and many states moved rapidly from outright prohibition of gambling to legalization of lotteries, horse racing, and various other forms of gaming. In 1988, Congress passed the Indian Gaming Regulatory Act, which gave rise to tribal casinos throughout the nation, including two in Mississippi.[74]

During the period of expansion, many states legalized lotteries but not casinos, perhaps because casinos had a faint historical odor of seediness and disrepute that state-run lottery games do not. Mississippi followed an opposite course, for constitutional rather than cultural reasons. In 1990, Governor Ray Mabus proposed a lottery to provide funding for the educational reforms the legislature had instituted a decade earlier, but he faced an obstacle: a lottery could only be created through a constitutional amendment. The 1890 constitution made that process difficult: the legislature must first approve an amendment, voters must then approve it in a referendum, and if the amendment affected state revenues (as a lottery amendment would), the legislature must then enact an implementing bill by a three-fifths majority.[75]

Mabus persuaded the 1992 legislature to approve a lottery amendment and voters narrowly approved the amendment after an intense campaign, but supporters were never able to assemble the legislative supermajority needed for implementation.[76] As the lottery debate raged in 1990–91, pro-casino business groups in the Delta and on the Gulf Coast quietly obtained passage of a bill permanently legalizing casinos. They carefully avoided discussion of the moral aspects of casinos and presented the bill as a means of creating badly needed businesses and jobs. To date, Mississippi's casinos, though closely regulated, have fended off efforts to repeal the law. The appeal of gambling as a means of personal expression and fulfillment has proven stronger than religious scruples. In 1990, the supreme court created a narrow window of opportunity for bingo games by holding that they did not fall within the constitution's anti-lottery clause, but casinos remain Mississippi's gaming recreation of choice.[77]

Gay rights and gay marriage. The change of popular attitudes toward the rights of gay and lesbian Americans, particularly their right to marry, may be the most dramatic example of expressive individualism's modern ascendance. The gay-rights movement began in earnest in the early 1970s. Activists first focused on prohibiting employment discrimination based on sexual orientation; by 2010, thirty-one states had enacted laws or published executive orders against discrimination, but Mississippi was not among them.[78]

After an unsuccessful effort in the early 1970s to persuade several state courts to legalize gay marriage, activists renewed their campaign in the early 1990s. They gained their first success in Hawaii, whose supreme court held in 1993 that the state's equal-protection clause supported their position, but Hawaii voters promptly enacted a defense-of-marriage (DOMA) amendment to the state constitution that nullified the court's decision and limited marriage to heterosexual couples.[79] The campaign then moved to New England and quickly gained ground. Vermont's supreme court held in 1999 that its state constitution mandated that gay couples be allowed to form civil unions comprising the same legal rights given to married couples, although it did not give them the right to label such unions as marriage. In 2003, Massachusetts's supreme court held that its state constitution extended full marriage rights to gay couples.[80] Between 2003 and 2010 several other New England and mid-Atlantic state courts extended civil unions or full marriage rights to gay couples, as did California and Iowa.[81]

But other courts refused to do so, and there was a broader backlash. In 1996, Mississippi Governor Kirk Fordice issued an executive order prohibiting recognition of gay marriages, and the following year the legislature enacted a similar statute. The early court decisions in favor of gay marriage also prompted more than half the states, including Mississippi (2004), to enact DOMAs. Mississippi's DOMA was comparatively narrow in scope: it applied only to marriage, whereas other DOMAs also prohibited civil unions and other relationships comprising marital rights.[82]

A turning point came in 2010, when activists turned to the federal courts. After a nationally publicized trial in which gay-marriage opponents attempted to prove their contention that laws prohibiting gay marriage were a legitimate exercise of the police power because they promoted procreation and children's welfare, California federal district judge Vaughn Walker ruled in *Perry v. Schwarzenegger* (2010) that opponents had not made their case and that California's DOMA violated the federal equal-protection clause.[83] During the next five years, federal courts in numerous states followed Walker's ruling. Only the South held out, and even there courts were divided: federal judges in North Carolina and Florida agreed with Walker, but judges in Louisiana and Alabama rejected his decision in strongly worded opinions.[84]

Mississippi's turn came in 2014. In *Campaign for Southern Equality v Bryant*, Judge Carlton Reeves agreed with Walker and invalidated Mississippi's DOMA. Reeves, knowing that his opinion would be unpopular, went out of his way to explain himself to fellow Mississippians. "[T]he 86% of Mississippians who voted against same-sex marriage in 2004," he said, "did [not do] so with malice, bigotry, or hatred in their hearts. Many were simply trying to preserve their view of what a marriage should be, whether by religion or tradition." Reeves then explained at length why he believed Walker's reasoning was constitutionally sound. State officials appealed Reeves's decision but shortly before the appeal was decided, the Supreme Court held by a 5–4 vote in *Obergefell v. Hodges* (2015) that gay couples had a constitutional right to marry, thus ending the legal battle.[85] Dissenting judges at all levels have argued that gay marriage cannot endure unless it is endorsed by the people as well as by their judges, but polls indicate that popular as well as judicial opinion has swung in favor of gay marriage, and that may also be true in Mississippi. The massive reaction and resistance that swept the state in the wake of *Brown* did not recur after the *Southern Equality* and *Obergefell* decisions, even though in their own way those decisions were as revolutionary as *Brown*.[86]

Women's rights. The rise of expressive individualism was closely linked to a phase of the women's rights movement that began in the mid-1960s. The modern era of the movement had begun in 1920, immediately after ratification of the federal Nineteenth Amendment giving women the right to vote. Suffragists, speaking through the National Woman's Party (NWP), launched a campaign for an Equal Rights Amendment (ERA) that would guarantee women full civil rights much as the Fourteenth Amendment had done for black males. The NWP also worked to eliminate remaining restrictions on women's rights at the state level, such as restrictions on jury service. In 1921, Wisconsin's legislature enacted a broad equal-rights law eliminating nearly all such restrictions and granting women legal equality "in all other respects." The NWP used the Wisconsin law as a model and lobbied other states to adopt it.[87]

The NWP took its campaign to Mississippi in 1922, but met with little success. Mississippi had a long tradition of liberality as to women's rights in the private sphere, exemplified by the state's 1839 married women's property law (1839), but lawmakers were considerably less inclined to extend rights in the public sphere. This was due partly to certain conservative strains in the state's culture and partly to differences of opinion among women in Mississippi and throughout the United States. Many women feared that further expansion of their legal rights would result in the elimination of legal privileges they had previously enjoyed, such as dower rights and exemption from military and jury service. In the end, Mississippi's 1922 legislature expanded women's right to claim custody of their children and a share of children's earnings but would go no further.[88]

From the 1930s to the early 1960s, there was little advance in women's legal rights in Mississippi or elsewhere. Social pressure for further change began to build after World War II. Wartime labor shortages had impelled millions of women to work outside the home for the first time; many remained in the workforce after the war, and complaints about employment discrimination grew. Rising postwar divorce rates also led women to question whether they received fair treatment under existing divorce laws. In the early 1960s, the federal government and many states, including Mississippi, created commissions on the status of women. Some state commissions advocated sweeping expansion of rights but Mississippi's commission took a conservative tack, recommending only elimination of restrictions on jury service and modest employment-practices reforms. After Mississippi's supreme court declined to strike down jury-service restrictions as violative of constitutional equal-protection rights, the legislature eliminated all restrictions in 1968.[89]

In the early 1970s, several feminist groups resurrected the ERA, and in 1972, Congress approved it and sent it to the states for ratification. The new ERA movement elicited a powerful reaction from traditionalist women who believed that equal-rights feminists were denigrating the value of work in the home and motherhood, activities central to their identity and sense of self-worth. Like their predecessors in the 1920s, traditionalists feared that the ERA would result in the loss of legal privileges and exemptions they had enjoyed. Traditionalist leaders, most notably Phyllis Schlafly, organized lobbying efforts against ERA. The contest in Mississippi was not close: the legislature never even voted on the proposed amendment, and in the end ERA fell just short of securing the thirty-eight states needed for ratification. The ERA's failure in Mississippi perhaps was due to residual conservative hostility to the desegregation movement as well as Mississippi traditions of cultural conservatism. The federal 1964 Civil Rights Act, which was at the center of the desegregation movement, included pioneering provisions against gender discrimination which received increasing attention as the 1960s phase of the women's movement went forward;[90] and in Mississippi the anti-ERA movement operated chiefly through Women for Constitutional Government (WCG), which had arisen in the mid-1960s to sustain the fight against desegregation and federal incursion into Mississippi. Racial overtones aside, the failure of ERA sent a strong message that traditional feminine roles and legal privileges have enduring value to many Mississippians and likely will continue to influence the course of women's rights in the state.[91]

Abortion rights. Abortion rights have given rise to one of the most intense social conflicts of the late twentieth and early twenty-first centuries, in large part because they provide an unusually stark example of the gulf between supporters and opponents of expressive individualism. Abortion-rights supporters focus on a woman's right to choose whether motherhood will be a part of her life; opponents believe that by conceiving, a woman cedes her individual interest and assumes a societal duty to care for a new member of a larger community.[92] In the late nineteenth century, many states, including Mississippi, outlawed abortion except when necessary to protect the mother's life. Some states relaxed their abortion laws after World War II, but with *Roe v. Wade* (1973), the US Supreme Court gave abortion rights constitutional status for the first time. The high court balanced women's constitutional right to liberty and privacy against societal interests in preserving life by holding that during the first trimester of pregnancy, states could not interfere with the choice to have an abortion; from the end of the first trimester until quickening, states could regulate abortion but only to protect maternal health; and from that point until birth, states could regulate abortion in order to protect "potential life." [93]

Abortion opponents then launched a dual campaign: they attempted to overturn *Roe* through new appointments to the Supreme Court, and they went to state legislatures seeking passage of a variety of laws that would cabin abortion at the state level.[94] In 1986, Mississippi's legislature required that minors obtain parental consent for an abortion except in case of medical emergency, and in 1991, it established a twenty-four-hour waiting period and enacted an informed-consent law requiring physicians to provide women with information about possible adverse medical consequences and alternatives to abortion. A Mississippi federal district judge indicated that the 1991 law might violate *Roe*, but while his decision was on appeal the Supreme Court decided *Planned Parenthood of Southeastern Pennsylvania v. Casey* (1992). In *Casey*, the high court declined to overturn *Roe* but did revise *Roe*'s three-part test, holding that states could not impose an "undue burden" on the right to an abortion but that not all laws making abortion more difficult would be deemed an undue burden. [95]

The *Casey* court indicated that reasonable informed-consent and waiting-period requirements would pass constitutional muster, and in *Barnes v. Moore* (1992), the Fifth Circuit upheld Mississippi's requirements in reliance on *Casey*.[96] In 1998, a divided Mississippi Supreme Court rejected challenges to the law's waiting-period and parental-consent provisions under the state constitution. Mississippi's justices also relied heavily on *Casey*, although they concluded that Mississippi's constitution created a right to privacy separate from the federal right that *Roe* had recognized. Three dissenting justices argued that the waiting-period requirement effectively denied rural Mississippi women access to abortion because the state had only two abortion clinics; two other justices argued that there was no state constitutional right of privacy.[97]

After *Casey*, abortion opponents dropped active efforts to overturn *Roe* and expanded their campaign for restrictive state laws. Although many polls show that a majority of Americans support access to abortion in principle, opponents' fervor for their cause has won them success out of proportion to their numbers, particularly since 2010.[98] The most common restrictive laws have included: (i) informed-consent laws such as Mississippi's 1986 law; (ii) waiting-period laws such as Mississippi's 1991 law; (iii) targeted regulation-of-abortion-provider (TRAP) laws that require doctors who perform abortions to have admitting privileges at a nearby hospital or require abortion clinics to have facilities and staff equivalent to a full-service surgical center; (iv) laws prohibiting use of federal and state funds to pay for abortions; and (v) laws testing the limits of *Roe* by prohibiting all abortions after a period of time close to (and sometimes before) the end of the first trimester.[99] The laws in each category have elicited numerous challenges under state and federal constitutions, with mixed results.[100]

Mississippi generally has been in the mainstream of the abortion-restriction movement. The legislature enacted a public-funding ban in 2002 but made limited exceptions for cases involving rape, incest, a risk of death for the mother, and fetuses carrying fatal defects. To date, the law has not been challenged.[101] TRAP laws have proved considerably more controversial, and Mississippi's law has been no exception. In 2004, the legislature required that all abortions after the first trimester be performed at licensed ambulatory facilities or hospitals. Federal judge Tom S. Lee struck down the law because no licensed facilities in Mississippi would perform such abortions, thus, the law effectively eliminated all right to later abortions and was in violation of *Roe*.[102] In 2012, the legislature enacted a new TRAP law that required all doctors performing abortions to have admitting privileges at a local hospital; only one doctor in the state met this qualification, and hospitals refused several others who tried to gain privileges. Judge Daniel Jordan ruled that the new law was unconstitutional because, like the 2004 law, it shut off access to abortion in Mississippi. Jordan rejected the state's argument that women who wanted abortions could go to Memphis or New Orleans, holding that Mississippi could not look to other states to meet its constitutional obligations. On appeal, a divided Fifth Circuit agreed.[103]

In 2014, the legislature tried a new line of attack: it prohibited performance of abortions more than twenty weeks after conception, even though nearly all such laws have been struck down as violative of *Roe*.[104] Like many abortion foes, Mississippi lawmakers have held onto the hope that one day *Roe* will be overturned, as evidenced by a 2007 "placeholder" law that gives a preview of what post-*Roe* life in Mississippi would look like. The law, designed to go into effect automatically if *Roe* is ever overturned, would completely prohibit abortions except where necessary to save a mother's life and in cases of rape, and even then only when the mother agrees to press criminal charges against the rapist.[105] It remains to be seen whether the protective shield that the *Casey* court built around the core of *Roe* will eventually wear away as the anti-abortion winds continue to blow in Mississippi and elsewhere.

Tort reform. Another battle that has implicated expressive individualism is the debate over the extent to which costs of accidents should be socialized through insurance, government compensation programs, or other means. That debate is nearly two hundred years old and has taken various forms over time, including legislative efforts to eliminate railroads' and industrial employers' common-law defenses to liability in the late 1800s; replacement of common-law liability rules in the workplace with no-fault workers compensation systems during the Progressive era; and a renewed effort in the mid-twentieth century to create a more socialized system by eliminating traditional limits on liability of municipalities and charities, liberalizing comparative negligence rules, and making manufacturers and distributors strictly liable for hazardous products. Since the mid-1970s, the tort-reform movement has served as the principal forum for the debate. Insurers and business groups have attacked liberalized tort recovery rules for causing steep increases in professional malpractice insurance premiums and for being generally inimical to economic development, and they have persuaded many state legislatures and courts to cut back mid-twentieth-century liberalization. Injury victims and their attorneys, together with the American Bar Association, have questioned whether there is a true insurance crisis and have argued that most of the recent reforms deny victims their due-process right to a fair recovery.[106]

The debate has raged with particular intensity in Mississippi. Beginning in the early 1990s, the state experienced a wave of tort claims by asbestosis victims, many of whom worked at the Ingalls shipyard, and tobacco smokers. As smokers' lawsuits multiplied, tobacco companies responded with an intensive public-relations campaign: they argued that smokers should take responsibility for their own health, painted plaintiffs' lawyers as parasites who wanted to enrich themselves at the victims' expense, and raised the specter of economic ruin that mass verdicts against them might bring.[107] In response, the 1993 legislature approved changes to Mississippi's products liability law. Manufacturers and suppliers would remain liable for defective products, but only if some negligence on their part was shown; they could no longer be held liable simply because their products were inherently dangerous.[108]

Lawsuits involving asbestosis and other industrial health problems continued. Mississippi gradually gained a reputation as plaintiff-friendly state, and after two juries in Natchez-region counties awarded damages exceeding $100 million in 1998–99, business groups in Mississippi and throughout the nation took note. They criticized Mississippi as a "jackpot justice" state, called for new laws limiting recoveries, supported business-friendly candidates in the state's 2000 Supreme Court election with some success, and gained a major success when the 2002 and 2004 legislatures made sweeping changes to Mississippi's tort system. The new laws' most-publicized features were limits on the amounts of punitive damages juries could award and caps on non-economic damages, that is, awards for a victim's pain and suffering, the amounts of which had traditionally been left to juries' discretion. The legislature imposed a cap of $500,000 in medical-malpractice cases and $1 million in other civil cases.[109]

The non-economic damages cap was soon challenged, and the courts' divided reaction underscored the controversy attending tort reform in Mississippi. In *Learmonth v. Sears, Roebuck & Co.* (2011), a federal jury awarded an auto-accident victim $4 million in damages but did not specify what part of that sum was for non-economic damages. The trial court reduced the award by $1.2 million based on its understanding that the non-economic portion of the award was about $2.2 million. Learmonth then challenged the constitutionality of the cap, arguing that it violated her rights to trial by jury and due process of law and constituted improper legislative interference with the judicial branch of government. The Fifth Circuit asked Mississippi's supreme court to opine whether the cap was unconstitutional, but the supreme court demurred: it concluded that the issue was not presented because the defendants had not asked the jury to determine the amount of non-economic damages, and it strongly hinted that because of that failure the victim should receive her full award. [110]

The Fifth Circuit ignored the hint. It concluded that the parties had agreed on the amount of the verdict attributable to non-economic damages even though the jury had not addressed that issue. The court also rejected Learmonth's constitutional challenges: it noted that the legislature's power to modify tort recovery rules and judges' power to reduce awards were both long-established features of Mississippi law and held that, accordingly, the cap was valid. The cap is now uniformly enforced in Mississippi's federal courts but not in its state courts: Mississippi's supreme court has not yet determined whether the cap is constitutional, and state courts (which are not bound by federal decisions) are divided over the issue.[111]

The tort reform controversy does not fit neatly into a paradigm of expressive individualism versus traditionalism and communitarianism. Tort-reform supporters could be viewed either as communitarians who believe that verdicts must be limited for the common economic good, or as individualists who believe that the right of individual expression carries with it an obligation of individual responsibility; accident victims should not try to spread the burden of their loss among others. Tort-reform opponents could be viewed as individualists who support accident victims' right to a full affirmation of their personal worth, or as communitarians who want to preserve socialization of accident costs. Despite this ambiguity, the tort-reform controversy has highlighted the tensions between expressive individualism, communitarianism, and traditionalism in Mississippi and elsewhere, and likely will continue to do so for some time.

Expressive individualism in the Mississippi Supreme Court. Prior to the 1960s, state supreme courts placed a premium on consensus for both practical and cultural reasons. Most state courts were required to decide all appeals of trial court decisions; few intermediate appellate courts existed to ease their burden. State justices had to write and issue hundreds of decisions each year; they had little time for lengthy opinions setting out reasons for dissent. Just as important, consensus and collegiality were prized as a means of presenting a united front in a largely communitarian society which looked to courts as sources of moral as well as legal authority.[112]

After 1960, judicial consensus began eroding, although the pace of erosion varied from state to state. Mississippi's supreme court largely preserved a culture of consensus until the 1990s, when its caseload became so large that the legislature created an intermediate court of appeals and gave the supreme court authority to hear only appeals of its choosing.[113] The proportion of cases decided unanimously by the supreme court then fell from more than 90 percent to approximately 50 percent, and at the same time it became common even for judges who agreed with a decision to write separate opinions explaining their view of the case. Mississippi judicial elections have long been vigorously contested, sometimes indecorous affairs which often reward the most outspoken candidates. So long as that continues to be so and so long as the age of expressive individualism continues, the current high rate of dissensus is likely to continue.[114]

Judicial expressive individualism has also manifested itself in the "new federalism" movement. State courts have challenged federal authority regularly since the early nineteenth century, and between 1875 and 1925, they built an extensive body of case law guaranteeing criminal procedural rights under state constitutions at a time when federal courts were disinclined to address such rights.[115] After 1925, the US Supreme Court replaced state courts as the primary delineator of procedural rights, a shift felt by Mississippi when the high court focused on the plight of black criminal defendants in the 1930s and 1940s. After Chief Justice Earl Warren retired in 1969, many observers worried that the court would retreat from its expansion of constitutional rights. In 1977, Justice William Brennan, a Warren ally, suggested in an influential article that state supreme courts could counter any such retreat by interpreting state bill-of-rights provisions more expansively than their counterpart federal provisions. Brennan's suggestion attracted nationwide attention and support from several prominent state justices.[116]

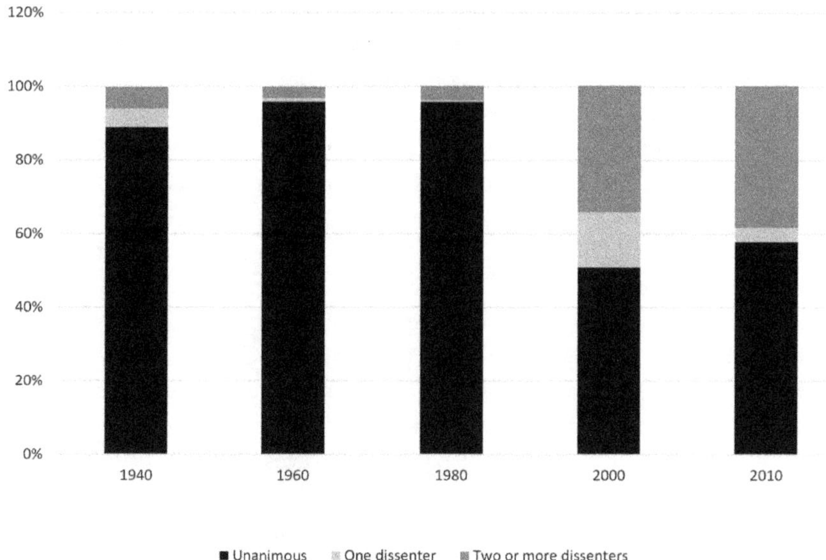

Figure 6.2. Mississippi Supreme Court: The Rise of Dissensus, 1940–2010

Nearly all state courts gave nominal support to the new federalism: to renounce it would be to cede authority over a large part of their state constitutions to the federal courts, a step they were unwilling to take. But most courts applied the doctrine sparingly, particularly after judicial decisions in California and other states expanding criminal procedural rights and limiting use of the death penalty under state constitutions elicited voter backlash in the form of corrective constitutional amendments and ouster of justices who had supported the decisions. At least two Mississippi Supreme Court judges, Joel Blass (1990) and James Robertson (1992), lost bids for reelection to the court amid charges that they were insufficiently supportive of the death penalty.[117] Mississippi's supreme court has affirmed its right to interpret the Mississippi constitution independent of analogous federal provisions, but in almost all cases it has followed federal precedent in the interest of maintaining judicial consistency and efficiency.[118] The court asserted the new federalism most prominently in *Stringer v. State* (1986), where it adhered to Mississippi's longstanding rule that evidence obtained in a criminal investigation without a proper warrant may not be used at trial, and it declined to adopt a recent US Supreme Court decision creating an exception for investigators who believe in good faith that they have a valid warrant. But nearly two decades later, in *White v. State* (2003), the court changed course and adopted the federal exception.[119]

White is emblematic of the extent to which the federal presence has dominated Mississippi law since the 1940s. It is not surprising that federal courts shaped Mississippi's civil rights revolution. The Jim Crow system was deeply entrenched in state law, a body of law which Mississippi's supreme court was charged with enforcing. Ultimately it fell to the judges of the Fifth Circuit to force the birth of a new society in Mississippi, a prolonged and difficult process. After school desegregation began in earnest in 1970, the federal courts turned their attention to the birth pangs of Mississippi's new political order as the white Democratic hegemony of the Jim Crow era gave way to an unstable three-cornered balance of power between newly enfranchised black citizens, white Democrats, and a resurgent Republican Party. Despite the Mississippi Supreme Court's lamentation of the legislature's failure to take back control of legislative apportionment from the federal courts, federal involvement likely will not end until the three-corner balancing process comes closer to a state of equilibrium.

Mississippi's new social and political order and the accompanying legal changes have brought the state into the national legal mainstream more than ever before. The BAWI system that Mississippi devised in the 1930s continues to serve, in modified form, as a pillar of Mississippi's economy and the economies of many other states. Mississippi's legal response to expressive individualism has often been oppositional but the state has expressed its opposition through the legal process, not extralegal violence, and its reaction to expressive individualism has mirrored that of many other states. Legislative and judicial defiance of national norms defined by Congress and the federal courts, a Mississippi hallmark during the 1950s and 1960s, has all but disappeared from the state's modern legal discourse.

If William Sharkey and Horatio Simrall could see their state today, they likely would approve of its movement toward the national mainstream. Despite his eventual support of the Confederacy, Sharkey made clear in several 1830s cases that deference to national authority in constitutional matters was a price well worth paying for membership in the larger union of states, and Simrall, when he came to recognize that his state could preserve much of its pre-Civil War racial order even in a changed postwar legal system, likewise counseled accommodation rather than defiance of national authority.[120] But others such as William Harris, who feared the threat that other parts of the Union posed to Mississippi's antebellum social order, and William Anderson and Ben Cameron, who resented federal intrusion into the state's affairs during the New Deal and civil rights years, would view Mississippi's entry into the national legal mainstream with alarm.[121] How should Mississippi complete the revolution begun in the 1950s and accommodate the new balance of power that the revolution has produced? How should Mississippians balance their desire for the right of self-expression and pride in their distinctiveness against the benefits of nationalization? These are the major questions that Mississippi's legal system will have to address as the state begins its third century. The answers will shape the state's larger history during the century to come.

NOTES

Introduction

1. Morris, "Delta Blues," *New York Times*, February 11, 1996. Morris attributed the words to William Faulkner but he did not cite a source, and others have been unable to find the words in Faulkner's writings. The words reflect Faulkner's spirit but they are Morris's.

Chapter One

1. Sargent to US Secretary of State Timothy Pickering, June 16, 1798, quoted in William N. Ethridge Jr., "An Introduction to Sargent's Code of the Mississippi Territory (1799–1800)," 11 *American Journal of Legal History* 148, 151 (1967). Adams initially selected George Mathews, a member of a prominent Georgia political family, for the governorship but later dropped Mathews due to his connection with potentially fraudulent land schemes in Georgia. Thomas P. Abernethy, *A History of the South, Vol. IV: The New Nation, 1789–1819* (1961), 158.

2. Ethridge, "Sargent's Code," 149–51; J. F. H. Claiborne, *Mississippi as a Province, Territory and State* (1880), 204; Robert V. Haynes, *The Mississippi Territory and the Southwest Frontier, 1795–1817* (2010), 28–33; Herbert James Lewis, *Clearing the Thickets: A History of Antebellum Alabama* (2013), 47 n.5.

3. Ethridge, "Sargent's Code," 149–51; *Haynes, Mississippi Territory*, 35–36; Lewis, *Clearing the Thickets*, 48–50.

4. Haynes, *Mississippi Territory*, 41–44, 47–50; Lewis, *Clearing the Thickets*, 48–57.

5. Haynes, *Mississippi Territory*, 263–64; Lewis, *Clearing the Thickets*, 63–65; see 2 U.S. Stats. at Large 298 (1804).

6. Haynes, *Mississippi Territory*, 263–64; Lewis, *Clearing the Thickets*, 63–65; Clarence E. Carter, ed., *Territorial Papers of the United States* (1937), 5:245, 268–69; http://congressional .proquest.com.ezproxy.library.wisc.edu/ congressional/ docview/537.d48.asp038_misc.300? accountid=465.

7. Harry Toulmin, *The Statutes of the Mississippi Territory, Revised and Digested by the Authority of the General Assembly* (1807); John D. W. Guice, "The Cement of Society: Law in the Mississippi Territory," 1 *Gulf Coast Historical Review* 76, 84–86 (1986); Haynes, *Mississippi Territory*, 264–80; Lewis, *Clearing the Thickets*, 63–76.

8. Christopher Morris, *Becoming Southern: The Evolution of a Way of Life, Warren County and Vicksburg, Mississippi, 1770–1860* (1999), xviii–xx; Haynes, *Mississippi Territory*, 77–78; Sven Beckert, *Empire of Cotton: A Global History* (2014), 202–203, 317–18.

9. Wesley F. Busbee Jr., *Mississippi: A History* (2005), 27–35; John A. Caruso, *The Mississippi Valley Frontier: The Age of French Exploration and Settlement* (1964), 234–40; Noel Polk, ed., *Natchez Before 1830* (1989), 92–101; see Charles J. Balesi, *The Time of the French in the Heart of North America, 1673–1818* (1991); Morris, *Becoming Southern*, 18–26.

10. Caruso, *Mississippi Valley Frontier*, 238–40; William Baskerville Hamilton, *Anglo-American Law on the Frontier: Thomas Rodney and his Territorial Cases* (1953), 119; see also Morris S. Arnold, *Unequal Laws unto a Savage Race: European Legal Tradition in Arkansas, 1686–1836* (1985), 1–112, and Roger L. Severns, *Prairie Justice: A History of Illinois Courts Under French, English and American Law* (2015), 1–49; Morris, *Becoming Southern*, 18–19, 24–25.

11. Haynes, *Mississippi Territory*, 7–20; Busbee, *Mississippi*, 45–50; 8 U.S. Stats. 138 (1795).

12. See Kermit L. Hall, *The Magic Mirror: Law in American History* (1989), 9–12; Roscoe Pound, *The Spirit of the Common Law* (1921), 17–31; James Kent, *Commentaries on American Law* (1826), 507.

13. See Pound, *Spirit of the Common Law*, 21–26, 29; Lawrence E. Friedman, *A History of American Law* (3rd ed. 2005), xvii.

14. The seven parts consisted of: (1) canon law, reflecting the fact that the Catholic Church was an integral part of the state; (2) public law, setting forth the government's powers and its mode of organization; (3) court procedures to be used in resolving civil (that is, non-criminal) disputes; (4) family law, enforcing husbands' and fathers' role as head of the family but also emphasizing that they held their power in trust to benefit the family as a whole; (5) contract law; (6) law governing wills and succession, which was designed to promote long-term retention of land and assets by family and to reject the idea of land as a commodity; and (7) criminal law, including control of social outsiders such as Jews, Moors, and slaves. Louis Moreau-Lislet and Henry Carleton, *Law of Las Siete Partidas, Which are Still in Force in the State of Louisiana* (1820), 1:ix–xii.

15. George Dargo, *Jefferson's Louisiana: Politics and the Clash of Legal Traditions* (1975), 23–51, 105–176; Richard H. Kilbourne Jr., *A History of the Louisiana Civil Code: The Formative Years, 1803–1839* (1987).

16. 1 U.S. Stats. 123 (1790).

17. 1785 Journals of Continental Congress 375 (May 20, 1785), available at Library of Congress Memory Project, http://memory.loc.gov./cgi-bin/query; 1 U.S. Stats. 123 (1790); Benjamin Perley Poore, *The Federal and State Constitutions, Colonial Charters and Other Organic Laws of the United States* (1877), 1:432; see particularly Northwest Ordinance §§ 3–8.

18. Northwest Ordinance, §§ 9–11; see Jack E. Eblen, *The First and Second United States Empires: Governors and Territorial Government, 1784–1912* (1968), 39.

19. Northwest Ordinance, § 14, art. 4 (navigation clause), art. 6 (prohibition of slavery); see Southwest Ordinance, 1 U.S. Stats. at 123.

20. 1 U.S. Stats. 549 (1798). The Mississippi Territory consisted of present-day Mississippi and Alabama except for the Gulf coast region south of 31° north latitude, which was still controlled by Spain.

21. Haynes, *Mississippi Territory*, 28–29, 35–36; Ethridge, "Sargent's Code," 150–52.

22. "A Law establishing Courts of Judicature" (February 28, 1799); "A Law establishing a court of probate" (February 28, 1799); "A Law Respecting Sheriffs, Coroners, Recorders

and Treasurers" (February 28, 1799); "A Law directing the manner in which money shall be raised and levied, to defray the charges which may arise without the several counties" (April 3, 1799); Ethridge, "Sargent's Code," 160–65, 173–75, 184–92, 198–204.

23. "A Law Respecting crimes and punishment" (February 28, 1799); Ethridge, "Sargent's Code," 166–72.

24. "A Law for the regulation of Slaves" (March 30, 1799); Ethridge, "Sargent's Code," 192–96.

25. "A Law regulating Marriages" (February 28, 1799); "A Law concerning Defalcation" (February 28, 1799); Ethridge, "Sargent's Code," 176–77, 178–79.

26. "A Law to regulate Taverns and retailers of Liquors, and concerning Indians" (February 28, 1799); Ethridge, "Sargent's Code," 179–83.

27. "A Law concerning Aliens and contagious Diseases" (March 18, 1799); Ethridge, "Sargent's Code," 191–92.

28. Claiborne, *Mississippi as a Province*, 209–219; John Wunder, "American Law and Order Comes to Mississippi Territory: The Making of Sargent's Code, 1798–1800," 38 *Journal of Mississippi History* 131, 142–54 (1976); Haynes, *Mississippi Territory*, 36–38, 47–50; Ethridge, "Sargent's Code," 151. For a detailed history of the subsequent evolution of Mississippi's territorial court system, see Michael H. Hoffheimer, "Mississippi Courts: 1790–1868," 65 *Mississippi Law Journal* 99 (1995).

29. Haynes, *Mississippi Territory*, 135.

30. Edward L. Ayers, *Vengeance and Justice: Crime and Punishment in the Nineteenth Century American South* (1984), 9–14, 18–19; John Hope Franklin, *The Militant South, 1800–1861* (1956), 44–60; Morris, *Becoming Southern*, 135; Bertram Wyatt-Brown, *The Shaping of Southern Culture: Honor, Grace and War, 1790s–1860s* (2001), 62–70; see also Joshua D. Rothman, "The Hazards of the Flush Times: Gambling, Mob Violence and the Anxieties of America's Market Revolution," 95 *Journal of American History* 651 (2008).

31. Lewis, *Clearing the Thickets*, 56 (Sargent); Haynes, *Mississippi Territory*, 191–93 (Bruin).

32. Carter, *Territorial Papers*, 5:245, 268–69 (Toulmin to Madison, February 17, 1812); Abernethy, *The New Nation*, 357–62; http://congressional.proquest.com.ezproxy.library.wisc.edu/congressional/docview/537.d48.asp038_misc.300?accountid=465.

33. Joseph G. Baldwin, *The Flush Times of Alabama and Mississippi* (1853), 58–59.

34. Reuben Davis, *Recollections of Mississippi and Mississippians* (1889, reprint 1972), 150–52.

35. Davis, *Recollections of Mississippi*, 159–61; see Wyatt-Brown, *Shaping of Southern Culture*, 67–70.

36. See John Ray Skates, *A History of the Mississippi Supreme Court, 1817–1848* (1973), 10.

37. See William F. Keller, *The Nation's Advocate: Henry Marie Brackenridge and Young America* (1956), 298–354; Frank B. Woodford, *Mr. Jefferson's Disciple: A Life of Justice Woodward* (1953); William Wirt Blume, "Legislation on the American Frontier," 60 *Michigan Law Review* 317, 348–53, 363–65 (1962); Alice E. Smith, *James Duane Doty: Frontier Promoter* (1954), 54–55, 374–85.

38. Lewis, *Clearing the Thickets*, 73; Paul M. Pruitt, *Taming Alabama: Lawyers and Reformers, 1804–1929* (2010), 11–13.

39. "A Law Respecting crimes and punishments—Maiming or disfiguring" (February 28, 1799); Ethridge, "Sargent's Code," 172; Miss. Act of June 14 1822, A. Hutchinson and V. Howard, *Code of Mississippi, Being an Analytical Compilation of the Public and General Statutes of*

the Territory and State, with Tabular References to the Local and Private Acts, from 1798–1848 (1848) (hereinafter "Hutchinson Code"), 945–50; Miss. Const. (1832), VII:2.

40. Hamilton, *Anglo-American Law*, 79–84, 92–103; Claiborne, *Mississippi as a Province*, 277–91; Guice, "Cement of Society," 87–88; *American Insurance Co. v. Canter*, 26 U.S. 511 (1828).

41. Busbee, *Mississippi*, 45–50, 59; Paul W. Gates, *History of Public Land Law Development* (1968), 54–55, 293–94; *Fletcher v. Peck*, 10 U.S. 87 (1810); Morris, *Becoming Southern*, 20–22; Abernethy, *The New Nation*, 446–50.

42. 1785 Journals of Continental Congress 375 (May 20, 1785), available at Library of Congress Memory Project, http://memory.loc.gov./cgi-bin/query; Gates, *History of Public Land Law*, 59–71.

43. 8 U.S. Stats. 138 (1795); Articles of Agreement and Cession (April 24, 1802), at http:// amindians.tripod.com/18022.htm; 2 U.S. Stats. 229 (1803); 3 U.S. Stats. 116 (1814); Hamilton, *Anglo-American Law*, 66–68; Claiborne, *Mississippi as a Province*, 137; Guice, "Cement of Society," 89.

44. 7 U.S. Stats. 98 (1805), 210 (1820), 333 (1830), 381 (1832) (Indian cession treaties); *Haynes, Mississippi Territory*, 95–97, 236–40; Busbee, *Mississippi*, 63–65; Carolyn Keller Reeves, ed., *The Choctaw Before Removal* (1985), 169–70; Kathleen S. Hutchison, *Red Book: American State, County and Town Sources* (1989).

45. Haynes, *Mississippi Territory*, 324–26.

46. Ibid.; see Carter, *Territorial Papers*, 5:584 (Toulmin to territorial Congressional delegate William Lattimore, December 1815); 5:641 (Toulmin to President Madison, January 20, 1816); Gates, *History of Public Land Law*, 59–71; 5 U.S. Stats. 382 (1841).

47. 8 U.S. Stats. 138, art. XX (1795); see *Chew v. Calvert*, Walker 54 (Miss. 1818); Gates, *History of Public Land Law*, 113.

48. Haynes, *Mississippi Territory*, 95–97, 236–40, 333–37; Busbee, *Mississippi*, 63–68; Francis P. Prucha, *American Indian Policy in the Formative Years* (1962), 161–63. The United States agreed in at least one cession treaty to provide funds to cover debts to white settlers. See 7 U.S. Stats. 98, art. II (1805).

49. 21 U.S. 543, 590–92 (1823).

50. 1 U.S. Stats. 187, § 1 (1790), 452 (1796); 2 U.S. Stats. 139, §§ 2–7, 12–15, 21 (1802); see Prucha, *American Indian Policy*, 85–93; Felix S. Cohen, *Cohen's Handbook of Federal Indian Law* (Nell Jessup Newton, ed., 1982), 109–114. The government-post system was unsuccessful and was abolished in 1822. 3 U.S. Stats. 682 (1822).

51. Ethridge, "Sargent's Code," 183; 2 U.S. Stats. 139 (1802); Prucha, *American Indian Policy*, 88–93, 133–35. Congress prohibited all liquor sales to Indians in 1832, but that law proved equally difficult to enforce. 4 U.S. Stats. 564 (1832).

52. 1 U.S. Stats. 187 (1790); 2 U.S. Stats. 139 (1802); 3 U.S. Stats. 332 (1816), 682 (1822); 4 U.S. Stats. 564 (1832); Prucha, *American Indian Policy*, 133–35.

53. *Cherokee Nation v. Georgia*, 30 U.S. 1, 16–17 (1831); see also *Worcester v. Georgia*, 31 U.S. 515, 559–61 (1834).

54. 1 U.S. Stats. 187, § 1 (1790), 452 (1796); Prucha, *American Indian Policy*, 188–212; Cohen, *Cohen's Handbook*, 188–93.

55. Haynes, *Mississippi Territory*, 224–27; Cohen, *Cohen's Handbook*, 193–98.

56. Carter, *Territorial Papers*, 5:69 (Holmes to Toulmin, June 5, 1810); 5:91 (Holmes to Toulmin, July 30, 1810).

57. Davis, *Recollections of Mississippi*, 61.

58. Davis, *Recollections of Mississippi*, 61–62. Davis suggests that the defendant was the Choctaw chief Pushmataha, but that is unlikely: Pushmataha died in 1824, and Davis states that the trial took place shortly before the Choctaw removal process began in 1831. Possibly the defendant was Pushmataha's son Hashitubbe, who was also a Choctaw leader.

59. Anna Lewis, *Chief Pushmataha: American Patriot: The Story of the Choctaws' Struggle for Survival* (1959), 97–100.

60. Haynes, *Mississippi Territory*, 212. The same was not true of the Tombigbee District, which never developed a true aristocracy. *Id.*, 213–15.

61. Dunbar Rowland, *Courts, Judges and Lawyers of Mississippi, 1798–1935* (1935), 16–17.

62. Haynes, *Mississippi Territory*, 333–41; see Figure 1.2.

63. Dunbar Rowland, "Mississippi's First Constitution and Its Makers," 6 *Publications of the Mississippi Historical Society* 79, 83–85 (1902); Winborne Magruder Drake, "The Framing of Mississippi's First Constitution," 29 *Journal of Mississippi History* 301, 304–307 (1967). The Natchez district is defined here to include Adams, Jefferson, Wilkinson, Claiborne, and Warren counties.

64. *Worcester (Mass.) Spy*, quoted in *Albany (N.Y.) Gazette*, October 11, 1817, cited in Drake, "Framing of Mississippi's First Constitution," 324 n.74 (other citations omitted).

65. *Reports of the Proceedings and Debates of the Convention of 1821 Assembled for the Purpose of Amending the Constitution of the State of New York* (1821), 220.

66. See, e.g., Mass. Const. (1780), ch. 2, art. 2, § 2 and ch. 3, art. 3, § 4; N.Y. Const. (1777), VII; N.J. Const (1776), IV; Md. Const. (1776), II; N.C. Const. (1776), VII-VIII; Pa. Const. (1790), III:1 (taxpayer qualification only); S.C. Const. (1790), I:4 (same); Ga. Const. (1798), IV:1 (same).

67. Some of the new states provided that only persons who had paid state or local taxes could hold office, but only Tennessee imposed a property requirement for officeholding. See Vt. Const. (1777), II:8, 17, 44; Ky. Const. (1792), III; Tenn. Const. (1796), III:1; Ohio Const. (1803), IV:1; La. Const. (1812), II:8; Ind. Const. (1816), VI:1.

68. 2 U.S. Stats. 455 (1808); Miss. Const. (1817), II:1.

69. Miss. Const. (1817), III:8–9, IV:3.

70. Drake, "Framing of Mississippi's First Constitution," 325–27. The official proceedings of the convention were published, *Journal of the Convention of the Western Part of the Mississippi Territory* (1831), reprinted at 29 *Journal of Mississippi History* 443 (1967), but the convention debates were not reported. Newspapers of the period contain fragmentary reports but those reports have never been compiled. See Drake, "Framing of Mississippi's First Constitution," 307–308 n.17.

71. Miss. Const. (1817), III:8–9.

72. Peter J. Coleman, *Debtors and Creditors in America: Insolvency, Imprisonment for Debt, and Bankruptcy, 1607–1900* (1974), 6–15, 39–42, 105–114, 191–99; Charles S. Sydnor, *A History of the South, Vol. V: The Development of Southern Sectionalism, 1819–1848* (1948), 97.

73. Ibid.; see also Jerome Mushkat and Joseph G. Rayback, *Martin Van Buren: Law, Politics, and the Shaping of Republican Ideology* (1997), 76–78.

74. Miss. Const. (1817), VI:9.

75. The population data in the table below is compiled from US Bureau of the Census, *Second Census of the United States* (1801); *Aggregate Amount of Each Description of Persons Within the United States of America and its Territories in the Year 1810* (1811); *Population Schedules of the Fourth Census of the United States* (1821); *Abstract of the Returns of the Fifth Census* (1831), 36; and *Compendium of the Enumeration of the Inhabitants and Statistics of the United States* (1841), 56–57.

76. See Miss. Laws, Act of June 7, 1822, §§ 1, 15; Hutchinson Code, 824, 896.

77. See Miss. Laws, Act of June 2, 1822; Act of January 27, 1824; Hutchinson Code, 543–45.

78. Skates, *Mississippi Supreme Court*, 609. The decisions at issue were unpublished.

79. Miss. Laws, Act of June 14, 1822, §§ 19–26; Miss. Laws, Act of December 16, 1831; Hutchinson Code, 938–39.

80. Miss. Laws, Act of June 18, 1822, §§ 1, 4, 6, 11; Hutchinson Code, 941–43.

81. Miss. Laws, Act of June 13, 1822. Between 1817 and 1832, the Mississippi legislature also devoted substantial attention to the law of slavery; it enacted a detailed slave code in 1822. See Chapter 2; see also Miss. Laws, Act of June 18, 1822; Hutchinson Code, 510–42.

82. Toulmin, *Statutes of the Mississippi Territory*; Edward Turner, *Statutes of the Mississippi Territory* (1816); George Poindexter, *The Revised Code of the Laws of Mississippi, In Which Are Comprised All Such Acts of the General Assembly of a Public Nature, As Were In Force at the End of the Year 1823* (1824); Hutchinson Code. Several updates of the code were also published in the 1830s without formal legislative authorization. See https://library.courts .ms.gov/MSCodes1799-1839.htm.

83. Frederick Hicks, *Men and Books Famous in the Law* (1921), 118–33; Wilfrid R. Prest, *William Blackstone: Law and Letters in the Eighteenth Century* (2008).

84. See G. Edward White, "The Chancellor's Ghost," 74 *Chicago-Kent Law Review* 229, 233–34 (1998); John T. Horton, *James Kent: A Study in Conservatism* (1939), 139≠263. Some states went to New York to have their own court reports published. See, e.g, Elihu H. Bay, *Reports of Cases Argued and Determined in the Superior Courts of Law in the State of South Carolina,* vols. 1–2 (1809, 1811), frontispiece; Thomas U. P. Charlton, *Reports of Cases Argued and Determined in the Superior Courts of the Eastern District of the State of Georgia* (1824), frontispiece. Robert Walker, the reporter for Mississippi's first volume of case reports (1818–33), selected a Jackson publisher but subsequent Mississippi volumes were published in Philadelphia, New Orleans, and Cincinnati. See Walker, *Reports of Cases Adjudged in the Supreme Court of Mississippi* (1834), frontispiece; see also *Howard's Mississippi Reports*, vols. 1–5.

85. Horton, *Kent*, 264–306; Hicks, *Men and Books*, 149–58.

86. For a description of the daily work life of one prominent antebellum Southern judge, see Paul D. Hicks, *Joseph Henry Lumpkin: Georgia's First Chief Justice* (2002). The statistics in Figure 1.3 are compiled from volumes of Mississippi case reports for the years in question; computations are on file with the author.

87. Skates, *Mississippi Supreme Court*, 17–26, 31.

88. *Natchez Gazette*, October 20, 1830, quoted in Winborne Magruder Drake, "The Mississippi Constitutional Convention of 1832," 23 *Journal of Southern History* 354, 369 (1957).

89. Drake, "Convention of 1832," 355–60; Morris, *Becoming Southern*, 150–53.

90. Drake, "Convention of 1832," 362; Morris, *Becoming Southern*, 148–52.

91. Miss. Const. (1817), VI:2; see Hicks, *Men and Books*, 75; 12 & 13 Will.3, ch. 2 (Eng.) (1700).

92. J. Willard Hurst, *The Growth of American Law: The Law Makers* (1950), 37–38, 140–41; Friedman, *History of American Law*, 110–11; Caleb Nelson, "A Re-Evaluation of Scholarly Explanations for the Rise of the Elective Judiciary in Antebellum America," 37 *American Journal of Legal History* 190, 203, 223 (1993).

93. Miss. Const. (1832) IV:2; Drake, "Convention of 1832," 359–60, 364.

94. Quitman to J. Fenwick Brent, March 22, 1845, letter reprinted in *Proceedings and Debates of the Convention of Louisiana Which Assembled at the City of New Orleans, January 14, 1844* (1845), 755; Drake, "Convention of 1832," 370. See also Nelson, "Rise of the Elective Judiciary," 190–92.

95. Miss. Const. (1832), VII:19.

96. Miss. Const. (1832), VII:2.

97. Prior to 1832, three states had enacted anti-dueling provisions. See Conn. Const. (1818), VI:3; Ala. Const. (1819), VI:3; Va. Const. (1830), III:12.

98. Tennessee (1834), Florida (1838), Louisiana and Texas (1845), Kentucky (1850), and Maryland (1851). See Poore, *Federal and State Constitutions*.

99. Pennsylvania (1838), Iowa (1846), Illinois and Wisconsin (1848), California and Michigan (1850), and Indiana and Ohio (1851). See *id.*

100. See Ayers, *Vengeance and Justice*, 18–19. Connecticut (1818), Louisiana (1845), Wisconsin (1848), and California and Michigan (1850) deprived duelists of the vote. See Poore, *Federal and State Constitutions*.

101. Beckert, *Empire of Cotton*, 117–18, 202–205; Haynes, *Mississippi Territory*, 133–35.

102. Busbee, *Mississippi*, 75–77, 83–85.

103. Miss. Const. (1832), VII:9.

104. Id., VII:8.

Chapter Two

1. *Oliver v. State*, 39 Miss. 526, 539 (1860).

2. Charles S. Sydnor, *Slavery in Mississippi* (1933), 89–90, 224–30; Alan Huffman, *Mississippi in Africa: The Saga of the Slaves of Prospect Hill Plantation and Their Legacy in Liberia Today* (2010), 23–30, 43–56.

3. Sydnor, *Slavery in Mississippi*, 89–90, 224–30; Huffman, *Mississippi in Africa*, 43–70, 83–94; *Ross v. Vertner*, 6 Miss. 305, 360 (1840). Slaves who chose not to go would be sold except for Ross's cook Grace and his valet Hannibal, who would be given to his granddaughter. *Vertner*, 6 Miss. at 305–306.

4. *Wade v. American Colonization Society*, 15 Miss. 663, 698 (1846); Sydnor, *Slavery in Mississippi*, 227–30; Huffman, *Mississippi in Africa*, 83–94; Norwood Allen Kerr, "The Mississippi Colonization Society (1831–1860), 43 *Journal of Mississippi History* 1, 21–22 (1981); Michael P. Mills, "Slave Law in Mississippi from 1817–1861: Constitutions, Codes and Cases," 71 *Mississippi Law Journal* 153, 182–87 (2001); 1842 Miss. Laws, ch. 4, § 9.

5. Sydnor, *Slavery in Mississippi*, 229–30; Huffman, *Mississippi in Africa*, 69–70, 83–85; 37 Miss. 235, 252 (1859).

6. Code Noir, arts. 9 (concubinage), 18–19 (economic activities), 47 (separation of slave families), 50–51, 58 (manumission), available at http://chmn.gmu.edu/revolution/d/335/; Moreau-Lislet and Carleton, *Siete Partidas*, IV, Tit. 21, §§ 5–6, Tit. 22, § 2.

7. Code Noir, art. 33 (punishment); 1740 S.C. Laws, no. 670, arts. 5–6, 21, 37 (punishment), 7 (slave meetings), 9–10 (criminal trial system), 23 (hunting), 33, 36, 43 (assembly and travel), 34 (keeping boats), 40 (clothing), 45 (learning to write), 46 (white presence on plantations). The South Carolina Code is available at https://en.wikipeda.org/wiki/Negro_Act_of_1740. See also Darold D. Wax, "'The Great Risque We Run': The Aftermath of Slave Rebellion at Stono, South Carolina, 1739–1745," 67 *Journal of Negro History* 136 (1982); Mark M. Smith, "Remembering Mary, Shaping Revolt: Reconsidering the Stono Rebellion," 67 *Journal of Southern History* 513 (2001).

8. See David J. Libby, *Slavery in Frontier Mississippi, 1720–1835* (2004), 7–30; John Hebron Moore, *The Emergence of the Cotton Kingdom in the Old Southwest: Mississippi, 1770–1860* (1988), 17–18.

9. "A Law for the regulation of Slaves" (March 30, 1799), reprinted in Ethridge, "Sargent's Code," 192; Morris, *Becoming Southern*, 67–78.

10. Libby, *Slavery and Frontier Mississippi*, 49–50, 53–61; Miss. Terr. Laws, Act of December 28, 1812.

11. See Pauline Maier, *American Scripture: Making the Declaration of Independence* (1998), 191–99; Ronald Hoffman and Peter J. Albert, eds., *The Transforming Hand of Revolution: Reconsidering the American Revolution as a Social Movement* (1996), 73–74, 84–85, 207–208; 1782 (May) Va. Laws, ch. 21; St. George Tucker, *Blackstone's Commentaries: With Notes of Reference to the Constitution and Laws of the Federal Government of the United States and the Commonwealth of Virginia* (1996 ed.), 68–86.

12. Kerr, "Mississippi Colonization Society," 2–6; Sydnor, *Slavery in Mississippi*, 203–214.

13. Miss. Const. (1817), VI, "Slaves," § 1. Figure 2.1 is compiled from information in Ira Berlin, *Slaves without Masters: The Free Negro in the Antebellum South* (1975), 396–99.

14. 1 Miss. 36, 42 (1818); see Mills, "Slave Law in Mississippi," 176–79. Other leading cases that applied a liberal sojourn rule included *Lunsford v. Coquillon*, 2 Martin N.S. 401 (La. 1824); *Winny v. Whitesides*, 1 Mo. 472 (1824); *Hunter v. Fulcher*, 1 Leigh 172 (Va. 1829); and *Blackmore v. Negro Phill*, 15 Tenn. 452 (1835). See generally Paul Finkelman, *An Imperfect Union: Slavery, Federalism and Comity* (1980), 181–235, 285–312.

15. Miss. Act of June 18, 1822, §§ 75 (emancipation), 80 (prohibiting entry of free blacks).

16. Miss. Act of June 18, 1822, §§ 8 (pass to travel), 10 (firearms); Miss. Act of January 16, 1823, §§ 1 (assembly), 3 (worship assembly). According to one historian, George Poindexter, one of the principal authors of the code, had proposed more drastic restrictions on worship by slaves. His proposal met with substantial resistance from white religious leaders, and its unpopularity contributed to his defeat for reelection as governor in 1822. Claiborne, *Mississippi as a Territory*, 385.

17. Miss. Act of June 18, 1822, §§ 32 (disputes with owner), 50 (conspiracy to rebel).

18. Miss. Act of June 26, 1822 (patrol); Miss. Act of January 16, 1823 (assembly for educational instruction). For a description of the code's harsh punishment of slave infractions, see Mills, "Slave Law in Mississippi," 168–69.

19. Miss. Act of June 18, 1822, §§ 9 (trading on own account), 26 (working for wages on own account), 42 (livestock), 43 (cotton), 8 (pass to travel), 10 (firearms); Miss. Act of January 16, 1823, §§ 1 (assembly), 3 (worship assembly).

20. See, e.g., Miss. Act of June 18, 1822, §§ 9–10, 31–32, 56–57.

21. U.S. Const. art. I, § 9; see Herbert J. Klein and Jacob Klein, *The Atlantic Slave Trade* (1999); Ronald Segal, *The Black Diaspora: Five Centuries of the Black Experience Outside Africa* (1995); see also *The Federalist*, no. 42 (James Madison) (Modern Library ed. 1937). Madison stated that although an immediate end to the trade "were doubtless to be wished," at least 1808 would see the end of "a traffic which has so long and so loudly upbraided the barbarism of modern policy." The Southwest Ordinance prohibited international slave trade in the territory, but the ban was widely ignored. 1 U.S. Stats. 123 (1790); Libby, *Slavery and Frontier Mississippi*, 52.

22. Sydnor, *Slavery in Mississippi*, 161–62; *Green v. Robinson*, 6 Miss. 80 (1840).

23. Miss. Terr. Laws, Act of March 1, 1808; Sydnor, *Slavery in Mississippi*, 162.

24. Miss. Const. (1817), Slaves, § 1; Brandon message to 1828 legislature, quoted in Sydnor, *Slavery in Mississippi*, 161–62; *Green*, 6 Miss. at 101; Libby, *Slavery in Frontier Mississippi*, 87–90.

25. *Green; Groves v. Slaughter*, 40 U.S. 449 (1841); *Brien v. Williamson*, 8 Miss. 14 (1843).

26. Sydnor, *Slavery in Mississippi*, 170.

27. See *Jincey v. Winfield's Administrator*, 9 Gratt. 708 (Va. 1853).

28. *See* Thomas D. Morris, *Southern Slavery and the Law, 1619–1860* (1996), 371–423; Wyatt-Brown, *Shaping of Southern Culture*, 141–46; see also, e.g., 1831 Tenn. Laws, ch. 52; *Fisher's Negroes v. Dabbs*, 14 Tenn. 119 (1834); *Thompson v. Newlin*, 3 Ired. Eq. 338 (N.C. 1844) and 8 Ired. Eq. 32 (1851).

29. 1801 Ga. Laws, p. 71; 1820 S.C. Laws, p. 22.

30. *Frazier v. Executors of Frazier*, 2 Hill Eq. 304 (S.C. 1835); *Vertner*, 6 Miss. at 361–62; Mills, "Slave Law in Mississippi," 185–86. In 1841, South Carolina's legislature enacted a law overruling *Frazier*, just as Mississippi's legislature overruled *Vertner*. 1841 S.C. Laws, p. 154. But O'Neall did not give up: the following year, he persuaded his colleagues to approve a stratagem allowing owners to bequeath slaves to others on condition that the slaves be "held to their own benefit and advantage," that is, free in all but name. *Carmille v. Carmille's Administrator*, 2 McMullen 454 (S.C. 1842).

31. See Edwin A. Miles, "The Mississippi Slave Insurrection Scare of 1835," 42 *Journal of Negro History* 48 (1957); Davidson B. McKibben, "Negro Slave Insurrections in Mississippi, 1800–1865," 34 *Journal of Negro History* 73 (1949).

32. *A Report and Resolution to the Gradual Emancipation of People of Color Held in Servitude in the United States*, 1826 Miss. Laws 125, quoted in Mills, "Slave Law in Mississippi," 173; *Report of the Legislature on the Annexation of Texas* (1837), in Herman V. Ames, ed., *State Documents on Federal Relations: The States and the United States* (1900; reprint 1970), 225; Sydnor, *Slavery in Mississippi*, 240–42, quoting George L. Prentiss, *Memoir of S. S. Prentiss* (1856), 1:107 and *Woodville (Miss.) Republican*, April 21, 1838. See also William W. Fisher, "Ideology and Imagery in the Law of Slavery," 68 *Chicago-Kent Law Review* 1051, 1075–77 (1993); Mills, "Slave Law in Mississippi," 156–61. The court had already begun to shift in the wake of the state's 1842 law prohibiting manumission: in 1848, it upheld that law and made clear that Mississippi policy did not permit recognition even of testamentary manumissions made in states that permitted them. *Mahorner v. Hooe*, 17 Miss. 247 (1848).

33. *Shaw v. Brown*, 35 Miss. 246, 317 (1858); *Scott v. Sandford*, 60 U.S. 393 (1857).

34. 37 Miss. 209 (1859), 232 (Harris), 233 (Handy dissent).

35. *Mitchell v. Wells*, 37 Miss. 235, 252 (1859), citing *Hinds v. Brazealle*, 3 Miss. 837 (1838).

36. 18 Pick. 193 (Mass. 1836); see also *Jackson v. Bulloch*, 12 Conn. 38 (1837); *State v. Farr* (Ohio, 1841), reported in *Cincinnati Gazette*, May 21 and June 1, 1841; Finkelman, *Imperfect Union*, 164–72; *Lemmon v. People*, 20 N.Y. 562 (1860).

37. *In re Booth*, 3 Wis. 1 (1854), *reversed*, 62 U.S. 506 (1859); *Ableman v. Booth*, 11 Wis. 501 (1859); *Ex parte Bushnell*, 9 Ohio St. 77 (1859); see Thomas D. Morris, *Free Men All: The Personal Liberty Laws of the North, 1780–1861* (1974), 42–106, 166–201.

38. 37 Miss. at 264.

39. On the eve of the Civil War, O'Neall persuaded South Carolina's supreme court to adhere to the spirit of *Frazier* and *Vertner*, notwithstanding his state's 1841 anti-*Frazier* law: the court held that the 1841 law did not apply to slaves manumitted by taking them to freedom outside South Carolina. When one of O'Neall's colleagues protested in dissent that the state should retaliate against recent efforts of Northern courts to encourage fugitive slaves, O'Neall rejoined: "I should feel myself degraded, if, like some in Ohio and other abolition States, I trampled on law and constitution, in obedience to popular will." *Willis v. Jolliffe*, 11 Rich. Eq. 447, 515 (S.C. 1860); see A. E. Keir Nash, "Negro Rights, Unionism, and Greatness on the South Carolina Court of Appeals: The Extraordinary Chief Justice John Belton O'Neall," 21 *South Carolina Law Review* 141, 160 (1969).

40. 37 Miss. at 286 (Handy dissent); Mills, "Slave Law in Mississippi," 216–29.

41. *State v. Mann*, 13 N.C. 263, 266 (1829); see Morris, *Southern Slavery and the Law*, 189–92; A. E. Keir Nash, "Reason of Slavery: Understanding the Judicial Role in the Peculiar Institution," 32 *Vanderbilt Law Review* 1, 74–79 (1979); *Jacob v. State*, 22 Tenn. 493 (1842); *Craig's Administrator v. Lee*, 53 Ky. 119 (1853).

42. "A Law for the regulation of Slaves" (March 30, 1799); Ethridge, "Sargent's Code," 192–96; Miss. Laws, Act of June 18, 1822, § 44 (no cruel and unusual punishment), 1822 Code §§ 58, 68–74 (jury trial of slaves, appointment of counsel).

43. 1822 Code, § 58; George M. Stroud, *A Sketch of the Laws Relating to Slavery in the Several States of the United States of America* (1856), 27.

44. *Peter v. State*, 12 Miss. 31 (1844); *Van Buren v. State*, 24 Miss. 512 (1852); 30 Miss. 593 (1856); *Simon v. State*, 37 Miss. 288 (1858); Daniel J. Flanigan, "Criminal Procedure in Slave Trials in the Antebellum South," 40 *Journal of Southern History* 537, 562–64 (1974); Morris, *Southern Slavery and the Law*, 215–28.

45. *State v. Jones*, 1 Miss. 83 (1821); *Kelly v. State*, 11 Miss. 518 (1844). See also *Scott v. State*, 31 Miss. 473 (1856) (upholding conviction of overseer for cruel treatment of slaves).

46. 26 Miss. 410 (1853).

47. *George v. State*, 37 Miss. 316, 320 (1859); 1860 Miss. Laws, ch. 62. One scholar has also argued that *George* marked the end of a long period during which the court had gradually concluded that common-law rights did not extend to slaves: it was strictly for the legislature to determine what protections they would have. Mark Tushnet, "The American Law of Slavery, 1810–1860: A Study in the Persistence of Legal Autonomy," 10 *Law and Society Review* 119, 123–24 (1975).

48. 39 Miss. 526, 540 (1860); see also Morris, *Becoming Southern*, 174–76. During the 1850s, the court preserved some additional, if minimal, protection for slaves. It did not interfere with the rule laid down in *Kelly* that slaves could lawfully resist an owner's attempt to kill them, and in *Thompson v. Young*, 30 Miss. 17, 18 (1855), it held that fugitives could lawfully be killed only if they threatened to kill or harm their pursuers. "The law," proclaimed Chief Justice Smith, "is careful of the safety of the slave within his prescribed sphere." Evidence of an owner's bad character, however, could not be considered in determining whether he had used excessive force against a slave. *Wesley v. State*, 37 Miss. 327 (1859).

49. Moore, *Emergence of the Cotton Kingdom*, 79–81, 98 (quoting John Gilmer of Lowndes County); Libby, *Slavery and Frontier Mississippi*, 53–54, 58–59, 99.

50. Moore, *Emergence of the Cotton Kingdom*, 83–85, 101–105, 270–72; Libby, *Slavery and Frontier Mississippi*, 58, 99; J. Michael Crane, "Controlling the Night: Perceptions of the Slave Patrol System in Mississippi," 61 *Journal of Mississippi History* 119, 135 (1999); Morris, *Becoming Southern*, 78–80.

51. See Joseph A. Ranney, "'This New and Beautiful Organism': The Evolution of American Federalism in Three State Supreme Courts," 87 *Marquette Law Review* 253, 255, 259–60, 267 (2003); Hicks, *Lumpkin*, 8–28, 107–110.

52. See *Federalist*, no. 46 (James Madison); see also no. 9 (Hamilton) and no. 40 (Madison). Hamilton revealed his feelings in the context of threats of intramural secession (that is, boycotts) by legislative factions that could not get their way: such secession was "a baneful practice . . . which leads more directly to public convulsions, and the ruin of popular governments, than any other which has yet been displayed among us." *Federalist*, no. 58 (Hamilton).

53. Forrest McDonald, *States' Rights and the Union: Imperium in Imperio, 1776–1876* (2000), 40–41; Ames, *State Documents*, 15–25. The Alien and Sedition Acts provided criminal

penalties against persons who published "false, scandalous or malicious" statements about the government, the president, or Congress. 1 U.S. Stats. 566, 570, 577, 596 (1798).

54. Leonard W. Levy, ed., *The Virginia Report of 1799–1800: Touching the Alien and Sedition Laws* (1970), 22.

55. *Hunter v. Martin*, 18 Va. 1 (1813), *reversed*, 14 U.S. 304 (1816); see also McDonald, *States Rights and the Union*, 76–79; Timothy S. Huebner, *The Southern Judicial Tradition: State Judges and Sectional Distinctiveness, 1790–1890* (1999), 10–39.

56. *Green v. Biddle*, 21 US. 18 (1823); Mc Donald, *States' Rights and the Union*, 79–84; Desha, Message to Kentucky Legislature; November 7, 1825, reprinted in Ames, *State Documents*, 113; *Bodley v. Gaither*, 19 Ky. 57 (1825).

57. *State ex rel. McCready v. Hunt*, 2 Hill 1 (S.C. 1834).

58. See *Flint River Steamboat Co. v. Foster*, 5 Ga. 194, 204–205 (1848); *Beall v. Beall*, 8 Ga. 210, 216 (1850); *Campbell v. State*, 11 Ga. 353, 366 (1852).

59. *Padelford, Fay & Co. v. Mayor of Savannah*, 14 Ga. 438, 499–501 (1854). Georgia had two major antebellum clashes with federal authorities. In the mid-1790s, it resisted efforts to enforce a US Supreme Court decision holding that creditors of British loyalists whose lands had been confiscated during the Revolution could sue the state for redress, and in the 1830s, it took control of the gold-rich Cherokee lands in north Georgia in defiance of the federal high court. See *Chisholm v. Georgia*, 2 U.S. 419 (1792); *Cherokee Nation v. Georgia*, 30 U.S.1 (1831); *Worcester v. Georgia*, 31 U.S. 515 (1832); McDonald, *States Rights and the Union*, 35–36, 98–103; Ames, State Documents, 9–11; Tim A. Garrison, *The Legal Ideology of Removal: The Southern Judiciary and the Sovereignty of Native American Nations* (2002), 103–124, 229–32.

60. 1829 Miss. Laws, pp. 108–109; 1833 Miss. Laws, pp. 246–48; Ames, *State Documents*, 51–52, 108–109; Lucie Robertson Bridgeforth, "Mississippi's Response to Nullification, 1833," 45 *Journal of Mississippi History* 1, 3–4, 7–8, 14–15 (1983).

61. *Brien v. Williamson*, 8 Miss. at 16; Mills, "Slave Law in Mississippi," 207–211.

62. In 1837, the legislature, reacting to Northern opposition to annexation of Texas as a slave state, supported annexation as necessary to preserve the institution "with which the affections of her people are so closely entwined and so completely enfibered," one which was being "violently assailed and boldly threatened." Four years later, the legislature denounced Northern resistance to extradition of fugitive slaves and vowed to pursue "any mode or measure of resistance necessary for . . . our protection." 1841 Miss. Laws, p. 155; Ames, *State Documents*, 225–26; Wyatt-Brown, *Shaping of Southern Culture*, 199–200 .

63. The Compromise provided for admission of California as a free state but also gave concessions to the South, including a strengthened federal fugitive slave law and permission for the people of Utah and New Mexico to adopt slavery if they desired. 9 U.S. Stats. 446, 452–53, 462, 467 (1850).

64. *Journal of the Convention of the State of Mississippi* (1851), 29–30 (Harris report), 47–49 (majority report).

65. Bradley G. Bond, *Political Culture in the Nineteenth-Century South: Mississippi, 1830–1900* (1995), 99–107.

66. 1850 Miss. Laws, ch. 31; 1861 Miss. Laws, ch. 40; see also 1854 Miss. Laws, ch. 36 (revising procedures for slave trials).

67. 60 U.S. 393 (1857). One modern Mississippi jurist and historian has concluded that the importance of the *Dred Scott* decision to the hardening of popular and judicial attitudes about slavery in the last years before the Civil War "cannot be overstated." Mills, "Slave Law in Mississippi," 175–76, 212–14.

68. 1860 (November) Miss. Laws, ch. 13.

69. See http://civilwarcauses.org/wharris.htm (Harris speech to Georgia legislature, December 17, 1860); Dunbar Rowland, *Courts, Judges and Lawyers of Mississippi, 1798–1935* (1935), 94–95.

Chapter Three

1. *The Flush Times of Alabama and Mississippi* (1853), 83.

2. Sandra Moncrief, "The Mississippi Married Women's Property Act of 1839," 47 *Journal of Mississippi History* 110, 116–17 (1985); Elizabeth Gaspar Brown, Note, "Husband and Wife—Memorandum on the Mississippi Woman's Law of 1839," 42 *Michigan Law Review* 1110 (1944); 1839 Miss. Laws, ch. 46.

3. Moncrief, "Married Woman's Property Act," 116–18; Brown, "Memorandum on Mississippi Woman's Law," 1113–14; 1837 Miss. Laws, p. 34.

4. Brown, "Memorandum on Mississippi Woman's Law," 1117; *Fisher v. Allen*, 3 Miss. 611 (1837).

5. Brown, "Memorandum on Mississippi Woman's Law," 1111–12; 1835 Ark. Terr. Laws, pp. 34–35; Richard H. Chused, "Married Women's Property Law: 1800–1850," 71 *Georgetown Law Journal* 1359, 1397–1404 (1983).

6. 1839 Miss. Laws, ch. 46, § 1; Moncrief, "Married Woman's Property Act," 115–20; Brown, Memorandum on Mississippi Woman's Law," 1113–16; Claiborne, *Mississippi as a Province*, 475.

7. Moncrief, "Married Woman's Property Act," 115–24; Brown, "Memorandum on Mississippi Woman's Law," 1113–16.

8. Moore, *Emergence of the Cotton Kingdom*, xii, 232–35, 242–43; Beckert, *Empire of Cotton*, xx, 202–203, 317–18; Bond, *Political Culture*, 18–21, 66–68; Sydnor, *Development of Southern Sectionalism*, 260–62.

9. Bond, *Political Culture*, 83–89; Skates, *Mississippi Supreme Court*, 14–20; Harold Woodman, *King Cotton and His Retainers: Financing and Marketing the Cotton Crop of the South, 1800–1915* (1968).

10. Message to United States Congress, July 10, 1832, available at www.avalon.law.yale.edu/19th_century/ajveto01.asp; Arthur M. Schlesinger Jr., *The Age of Jackson* (1950 ed.), 74–143, 171–209, 306–349; Marvin Meyers, *The Jacksonian Persuasion: Politics and Belief* (1957), 17–23, 92–107, 172–75.

11. See, e.g., Ky. Const. (1792), III; Tenn. Const. (1796), III:1; Ohio Const. (1803), IV:1; La. Const. (1812), II:8; Ind. Const. (1816), VI:1.

12. See Md. Const. (1810), amdt. XIV; N.Y. Const. (1821), II:1; Va. Const. (1830), III:14; Del. Const. (1831), IV:1; R.I. Const. (1843), I:1–2; N.J. Const. (1844), II:1.

13. Miss. Const. (1817), III:8–9, IV:3; Miss. Const. (1832), I:20; Drake, "Framing of Mississippi's First Constitution," 325–27 (1967); Drake, "Convention of 1832," 362; see also Chapter 1.

14. Coleman, *Debtors and Creditors*, 6–15, 39–42, 105–114, 191–99; Jerome Mushkat and Joseph G. Rayback, *Martin Van Buren: Law, Politics, and the Shaping of Republican Ideology* (1997), 76–78; Miss. Const. (1817), VI:9. The 1817 Constitution required debtors to make their existing assets available to creditors in order to avoid prison, and it allowed imprisonment of debtors who fraudulently concealed their assets. Id. Mississippi did not completely abolish imprisonment for debt until the Reconstruction era. Miss. Const. (1868), I:11.

15. John W. Cadman, *The Corporation in New Jersey: Business and Politics, 1791–1875* (1949), 3–110; George J. Kuehnl, *The Wisconsin Business Corporation* (1959), 6–13.

16. Leggett in the *(New York) Plaindealer*, December 24, 1836, reprinted in Theodore Sedgwick Jr., *A Collection of the Political Writings of William Leggett* (1840), II:138.

17. Leggett in the New York Evening Post, August 6, 1834, reprinted in Sedgwick, *Writings of Leggett*, I:41.

18. Schlesinger, *Age of Jackson*, 74–102; Robert V. Remini, *The Life of Andrew Jackson* (1988), 220–32, 272–77.

19. Miss. Const. (1817), VI:9; 1817 Miss. Laws, pp. 124, 212; Sydnor, *Development of Southern Sectionalism*, 260–61; Busbee, *Mississippi*, 83–84.

20. 1830 Miss. Laws, p. 92; Miss. Const. (1832), VII:9; Sydnor, *Development of Southern Sectionalism*, 260–61; Busbee, *Mississippi*, 83–84.

21. Davis, *Recollections of Mississippi*, 105, 137; Bond, *Political Culture*, 69, 83; Busbee, *Mississippi*, 75–76.

22. 1837 Miss. Laws, pp. 34, 39; 1838 Miss. Laws, pp. 9, 33; Bond, *Political Culture*, 83–89.

23. Bond, *Political Culture*, 83–84; Carter Goodrich, *Government Promotion of American Canals and Railroads* (1960), 63–87, 102–120, 123–52, 162–65.

24. Bond, *Political Culture*, 85–86, quoting *Mississippi Senate Journal* (1841), 21.

25. Skates, *Mississippi Supreme Court*, 19–20.

26. 35 Miss. 625 (1853).

27. Bond, *Political Culture*, 85–86; Busbee, *Mississippi*, 95–98; J. A. P. Campbell, "Planters and Union Bank Bonds," 4 *Publications of the Mississippi Historical Society* 493 (1901); 1840 Miss. Laws, p. 13; Miss. Const. (1876), XII:5; Miss. Const. (1890), § 258.

28. 17 U.S. 518, 628–29 (1819); see also G. Edward White and Gerald Gunther, *The Marshall Court and Cultural Change, 1815–1835* (1988), 612–28.

29. See, e.g., Del. Const. (1831) II:17; Pa. Const. (1838), I:25; Iowa Const. (1846), VIII:12; Wis. Const. (1848), XI:1; Mich Const. (1850), XV:1; Ohio Const. (1851), XIII:2; Kuehnl, *Wisconsin Business Corporation*, 14–17, 148–49.

30. 36 U.S. 420, 536–38, 549–50 (1837).

31. 1820 Miss. Laws, p. 33. Figure 3.1 is derived from a tabulation of corporate charters listed in the indexes to volumes of session laws from 1838 to 1890. Laws incorporating municipalities and organizations created to perform public functions such as fire brigades are not included in the figures. Tabulations are in the author's possession.

32. 11 Miss. 661 (1844), *reversed*, 47 U.S. 301 (1848).

33. Bond, *Political Culture*, 82–83; 1840 Miss. Laws, pp. 13, 15.

34. *Payne*, 11 Miss. at 679.

35. 1840 Miss. Laws, p. 22; *Planters Bank v. Sharp*, 12 Miss. 17 (1844), *reversed*, 47 U.S. 301 (1848); Meredith Lang, *Defender of the Faith: The High Court of Mississippi, 1817–1875* (1977), 30–45.

36. *Grand Gulf Railroad & Banking Co. v. State*, 18 Miss. 428 (1848); *Montgomery v. Galbraith*, 19 Miss. 555 (1848); *McIntyre v. Ingraham*, 35 Miss. 525 (1858).

37. *Nevitt v. Bank of Port Gibson*, 14 Miss. 513, 525 (1846); *Collins v. Sherman*, 31 Miss. 679, 699–700 (1856).

38. Miss. Const. (1817) VI:2; Hicks, *Men and Books*, 75; 12 & 13 Will.3, c. 2 (Eng.) (1700); see Chapter 1.

39. Miss. Const. (1832), IV:2; Drake, "Convention of 1832," 359–60, 364, 370 (1957); Quitman to J. Fenwick Brent, March 22, 1845, letter reprinted in Louisiana Constitutional Convention, *Proceedings and Debates* (1845), 755; see Chapter 1.

40. Frederick Grimke, *Considerations on the Nature and Tendency of Free Institutions* (1848; 1871 ed.), 138, 478.

41. Milo M. Quaife, *The Convention of 1846* (1919), 289 (Charles Baker of Wisconsin); *Report of the Debates and Proceedings of the Convention for the Revision of the Constitution of the State of New York, 1846* (1846), 719 (Levi Chatfield).

42. William Blackstone, *Commentaries on the Law of England* (1765), I:430; Marylynn Salmon, *Women and the Law of Property in Early America* (1986), 159–60, 199–201; Norma Basch, *In the Eyes of the Law: Women, Property and Marriage in Nineteenth-Century New York* (1982), 51–55.

43. Salmon, *Women and the Law of Property*, 28–30, 41–44, 112–15, 504; Basch, *In the Eyes of the Law*, 72–75; Hamilton, *Anglo-American Law*, 129–31; Guice, "Cement of Society," 88–89.

44. *Journal of the Senate of the State of Mississippi* (1839), 260–61, quoted in Brown, "Mississippi Woman's Law," 1114–15.

45. Kyle G. Volk, *Moral Minorities and the Making of American Democracy* (2014), 70–81; Ian R. Tyrrell, *Sobering Up: From Temperance to Prohibition in Antebellum America, 1800–1860* (1979), 6–11, 34–38, 179–82, 216–18.

46. *Journal of the Senate of the State of Mississippi* (1839), 260–61, quoted in Brown, "Mississippi Woman's Law," 1115.

47. 1839 Miss. Laws, ch. 46, § 1; Joan Hoff, *Law, Gender and Injustice: A Legal History of U.S. Women* (1991), 377–82. The national movement to adopt married women's property laws began in earnest in the mid-1840s: between 1843 and 1852, seventeen states enacted separate-estate laws and five additional states and territories enacted debt-free laws only.

48. *Grand Gulf Bank v. Barnes*, 10 Miss. 165 (1844); 1846 Miss. Laws, ch. 13; *Ratliffe v. Dougherty*, 24 Miss. 181 (1851) (holding that the 1839 and 1846 laws did not limit traditional equitable rights married women had had with respect to their property); *Warren v. Brown*, 25 Miss. 66 (1852) (same); *Wells v. Treadwell*, 28 Miss. 717 (1855) (holding that husbands could not impair wives' right to dispose of their slaves freely by selling the husband's lifetime interest in use of the slaves).

49. 1846 Miss. Laws, ch. 13; Miss. Rev. Code (1857), art. 25; Miss. Rev. Code (1871), § 1778; Miss. Const. (1890), § 94. See also Brown, "Mississippi Woman's Law," 1118; *Netterville v. Barber*, 52 Miss. 168 (1876) (affirming that plaintiff, a wife who had founded a sawmill and forestry operation, had individual control of all aspects of the operation under the 1871 code).

50. Florida, Alabama, and Texas enacted separate-estate laws and Kentucky and Tennessee enacted debt-free laws between 1845 and 1850. Among the older states, North Carolina enacted a separate-estate law in 1850, but Virginia (1877), South Carolina (1868), and Georgia (1868) did not do so until the Reconstruction era. Hoff, *Law, Gender and Injustice*, 381; Suzanne D. Lebsock, "Radical Reconstruction and the Property Rights of Southern Women," 43 *Journal of Southern History* 195 (1977).

51. Early Mississippi divorce law presented a more ambiguous picture. Like most states created after the Revolution, Mississippi allowed divorce more liberally than older states, where divorce often was available only for adultery and, in some cases, only with legislative consent. In 1822, Mississippi's legislature authorized courts to grant final divorces based on desertion for a period of five years or more, and to grant decrees of legal separation, which would allow wives to receive alimony, for "extreme cruelty." Miss. Laws, Act of June 14, 1822, §§ 3, 6. One historian has argued that lawmakers allowed separation for cruelty because they recognized that as Mississippi moved from a subsistence farm economy to a slave-based and highly commercialized cotton economy, planters' wives had less economic importance and power than formerly and, thus, needed more legal protection. Morris, *Becoming Southern*, 57–59. Another historian has argued that Mississippi courts limited wives' power by

interpreting the term "extreme cruelty" more narrowly than other courts. Jane Turner Censer, "'Smiling Through Her Tears': Ante-Bellum Southern Women and Divorce," 25 *American Journal of Legal History* 24, 34, 40, 57 (1981), citing *Waskam v. Waskam*, 31 Miss. 154 (1856).

52. Coleman, *Debtors and Creditors*, 39–48, 103–114, 191–200; Paul Goodman, "The Emergence of the Homestead Exemption in the United States: Accommodation and Resistance to the Market Revolution, 1840–1880," 80 *Journal of American History* 470, 490 (Sept. 1993); 2 H. Gammel, *Laws of Texas* (1898), 125 (Act of January 26, 1839); Tex. Const. (1845), VII:22.

53. Goodman, "Emergence of Homestead Exemption," 472–93. For examples of arguments made in favor of and against homestead exemptions, see *Report of the Debates and Proceedings of the Convention for the Revision of the Constitution of the State of Indiana* (1851), 751 (Alvan Hovey), 786 (Robert Dale Owen); Benjamin F. Shambaugh, ed., *Fragments of the Debates of the Iowa Constitutional Conventions of 1844 and 1846* (1900), 159–61, 408.

54. 1841 Miss. Laws, ch. 15; *Proceedings of 1850 Indiana Convention*, 747 (Schuyler Colfax).

55. Goodrich, *American Canals and Railroads*, 52–61.

56. Goodrich, *American Canals and Railroads*, 61–120, 123–65. Many canal and railroad ventures suspended construction or went out of business due to lack of funds, leaving leading investor states such as Maryland, Illinois, and Michigan deeply in debt. Other states continued to support construction through hard times, and most of the leading debtor states continued to encourage or at least tolerate municipal investment. Goodrich, 78–81, 141–46.

57. *Sharpless v. Mayor of Philadelphia*, 21 Pa. 147, 169 (1853).

58. N.J. Const. (1844), IV:65; Tex. Const. (1845), VII:33; N.Y. Const. (1846), VII:1; Iowa Const. (1846), VIII:3; Ill. Const. (1848), III:37; Wis. Const. (1848), VIII:4, 6; Ky. Const. (1850), II:35; Mich. Const. (1850), XIV:3–4; Calif. Const. (1850), VII; Ohio Const. (1851), VII:1; Ind. Const. (1851), X:5; Md. Const. (1851), III:22.

59. N.Y. Const. (1846), VII:9; Iowa Const. (1846), VII:3; Ill. Const. (1848), III:38; Wis. Const. (1848), VIII:10; Ky. Const. (1850), II:33; Mich. Const. (1850), XIV:6; Ohio Const. (1851), VIII:4.

60. See, e.g., *Goddin v. Crump*, 8 Leigh 120 (Va. 1837); *City of Bridgeport v. Hoosatonuc R. Co.*, 15 Conn. 475 (1843); *Nichol v. Town of Nashville*, 28 Tenn. 252 (1848); *Sharpless v. Mayor of Philadelphia*, 21 Pa. 147 (1853); *Cotton v. Leon County Commissioners*, 6 Fla. 610 (1856); *Caldwell v. Justices of County of Burke*, 4 Jones 323 (N.C. 1858); *Lowell v. City of Boston*, 111 Mass. 454 (1873).

61. Bond, *Political Culture*, 108–110; John F. Stover, "Colonel Henry S. McComb, Mississippi Railroad Adventurer," 17 *Journal of Mississippi History* 177 (1955).

62. *Hanson v. Vernon*, 27 Iowa 28 (1869); *People v. Township Board of Salem*, 20 Mich. 452 (1870); Thomas B. Cooley, *A Treatise on the Constitutional Limitations Which Rest Upon the Legislative Power of the States of the American Union* (1868), 175, 213–19, 282 n.1, 357–58.

63. Wisconsin's supreme court, speaking through its chief justice Luther Dixon, held that government subsidies were constitutional only if they were coupled with substantial government power to regulate railroad rates and business operations. *Whiting v. Sheboygan & Fond du Lac Railroad Co.*, 25 Wis. 167 (1870).

64. See Alan R. Jones, *The Constitutional Conservatism of Thomas McIntyre Cooley: A Study in the History of Ideas* (1987), 16–26, 48–53; Clyde Jacobs, *Law Writers and the Courts: The Influence of Thomas M. Cooley, Christopher G. Tiedeman, and John F. Dillon upon American Constitutional Law* (1973), 111–14.

65. Mark W. Summers, *Railroads, Reconstruction and the Gospel of Prosperity: Aid Under the Radical Republicans, 1865–1877* (1984), ix–xii, 10–12, 45–52.

66. 1871 Miss. Laws, ch. 745; Bond, *Political Culture*, 196–99; Summers, *Gospel of Prosperity*, 68–95, 250–54.

67. 1872 Miss. Laws, chs. 90, 101; 1873 Miss. Laws, ch. 118; 1874 Miss. Laws, ch. 53; Richard A. McLemore, ed., *A History of Mississippi* (1973), 554–66.

68. 50 Miss. 735, 757–58 (1874).

69. Miss. Const. (1890), §§ 95, 100, 183.

70. Bond, *Political Culture*, 200–101; Stover, "McComb."

71. Leggett in *New York Evening Post*, August 6, 1834, reprinted in Sedgwick, *Writings of Leggett*, 1:41.

72. Cadman, *The Corporation in New Jersey*, 160–201; Christopher Grandy, *New Jersey and the Fiscal Origins of Modern American Corporation Law* (1993).

73. 1871 Miss. Laws, ch. 142 (ice plants and waterworks); 1880 Miss. Laws, ch. 1; George H. Ethridge, *Mississippi Constitutions* (1938), 202.

74. Miss. Const. (1890), §§ 87–88 (general incorporation laws), § 178 (anti-Dartmouth clause, providing that "[t]he Legislature shall have power to alter, amend or repeal any charter of incorporation now existing and revocable, and any that may hereafter be created, whenever, in its opinion, it may be for the public interest to do so"); Eric C. Clark, "Regulation of Corporations in the Mississippi Constitutional Convention of 1890," 48 *Journal of Mississippi History* 31, 32–37 (1986).

75. Bond, *Political Culture*, 209–212; Busbee, *Mississippi*, 183–87.

76. Useful studies of the war's effect on Southern women's place in society include Lee Ann Whites, *The Civil War as a Crisis in Gender: Augusta, Georgia, 1860–1890* (1995); Anne Firor Scott, *The Southern Lady: From Pedestal to Politics, 1830–1930* (1995); Sally G. McMillen, *Southern Women: Black and White in the Old South* (2nd ed. 2002).

Chapter Four

1. *Donnell v. State*, 48 Miss. 661, 675 (1873).

2. William C. Harris, *The Day of the Carpetbagger: Republican Reconstruction in Mississippi* (1979), 220–22; Joseph A. Ranney, *In the Wake of Slavery: Civil War, Civil Rights and the Reconstruction of Southern Law* (2006), 23–24.

3. Harris, *Day of the Carpetbagger*, 122–32; William C. Harris, "Formulation of the First Mississippi Plan: The Black Code of 1865," 29 *Journal of Mississippi History* 181, 184–89, 193 (1967); Alfred H. Stone, "Mississippi's Constitution and Statutes in Reference to Freedmen, and Their Alleged Relation to the Reconstruction Acts and War Amendments," 4 *Proceedings of the Mississippi Historical Society* 143, 211–12 (1901); David G. Sansing, "The Failure of Johnsonian Reconstruction in Mississippi, 1865–1866," 34 *Journal of Mississippi History* 373 (1972).

4. The acts provided that only those who took an oath that they had never given "aid, countenance, counsel, or encouragement" to the Confederate war effort and had never served in the Confederate armies or held government office under the Confederacy were eligible to vote. Military rule would not end and the states would not be admitted to representation in Congress until they ratified the federal Fourteenth Amendment, which conferred full rights of citizenship on black Americans and required states to afford them due process and equal protection of the laws. 14 U.S. Stats. 428–30 (1867); 15 U.S. Stats. 2–5, 14–16, 41 (1867).

5. James A. Baggett, *The Scalawags: Southern Dissenters in the Civil War and Reconstruction* (2003), 253 (quoting Simrall); William C. Harris, *The Day of the Carpetbagger: Reconstruction in Mississippi* (1979), 207–209, 215–16.

6. Harris, *Day of the Carpetbagger*, 301–302; James W. Garner, *Reconstruction in Mississippi* (1901), 216–28; Ranney, *Wake of Slavery*, 23–24.

7. During the Restoration period Justices Harris and Handy held over as members of the supreme court, along with Henry Ellett, who was appointed during the war. All three resigned in protest against the Reconstruction Acts and General Edward Ord, Mississippi's military commander, appointed a Military Reconstruction court comprised of native Unionists Ephraim Peyton, Thomas Shackelford, and Elza Jeffords. Simrall's colleagues on the Domestic Reconstruction court were Peyton, whom Alcorn retained, and Jonathan Tarbell, a Union officer who had settled in Mississippi after the war and had become a Republican leader. Harris, *Day of the Carpetbagger*, 68–69; William C. Harris, *Presidential Reconstruction in Mississippi* (1967), 115–16; Skates, *Mississippi Supreme Court*, 31, 35–36.

8. See, e.g., *Thomas v. Taylor*, 42 Miss. 651, 710 (1869); *Buchanan v. Smith*, 43 Miss. 90 (1870).

9. See, e.g., *Berry v. Alsop*, 45 Miss. 1 (1871); *Cowan v. Stamps*, 46 Miss. 435 (1872); *Donnell v. State*, 48 Miss. 661 (1873).

10. Janet Sharp Hermann, *Pursuit of A Dream* (1999), 11–13, 17–18, 153–60; Steven J. Ross, "Freed Soil, Freed Labor, Freed Men: John Eaton and the Davis Bend Experiment," 44 *Journal of Southern History* 351, 358 (1978); Harris, *Day of the Carpetbagger*, 278; W. E. B. Du Bois, *Black Reconstruction* (1935), 434; Albert D. Kirwan, *Revolt of the Rednecks: Mississippi Politics, 1876–1925* (1951), 79–80; Christopher Waldrep, *Roots of Disorder: Race and Criminal Justice in the American South, 1817–80* (1998), 10–12.

11. Hermann, *Pursuit of a Dream*, 153–60; Harris, *Day of the Carpetbagger*, 661–74, 697–98; Skates, *Mississippi Supreme Court*, 37–39, 42; Stephen Cresswell, *Rednecks, Redeemers and Race: Mississippi after Reconstruction, 1877–1917* (2006), 70–75.

12. Kirwan, *Revolt of the Rednecks*, 58–78; J. S. McNeilly, "History of Measures Submitted to the Committee on Elective Franchise, Apportionment, and Elections in the Constitutional Convention of 1890," 6 *Proceedings of the Mississippi Historical Society* 129, 130–33 (1902); Cresswell, *Mississippi after Reconstruction*, 114–16; Ranney, *Wake of Slavery*, 137.

13. McNeilly, "History of Measures," 139; Kirwan, *Revolt of the Rednecks*, 67.

14. Cresswell, *Mississippi after Reconstruction*, 118–19; Neal R. McMillen, *Dark Journey: Black Mississippians in the Age of Jim Crow* (1989), 49–57, 257; Kirwan, *Revolt of the Rednecks*, 82; Leon F. Litwack, *Been in the Storm So Long: The Aftermath of Slavery* (1979), 52–63; Hermann, *Pursuit of a Dream*, 228–37.

15. Eric S. Foner, *Reconstruction: America's Unfinished Revolution, 1863–1877* (1988), 78–88; Ranney, *Wake of Slavery*, 35–45.

16. George M. Fredrickson, *The Black Image in the White Mind: The Debate on Afro-American Character and Destiny, 1817–1914* (1971); James L. Roark, *Masters without Slaves: Southern Planters in the Civil War and Reconstruction* (1977), 85–94, 104–108, 133–55; Wyatt-Brown, *Shaping of Southern Culture*, 232–33, 260–63; Litwack, *Been in the Storm So Long*, 52–62, 177–79; Foner, *Reconstruction*, 35–50.

17. *Journal of the Proceedings and Debates in the Constitutional Convention of the State of Mississippi, August, 1865* (1865), 55, 70–72, 90–93 (delegate expressions of hope that slavery would be preserved or that owners would be compensated for lost slaves); 107 (Robert M. Brown, "stigma upon the graves" remark), 115 (Jarnagin); Foner, *Reconstruction*, 66–67,

182–84; Mark W. Summers, *The Ordeal of the Reunion: A New History of Reconstruction* (2014), 69–70; Garner, *Reconstruction in Mississippi*, 82–94.

18. *Journal of 1865 Mississippi Convention*, 152 (Yerger), 215 (Goode); Miss. Const. (1865), VIII:1.

19. *Congressional Globe*, 37th Cong., 2d sess., 736–37 (February 11, 1862); "Our Domestic Relations," reprinted in Charles Sumner, *Works of Sumner* (1875–83), 7:493, 523, 527, 540; *id.*, 6:309; Ranney, *Wake of Slavery*, 67–76.

20. This philosophy prevailed most strongly in West Virginia, Tennessee, and Missouri during the years immediately after the war. See, e.g., 1865 Tenn. Laws, ch. 19; 1865–66 W.Va. laws, ch. 71; Mo. Const. (1865), XI:4; *Yost v. Stout*, 44 Tenn. 205 (1867); *Hedges v. Price*, 2 W.Va. 192 (1867); Ranney, *Wake of Slavery*, 33–34.

21. 1866–67 Miss. Laws, p. 403; *Ford v. Surget*, 46 Miss. 130, 156 (1871).

22. 40 Miss. 618, 627, 639 (1866). Reconstruction-era courts in Tennessee, West Virginia, Arkansas, and Texas adopted *ab initio*, but their post-Reconstruction successors generally repudiated the doctrine. Compare, e.g., *Luter v. Hunter*, 30 Tex. 688 (1868) with *San Patricio County v. McClane*, 44 Tex. 392 (1876); *Latham v. Clark*, 25 Ark. 574 (1870) with *Berry v. Bellows*, 30 Ark, 198 (1876); *Wright & Cantrell v. Overall*, 42 Tenn. 336 (1865) with *Sherfy v. Argenbright*, 48 Tenn. 128 (1870); and *Brown v. Wylie*, 2 W.Va. 502 (1867) with *Clay v. Robinson*, 7 W.Va. 348 (1874). See also Ranney, *Wake of Slavery*, 67–75.

23. *See* Chapters 1 and 2.

24. *Green v. Sizer*, 40 Miss. 530, 553, 560–61 (1866); *Murrell v. Jones*, 40 Miss. 465, 576 (1866).

25. *Marshall v. Grimes*, 41 Miss. 27 (1866); *State v. McGinty*, 41 Miss. 435 (1867); *Buchanan v. Smith*, 43 Miss. 90 (1870).

26. *Harlan v. State*, 41 Miss. 566 (1867) (criminal laws); *Cassell v. Backrack*, 42 Miss. 56 (1868) (foreclosure sale).

27. *Pickens v. Eskridge*, 42 Miss. 114 (1868).

28. *Thomas v. Taylor*, 42 Miss. 651, 710 (1869).

29. 74 U.S. 700, 725, 733, 735–36 (1869).

30. Ranney, *Wake of Slavery*, 67–75; Charles E. Fairman, *History of the Supreme Court of the United States, Vol. 6: Reconstruction and Reunion, 1864–1888* (1971), 852–53.

31. See, e.g., *Luter v. Hunter*, 30 Tex. 688 (1868); *Latham v. Clark*, 25 Ark. 574 (1870). Post-Reconstruction courts in Texas and Arkansas overturned their predecessors' decisions. *San Patricio County v. McClane*, 44 Tex. 392 (1876), *Berry v. Bellows*, 30 Ark, 198 (1876). See also Ranney, *Wake of Slavery*, 67–75.

32. 75 U.S. 1, 11 (1869); Fairman, *Reconstruction and Reunion*, 852–53; Ranney, *Wake of Slavery*, 67–75; *Beauchamp v. Comfort*, 42 Miss. 94 (1868); *Cowan v. McCutchen*, 43 Miss. 207 (1870); *Gray v. Harris*, 43 Miss. 421 (1870). In *Darcey & Wheeler v. Shotwell*, 49 Miss. 631 (1873), the domestic-Reconstruction court held that the value of an obligation in federal dollars must be scaled down as of the date the obligation was incurred, not the date it fell due.

33. *Ex parte Milligan*, 71 U.S. 2 (1866); *Ex parte McCardle*, 74 U.S. 506 (1869); Harris, *Day of the Carpetbagger*, 17–19; Garner, *Reconstruction in Mississippi*, 167–71.

34. *Ex parte Yerger*, 75 U.S. 85 (1869); Stanley I. Kutler, "Ex Parte McCardle, Judicial Incompetency? The Supreme Court and Reconstruction Reconsidered," 72 *American Historical Review* 835 (1967); Harris, *Day of the Carpetbagger*, 58–61.

35. *Welborn v. Mayrant*, 48 Miss. 652, 659 (1873) (Tarbell dissent); *Shattuck v. Daniel*, 52 Miss. 834, 837 (1876).

36. Summers, *Ordeal of the Reunion*, 73–76; Roark, *Masters without Slaves*, 86–94, 104–108, 133–55; Theodore B. Wilson, *The Black Codes of the South* (1965), 135–40; Litwack, *Been in the Storm So Long*, 265, 286–87, 521–24; Ranney, *Wake of Slavery*, 45–55.

37. 1865 Miss. Laws, ch. 4, §§ 1–4. Foner; *Reconstruction*, 204–205; Harris, *Presidential Reconstruction*, 82, 131; William C. Harris, "Formulation of the First Mississippi Plan: The Black Code of 1865," 29 *Journal of Mississippi History* 181, 186, 193–97 (1967); Ranney, *Wake of Slavery*, 50–51; Campbell quoted in Waldrep, *Roots of Disorder*, 112.

38. 1865 Miss. Laws, ch. 4, §§ 5–9.

39. 1865 Miss. Laws, ch. 5, §§ 1, 4 (apprentice law); ch. 6, §§ 1–2, 6 (vagrancy law).

40. Foner, *Reconstruction*, 167; Stone, "Mississippi's Constitution and Statutes in Reference to Freedmen," 167; 1866 *Miss. House Journal* 16, quoted in Stone, 162.

41. 1865 Miss. Laws, ch. 165.

42. Harris, *Presidential Reconstruction*, 141, quoting *Chicago Tribune*, December 1, 1865; Litwack, *Been in the Storm So Long*, 368–70; Wilson, *Black Codes*, 116–19; Justice Miller quoted in Fairman, *Reconstruction and Reunion*, 125.

43. 1865 Miss. Laws, ch. 270; Stone, "Mississippi's Constitution and Statutes in Reference to Freedmen,"212.

44. *Jack v. Thompson*, 41 Miss. 49 (1866).

45. 1866–67 *Miss. House Journal*, 77 (1867), quoted in Stone, "Mississippi's Constitution and Statutes in Reference to Freedmen," 214; Donald G. Nieman, "The Freedmen's Bureau and the Mississippi Black Code," 40 *Journal of Mississippi History* 91 (1978).

46. Harris, *Day of the Carpetbagger*, 115–49; Richard L. Hume, "Carpetbaggers in the Reconstruction South: A Group Portrait of Outside Whites in the 'Black and Tan' Constitutional Conventions," 64 *Journal of American History* 313 (1977); Hume, "Negro Delegates to the State Constitutional Conventions of 1867–69," in Howard N. Rabinowitz, ed., *Southern Black Leaders of the Reconstruction Era* (1982).

47. Harris, *Day of the Carpetbagger*, 130–37.

48. Ibid., 139–48; see also *Journal of the Proceedings in the Constitutional Convention of the State of Mississippi* (1868), 63–68, 295–323, 381–410, 543, 731–33.

49. Miss. Const. (1868), I:20, VII:3.

50. Miss. Const. (1868), IX:1 (militia), I:24 (public conveyances).

51. Miss. Const. (1868), VI:2 (appointive judiciary), I:16 (married women's property rights); Harris, *Day of the Carpetbagger*, 179.

52. Miss. Const. (1868), VIII:1, 5–7. Mississippi had enacted a statute authorizing common schools as early as 1846, but the law made schools and financing largely discretionary with local communities, and only a handful of common schools were created before Reconstruction. 1846 Miss. Laws, ch. 2; Harris, *Day of the Carpetbagger*, 149–51, 321–35; see also Elise Timberlake, "Did the Reconstruction Regime Give Mississippi Her Public Schools," 12 *Proceedings of the Mississippi Historical Society* 72 (1912) for an example of a white conservative's perspective on Reconstructionists' emphasis on universal education.

53. Harris, *Day of the Carpetbagger*, 190–217; Poore, *Federal and State Constitutions*, 1081.

54. 1870 Miss. Laws, chs. 73 (Black Code repeal), 95 (vagrancy law), 104 (public transportation), 132 (militia), 374 (apprenticeship), 631 (ratification of Fourteenth Amendment), 633 (Fifteenth Amendment).

55. 1870 Miss. Laws, ch. 59; Harris, *Day of the Carpetbagger*, 172–75; Allen W. Trelease, *White Terror: The Ku Klux Klan Conspiracy and Southern Reconstruction* (1971); Ranney, *Wake of Slavery*, 57–58.

56. 16 U.S. Stats. 140 (1870), 433 (1871), 17 U.S. Stats. 13 (1871); Stephen Cresswell, "Enforcing the Enforcement Acts: The Department of Justice in Northern Mississippi, 1870–1900," 53 *Journal of Southern History* 421 (1987); Edward Mayes, *Lucius Q. C. Lamar: His Life, Times, and Speeches, 1825–1893* (1896), 133; see also Robert Kaczorowski, *The Politics of Judicial Interpretation: The Federal Courts, Department of Justice and Civil Rights, 1866–1876* (1985), 53–78; Cresswell, "Enforcement Acts," 434, citing House Reports, 42nd Cong., 2d Sess., no. 22 (1872), XI, 48; XII, 934–87; 1161. Not surprisingly, Hill was popular with Mississippi conservatives. Claiborne, *Mississippi as a Province*, 472.

57. Fairman, *Reconstruction and Reunion*, 156–72; C. Vann Woodward, *The Strange Career of Jim Crow* (1966), 24–27.

58. Fairman, *Reconstruction and Reunion*, 165–84; 18:3 U.S. Stats. 335 (1875); *Civil Rights Cases*, 109 U.S. 3 (1883). The legislature originally passed the law in 1872, but the enrolled copy of the bill mysteriously disappeared, necessitating another vote the following year. Harris, *Day of the Carpetbagger*, 442–45.

59. Harris, *Day of the Carpetbagger*, 442–46.

60. *Donnell v. State*, 48 Miss. at 664 (Donnell), 672 (Morris), 675 (Simrall); William C. Harris, "The Creed of the Carpetbaggers: The Case of Mississippi," 40 *Journal of Southern History* 199 (1974); Harris, *Day of the Carpetbagger*, 448–49; McMillen, *Dark Journey*, 4.

61. *Berry v. Alsop*, 45 Miss. 1 (1871); *Cowan v. Stamps*, 46 Miss. 435 (1872); see also *Mitchell v. Wells*, 37 Miss. 235 (1859) and Chapter 2.

62. *Dickerson v. Brown*, 49 Miss. 357, 374–75 (1873); compare, e.g., 1865 N.C. Laws, ch. 99; 1865 S.C. Laws, p. 291; Ga. Const. (1865), V:1; *Scott v. State*, 39 Ga. 321 (1869); see also Ranney, *Wake of Slavery*, 52–54.

63. 1866–67 Miss. Laws, ch. 465; *Bain v. Brooks*, 46 Miss. 537 (1872); 1872 Miss. Laws, ch. 107; 1873 Miss. Laws, ch. 75; Harris, *Day of the Carpetbagger*, 605–15; Summers, *Ordeal of the Reunion*, 356–66; Ranney, *Wake of Slavery*, 97–99.

64. Harris, *Day of the Carpetbagger*, 636–49, 660–78, 684–98; Nicholas Lemann, *Redemption: The Last Battle of the Civil War* (2006), 65–105.

65. Late nineteenth-century Mississippians commonly referred to the conservatives as "Redeemers"; they were later called "Bourbons," connoting a retreat from Reconstruction-era ideals of equality and a return to the pre-Reconstruction social hierarchy. Neither label is accurate. From a twenty-first century perspective, the conservatives' actions were anything but redemptive, and the conservative resurgence was led not by antebellum elites but by younger Mississippians who had spent their early adulthood serving the Confederate cause and then waiting out Reconstruction. Nevertheless, the first generation of post-Reconstruction leaders is sometimes referred to here as Bourbons. See Foner, *Reconstruction*, 587–98; Kirwan, *Revolt of the Rednecks*, 8–9.

66. 1876 Miss. Laws, ch. 66; Foner, *Reconstruction*, 589– 93; Ranney, *Wake of Slavery*, 125–26, 128–31.

67. Kirwan, *Revolt of the Rednecks*, 33–39; C. Vann Woodward, *A History of the South, Vol. IX: Origins of the New South, 1877–1913* (1951), 103–105; Cresswell, *Mississippi after Reconstruction*, 9; S. S. Calhoon, "The Causes and Events that Led to the Calling of the Constitutional Convention of 1890," 6 *Publications of the Mississippi Historical Society* 105 (1902). Racial accommodation in the black belt even extended on occasion to deals that gave black residents a modest share of local offices. Kirwan, *Revolt of the Rednecks*, 16–17.

68. Stephen Cresswell, *Multiparty Politics in Mississippi, 1877–1902* (1995), 22–99; Kirwan, *Revolt of the Rednecks*, 3–57.

69. Kirwan, *Revolt of the Rednecks*, 3–57, 58 (quoting Chrisman); Woodward, *Origins of the New South*, 57–58; Cresswell, *Multiparty Politics in Mississippi*, 16–22, 48–50; Busbee, *Mississippi*, 169–71; Lemann, *Redemption*, 65–68.

70. Kirwan, *Revolt of the Rednecks*, 58–62; McNeilly, "History of Measures," 130–31.

71. See *Journal of the Proceedings of the Constitutional Convention, of the State of Mississippi, Begun at the City of Jackson on August 12, 1890* (1890), 704–708; Kirwan, *Revolt of the Rednecks*, 64–68; McNeilly, "History of Measures," 132–33.

72. Miss. Const. (1890), §§ 241, 243–44, 251; Albert D. Kirwan, "Apportionment in the Mississippi Constitution of 1890," 14 *Journal of Southern History* 234 (1948); Kirwan, *Revolt of the Rednecks*, 67–72; McNeilly, "History of Measures," 135.

73. Miss. Const. (1890), §§ 241–44; Kirwan, *Revolt of the Rednecks*, 79–82; Eric C. Clark, "Legislative Apportionment in the 1890 Constitutional Convention," 42 *Journal of Mississippi History* 298 (1980).

74. McNeilly, "History of Measures," 135, 137–38.

75. Kirwan, *Revolt of the Rednecks*, 72–73.

76. George B. Tindall, "The Question of Race in the South Carolina Convention of 1895," 37 *Journal of Negro History* 227, 288–90 (1952); *Journal of the Constitutional Convention of the State of South Carolina* (1895), 111, 319–30, 468–69, 727.

77. Michael Perman, *Struggle for Mastery: Disfranchisement in the South, 1888–1908* (2001), 129–221; Woodward, *Origins of the New South*, 330–38; Edward L. Ayers, *The Promise of the New South: Life after Reconstruction* (1992), 146–49; Kirwan, *Revolt of the Rednecks*, 78; Tindall, "South Carolina Convention of 1895"; Edward A. Miller, *Gullah Statesman: Robert Smalls from Slavery to Congress, 1838–1915* (1995), 204–214.

78. See Wyatt-Brown, *Shaping of Southern Culture*, 271. South Carolina Governor (and future US Senator) Benjamin Tillman delivered the one of the earliest and most widely publicized proclamations of the straight-out doctrine at his state's 1895 constitutional convention. "We are met . . . openly, boldly, without any pretense of secrecy," said Tillman, "to announce that it is our purpose, as far as we may, without coming in conflict with the United States Constitution, . . . to so restrict the suffrage and circumscribe it, that this infamy can never come about again." *South Carolina 1895 Convention Journal*, 463.

79. 20 So. 865, 868 (Miss. 1896).

80. *Williams v. Mississippi*, 170 U.S. 213, 225 (1898), *affirming Williams v. State*, 19 So. 826 (Miss. 1896).

81. Ranney, *Wake of Slavery*, 52–55. The pattern in the North was quite different. Following the Civil War, some Northern state courts upheld segregation laws, although they required that equal accommodations be offered to each race. See, e.g., *West Chester & Philadelphia R. Co. v. Miles*, 55 Pa. 198 (1867); *Cory v. Carter*, 48 Ind. 327 (1874); *People ex rel. King v. Gallagher*, 93 N.Y. 438 (1883). Others held that segregation violated due-process and equal-protection provisions in federal and state constitutions. See, e.g., *People ex rel. Workman v. Board of Education of Detroit*, 18 Mich. 400 (1869); *State ex rel. Stoutmeyer v. Duffy*, 7 Nev. 342 (1872); *Coger v. Northwestern Union Packet Co.*, 37 Iowa 145 (1873). After the US Supreme Court declared the 1875 federal accommodations law unconstitutional in 1883, many Northern states enacted accommodations laws modeled on the federal law. Gilbert T. Stephenson, *Race Relations in American Law* (1910), 112–51.

82. 1878 Miss. Laws, p. 103.

83. Kirwan, *Revolt of the Rednecks*, 141, 149–50; *Dawson v. Lee*, 83 Ky. 49 (1885); *Puitt v. Commissioners of Gaston County*, 94 N.C. 709 (1886). Prior to 1901, Mississippi school funds

were allocated among school districts based on the number of school-age children in each district; that same year, the state constitution was amended to provide a formula based on actual attendance. Miss. Const. (1890), § 206 (amended 1901); James C. Cobb and Michael Namorato, eds., *The New Deal and the South* (1984), 259–60.

84. *McFarland v. Goins*, 50 So. 493, 493–94 (Miss. 1909); *Cumming v. Richmond County Board of Education*, 175 U.S. 528 (1899); *Trustees of Walton School v. Board of Supervisors of Covington County*, 75 So. 833 (Miss. 1917); *Bryant v. Barnes*, 106 So. 113 (Miss. 1925); McMillen, *Dark Journey*, 86–88; Ayers, *Promise of the New South*, 136–46; Kirwan, *Revolt of the Rednecks*, 138–44; see also Andrew W. Kahrl, "The Power to Destroy: Discriminatory Property Assessments and the Struggle for Tax Justice in Mississippi," 82 *Journal of Southern History* 579 (2016).

85. 1888 Miss. Laws, ch. 26, §§ 2–3; Cresswell, *Mississippi after Reconstruction*, 56–57; McMillen, *Dark Journey*, 8–9. The 1888 law was worded to authorize rather than require railroads to segregate passengers, but in light of prevailing custom and culture it was effectively mandatory.

86. *Hall v. DeCuir*, 95 U.S. 485 (1878), *reversing* 27 La. Ann. 1 (1875); *Louisville, New Orleans & Texas Railroad Co. v. State*, 6 So. 203 (Miss. 1889), *affirmed*, 133 U.S. 587 (1890).

87. 1904 Miss. Laws, ch. 99; *Plessy v. Ferguson*, 163 U.S. 537 (1896); *Southern Light & Traction Co. v. Compton*, 38 So. 629 (Miss. 1905); see also *Waldauer v. Vicksburg Ry. & Light Co.*, 40 So. 751 (Miss. 1906); McMillen, *Dark Journey*, 294–97; Cresswell, *Mississippi after Reconstruction*, 56–57, 86–88.

88. 60 So. 11, 14 (Miss. 1912); see also *Southern Railway Co. v. Norton*, 73 So. 1 (Miss. 1916) and *Smith v. State*, 46 S.W. 666 (Tenn. 1898) (reaching the same conclusion). Cases interpreting *DeCuir* to prohibit application of segregation laws to interstate commerce include *State ex rel. Abbott v. Hicks*, 11 So. 74 (La. 1892); *Pullman Palace Car Co. v. Cain*, 40 S.W. 220 (Tex. Civ. App. 1897), and *Hart v. State*, 60 A. 457 (Md. 1905). The US Supreme Court finally made clear in *Morgan v. Virginia*, 328 U.S. 373 (1946), that segregation laws could not be enforced in interstate travel.

89. 1900 Miss. Laws, chs. 100, 101; 1904 Miss. Laws, ch. 144; see Benno C. Schmidt Jr., "Principle and Prejudice: The Supreme Court and Race in the Progressive Era, Part 2: The Peonage Cases," 82 *Columbia Law Review* 646, 674–76 (1982); Pete Daniel, *Shadow of Slavery: Peonage in the South, 1901–1969* (1972).

90. See, e.g., *State v. Williams*, 10 S.E. 876 (S.C. 1890); *Edge v. State*, 39 S.E. 889 (Ga. 1901); Cresswell, *Mississippi after Reconstruction*, 45–51.

91. 1900–01 Ala. Laws, ch. 1208; *Peonage Cases*, 123 F. 671, 686–88 (M.D. Ala. 1903); *Clyatt v. United States*, 197 U.S. 207 (1905); Brent J. Aucoin, *Thomas Goode Jones: Race, Politics and Justice in the New South* (2016), 120–42.

92. See, e.g., *State v. Murray*, 40 So. 930 (La. 1906); *Ex parte Hollman*, 60 S.E. 19 (S.C. 1908); *Bailey v. State*, 49 So. 886 (Ala. 1909), *reversed*, 219 U.S. 219 (1911); *Bailey*, 219 U.S. at 244–45.

93. 1900 Miss. Laws, chs. 101, 102; *State v. Armstead*, 60 So. 778, 780 (Miss. 1913); William Cohen, "Negro Involuntary Servitude in the South, 1865–1940: A Preliminary Analysis," 42 *Journal of Southern History* 31, 37–44, 50 (1976); Cresswell, *Mississippi after Reconstruction*, 45–52.

94. *Beale v. Yazoo Yarn Mill*, 88 So. 411 (Miss. 1921); *Thompson v. Box*, 112 So. 597 (Miss. 1927); *Hill v. Duckworth*, 124 So. 641 (Miss. 1929); McMillen, *Dark Journey*, 140–46.

Chapter Five

1. *Albritton v. City of Winona*, 178 So. 799, 806 (Miss. 1938).

2. Skates, *Mississippi Supreme Court*, 60–61; Richard C. Cortner, *A "Scottsboro" Case in Mississippi: The Supreme Court and Brown v. Mississippi* (1986), 52–53.

3. Skates, *Mississippi Supreme Court*, 78.

4. *Brown v. State*, 158 So. 339 (Miss. 1934), *on reconsideration*, 161 So. 465 (Miss. 1935), *reversed*, 297 U.S. 278 (1936); *on remand*, 167 So. 82 (Miss. 1936); *Albritton*, 178 So. 799 (Miss. 1938).

5. *Brown*, 161 So. at 470 (Griffith dissent); Cortner, *Scottsboro Case in Mississippi*, 4–31.

6. *Brown*, 158 So. at 343–44 (Anderson dissent).

7. Cortner, *Scottsboro Case in Mississippi* ,40–46, 65–69; Michael J. Klarman, *From Jim Crow to Civil Rights: The Supreme Court and the Struggle for Racial Equality* (2004), 128–34.

8. *Brown*, 161 So. at 470 (Griffith dissent).

9. *Brown*, 161 So. at 472 (Griffith dissent); 297 U.S. at 281–84; Cortner, *Scottsboro Case in Mississippi*, 121–36, 141–47; Klarman, *Jim Crow to Civil Rights*, 128–31.

10. Cortner, *Scottsboro Case in Mississippi*, 147–54; Michael J. Pfeifer, *Rough Justice: Lynching and American Society, 1874–1947* (2004), 64–70.

11. James C. Cobb, *The Selling of the South: The Southern Crusade for Industrial Development, 1936–1990* (2nd ed. 1993), 9–28; Connie Lester, "Balancing Agriculture with Industry: Capital, Labor and the Public Good in Mississippi's Home-Grown New Deal," 70 *Journal of Mississippi History* 225 (2008); Eric C. Clark, "Legislative Adoption of BAWI, 1936," 52 *Journal of Mississippi History* 283 (1990).

12. Miss. Const. (1890), § 183 (municipal subsidies), § 258 (state subsidies); Cobb, *Selling of the South*, 20–21; Lester, "Balancing Agriculture with Industry"; *Albritton*, 178 So. at 805–806.

13. *Albritton*, 178 So. at 812 (Anderson dissent), 811–12 (Griffith concurrence); Cobb, *Selling of the South*, 22–31.

14. Dewey Grantham, *Southern Progressivism: The Reconciliation of Progress and Tradition* (1983), 34–40; Kirwan, *Revolt of the Rednecks*, 123–33, 314–15.

15. Joseph A. Ranney, *Wisconsin and the Shaping of American Law* (2017), 120–35; see also, e.g., Charles E. Merriam and Louise Overacker, *Primary Elections* (1928); Randolph E. Paul, *Taxation in the United States* (1954), 9–17, 22–27, 65–70; *Magoun v. Illinois Trust & Savings Bank*, 170 U.S. 283, 287–88 (1898); Werner Troesken, "Regime Change and Corruption: A History of Public Utility Regulation," in Edward L. Glaeser and Claudia Goldin, eds., *Corruption and Reform: Lessons from America's Economic History* (2006); John R. Commons, ed., *History of Labor in the United States, 1896–1932* (1935), 3:410–21, 466–95, 554–56; Arthur S. Link and Richard L. McCormick, *Progressivism* (1983), 79–85.

16. Grantham, *Southern Progressivism*, 45–47, 119–25, 179–203; John Ray Skates Jr., "World War II as a Watershed in Mississippi History," 37 *Journal of Mississippi History* 131 (1975).

17. *Slaughterhouse Cases*, 83 U.S. 36 (1873), 83, 93–100 (Field), 111, 122 (Bradley). See also Edward Keynes, *Liberty, Property, and Privacy: Toward a Jurisprudence of Substantive Due Process* (1996), 97–115; Michael Les Benedict, "Laissez-Faire and Liberty: A Re-Evaluation of the Meaning and Origins of Laissez-Faire Constitutionalism," 3 *Law & History Review* 293, 328–30 (1985).

18. *See* Chapter 3; *Hanson v. Vernon*, 27 Iowa 28 (1869); *People v. Township Board of Salem*, 20 Mich. 452 (1870); Cooley, *Constitutional Limitations*, 175, 357–58; John F. Dillon, *Law of Municipal Corporations* (1873 ed.), § 105; Jacobs, *Law Writers and the Courts*.

19. See Eric S. Foner, *Free Soil, Free Labor, Free Men: The Ideology of the Republican Party before the Civil War* (1971); Library of America, *Abraham Lincoln: Speeches and Writings, 1859–1865* (1989), 96–97; Message of Governor Jeremiah Rusk to Wisconsin Legislature, 1887 *Wis. Assembly Journal* 15–16 (January 13, 1887).

20. The delegation doctrine first came into existence about 1850. See *Cincinnati, Wilmington & Zanesville Railroad Co. v. Commissioners of Clinton County*, 1 Ohio St. 77, 88 (1852).

21. *See* Owen M. Fiss, *History of the Supreme Court of the United States, Vol. 8: Troubled Beginnings of the Modern State, 1888–1910* (1993), 155–222; Russel B. Nye, *Midwestern Progressive Politics: A Historical Study of Its Origins and Development, 1870–1958* (1959); Grantham, *Southern Progressivism*; Robert F. Wesser, *Charles Evans Hughes: Politics and Reform in New York, 1905–1910* (1967); Keynes, *Jurisprudence of Substantive Due Process*, 97–115; Benedict, "Laissez-Faire and Liberty," 328–30. For a summary of early uses of substantive due process in state courts, see Ranney, *Wisconsin and the Shaping of American Law*, 135–38.

22. Grantham, *Southern Progressivism*, 11–13, 119–24; Cresswell, *Mississippi after Reconstruction*, 191–94.

23. Merriam and Overacker, *Primary Elections*, 24–25, 60–66; 1902 Miss. Laws, ch. 66; *McInnis v. Thames*, 32 So. 286, 287 (Miss. 1902); Kirwan, *Revolt of the Rednecks*, 123–33. In 1912, the legislature, apparently worried that its decision to leave a substantial degree of control with party officials had worked against its goal of eliminating insider power, passed a resolution urging the party to use primaries for all party offices. 1912 Miss. Laws, ch. 424.

24. See, e.g., Ore. Const. (1908), II:18; Cal. Const. (1911), II:8–11, 13–15; Ellis P. Oberholtzer, *The Referendum in America* (1912).

25. *Power v. Robertson*, 93 So. 769, 776 (Miss. 1922). The court took a twisting path to that result: in 1917, it rejected a challenge based on an argument that under the state constitution each device should have been submitted to voters separately. *State v. Brantley*, 74 So. 662 (Miss. 1917).

26. Woodward, *Origins of the New South*, 372. In 1900, Mississippi's supreme court struck down an initial attempt to amend the state's constitution to return to an elective judiciary on technical grounds, but the legislature eventually corrected the defect and voters again ratified the elective-judiciary amendment in 1916. See 1898 Miss. Laws, ch. 83; *State ex rel. McClurg v. Powell*, 27 So. 927 (Miss. 1900); 1914 Miss. Laws, chs. 514–15; 1916 Miss. Laws, chs. 158–59 (noting voter ratification of the corrected amendment).

27. Paul, *Taxation*, 9–17, 22–27, 65–70; Grantham, *Southern Progressivism*, 54–57, 74–76, 98–101.

28. Mississippi first enacted an income tax in 1934. 1934 Miss. Laws, ch. 120.

29. See 1908 Miss. Laws, chs. 82, 83, 85, 88 (conferring investigative and subpoena powers on railroad commission and authorizing it to require the building of side tracks).

30. Grantham, *Southern Progressivism*, 310–12; see George Rosen, *A History of Public Health* (1977).

31. 1897 (Ex. Sess.) Miss. Laws, ch. 15. See also 1898 Miss. Laws, ch. 79 (creating physician licensure system); 1900 Miss. Laws, chs., 108, 123 (authorizing counties to impose quarantines and provide for compulsory smallpox vaccination); 1904 Miss. Laws, ch. 145 (dentistry licensure system); 1906 Miss. Laws, ch. 112 (board of health given broad powers to disinfect public places); 1918 Miss. Laws, ch. 203 (municipalities authorized to appropriate funds to combat contagious diseases).

32. 1910 Miss. Laws, ch. 132; James C. Cobb, *Redefining Southern Culture: Mind and Identity in the Modern South* (1999), 15–16, 21–24.

33. Grantham, *Southern Progressivism*, 179–85; Commons, *History of Labor*, 410–37, 466–95; Cresswell, *Mississippi after Reconstruction*, 153–56.

34. Grantham, *Southern Progressivism*, 182–91; Commons, *History of Labor*, 410–37, 466–95.

35. 1908 Miss. Laws, ch. 99; 1912 Miss. Laws, chs. 141, 157, 165; 1914 Miss. Laws, chs. 164, 165; Grantham, *Southern Progressivism*, 44, 191–99; Charles G. Hamilton, *Progressive Mississippi* (1948), 61, 66.

36. Price V. Fishback and Shawn E. Kanter, "The Adoption of Workers' Compensation in the United States, 1900–1930," 41 *Journal of Law and Economics* 305, 320 (1998); Ayers, *Promise of the New South*, 415–17; 1948 Miss. Laws, ch. 354. During the Progressive era, the legislature did eliminate certain common-law defenses that employers had used to escape liability for claims of injured workers. See 1896 Miss. Laws, ch. 87 (abolishing fellow-servant doctrine, which had provided that employers were not liable for injuries caused by acts of co-workers).

37. See Ranney, *Wisconsin and the Shaping of American Law*, 78–81, 135–38; Hoyt L. Warner, *Progressivism in Ohio, 1897–1917* (1964), 295–319; Wesser, *Charles Evans Hughes*, 314; Franklin A. Smith, *Judicial Review of Legislation in New York, 1906–1938* (1952), 151–56; R. M. Wanamaker, "Recall of Judges—A Judicial Affirmative," *Illinois State Bar Proceedings* (1912), 174, in Edith M. Phelps, ed., *Selected Articles on the Recall: Including the Recall of Judges and Judicial Decisions* (2nd ed. 1915), 60.

38. See, e.g., Sidney M. Milkis, *Theodore Roosevelt, the Progressive Party, and the Transformation of American Democracy* (2009), 56–63, 89–97; Theodore Roosevelt, "Charter of Democracy," 100 *Outlook* 390 (February 24, 1912), in Phelps, *Selected Articles on the Recall*, 147–48; Elihu Root, "Judicial Decisions and Public Feeling," 35 *Proceedings of the New York State Bar Association* 148 (1912), in Phelps, *Selected Articles on the Recall*, 179–84.

39. Warner, *Progressivism in Ohio*, 295–319, 336; see also, e.g., *People ex rel. Rodgers v. Coler*, 59 N.E. 716 (N.Y. 1901) (striking down a law that required payment of the prevailing local wage rate on public works projects); N.Y. Const. (1894), XII:9 (1905 amendment overturning *Coler*); *Ives v. South Buffalo Railway Co.*, 94 N.E. 431 (N.Y. 1911) (striking down workers compensation law); N.Y. Const. (1894), I:19 (1913 amendment authorizing workers compensation law); Smith, *Judicial Review of Legislation in New York*, 151–56.

40. 59 So. 923 (Miss. 1912), *on rehearing*, 60 So. 215 (Miss. 1913).

41. *Ritchie v. People*, 40 N.E. 454 (Ill. 1895); *Holden v. Hardy*, 169 U.S. 366 (1898), *affirming* 46 P. 756 (Utah 1896); *Lochner v. New York*, 198 U.S. 45 (1904), *reversing* 69 N.E. 373 (N.Y. 1904); *Muller v. Oregon*, 208 U.S. 412 (1908), *affirming*, 85 P. 855 (Or. 1906).

42. 59 So. at 929 (Reed); 60 So. at 217 (Cook).

43. *State v. Brown & Sharpe Manufacturing Co.*, 25 A. 246 (R.I. 1892); *Leep v. St. Louis, Iron Mountain & Southern Railway Co.*, 25 S.W. 75 (Ark. 1894); *In re House Bill No. 1,230*, 40 N.E. 713 (Mass. 1895); *Commonwealth v. Hillside Coal Co.*, 58 S.W. 441 (Ky. 1900); *Commonwealtlh v. Reinecke Coal Mining Co.*, 79 S.W. 287 (Ky. 1904).

44. *Braceville Coal Co. v. People*, 35 N.E. 62 (Ill. 1893); *Johnson v. Goodyear Mining Co.*, 59 P. 304 (Cal. 1899); *Republic Iron & Steel Co. v. State*, 66 N.E. 1005 (Ind. 1903).

45. 197 U.S. 111 (1905), *affirming Commonwealth v. Pear*, 66 N.E. 719 (Mass. 1903); 1900 Miss. Laws, ch. 108. Pre-*Jacobson* cases upholding compulsory vaccination laws included *Abeel v. Clark*, 24 P. 383 (Cal. 1890); *Blue v. Beach*, 56 N.E. 90 (Ind. 1900); *Viemeister v. White*, 72 N.E. 97 (N.Y. 1904); and S*tate ex rel. Milhoof v. Board of Education of Village of Barberton*, 81 N.E. 568 (Ohio 1907). Cases striking down such laws included *Hurst v. Warner*, 60 N.W.

440 (Mich. 1894); *State ex rel. Adams v. Burdge*, 70 N.W. 347 (Wis. 1897); and *Potts v. Breen*, 47 N.E. 81 (Ill. 1897).

46. See *Coppage v. Kansas*, 236 U.S. 1 (1915) (holding anti-yellow-dog laws unconstitutional); *Adkins v. Children's Hospital*, 261 U.S. 525 (1923) (striking down minimum-wage law for women).

47. See, e.g., *Payne v. Baldwin*, 11 Miss. 661 (1844), *reversed*, 47 U.S. 301 (1848); see generally Chapter 3.

48. *Ex Parte Virginia*, 100 U.S. 339 (1880); *Virginia v. Rives*, 100 U.S. 313 (1880).

49. *Neal v. Delaware*, 103 U.S. 370 (1881); *Bush v. Kentucky*, 107 U.S. 110 (1883).

50. 100 U.S. 303 (1880); see 1894 Miss. Laws, ch. 69, 1906 Miss. Code § 2684 (providing that juries must consist of eligible voters who are literate).

51. Pfeifer, *Rough Justice*, 3–4, 45–69, 144–45; Pfeifer, *The Roots of Rough Justice: Origins of American Lynching* (2011), 15–21; Ashraf H. A. Rushdy, *American Lynching* (2012), 54; Ayers, *Promise of the New South*, 157; see also James Elbert Cutler, *Lynch-Law: An Investigation Into the History of Lynching in the United States* (1905), 99–101, 117–20. Cutler's book is a useful source of lynching's early history and of lynching statistics that unfortunately reflects the white racial attitudes of the period in which it was written.

52. Pfeifer, *Rough Justice*, 45–49, 141–43; Rushdy, *American Lynching*, 62–65; Cutler, *Lynch Law*, 179, 183, 188; Pete Daniel, *Standing at the Crossroads: The South Since 1900* (1986), 50–71; McMillen, *Dark Journey*, 220–49; Karlos K. Hill, "Black Vigilantism: The Rise and Decline of African American Lynch Mob Activity in the Mississippi and Arkansas Deltas, 1883–1923," 95 *Journal of African-American History* 26 (2010), 38–40; University of Missouri-Kansas City, "Lynching in America: Statistics, Information, Images," available at http://law2.umkc .edu/faculty/projects/trials/shipp/lynchstats.html (information from Tuskegee Institute Archives).

53. See, e.g., *White v. State*, 91 So. 903 (Miss. 1922); *Fisher v. State*, 110 So. 361 (Miss. 1926).

54. Pfeifer, *Rough Justice*, 67–69, 144–45; Cortner, *Scottsboro Case in Mississippi*, 11–13; *Brown*, 161 So. at 472 (Griffith dissent); Klarman, *Jim Crow to Civil Rights*, 119–22.

55. Klarman, *Jim Crow to Civil Rights*, 118–19, 130–34; Cortner, *Scottsboro Case in Mississippi*, 102–104, 144–46.

56. George C. Osborn, *James Kimble Vardaman: Southern Commoner* (1981), 63–64; McMillen, *Dark Journey*, 216–17; Lawrence E. Kight, "'The State Is On Trial': Governor Edmund F. Noel and the Defense of Mississippi's Legal Institutions against Mob Violence," 60 *Journal of Mississippi History* 191 (1998). DeKalb attorney John Clark represented the *Brown* defendants during their trial and in the initial appeal to Mississippi's supreme court. Both his health and his career suffered greatly as a result. Cortner, *Scottsboro Case in Mississippi*, 44–47, 155–56.

57. See, e.g., *Hampton v. State*, 40 So. 545 (Miss. 1906); *Funches v. State*, 87 So. 487 (Miss. 1921).

58. See, e.g., *Sykes v. State*, 42 So. 875 (Miss. 1907); *Story v. State*, 97 So. 806–807 (Miss. 1923) (overturning a black defendant's conviction for rape of a "bright mulatto" woman where the prosecutor had argued that the defendant was a "human gorilla" and that the victim was "almost white").

59. *Butler v. State*, 135 So. 357 (Miss. 1931).

60. *Fisher v. State*, 110 So. 361 (Miss. 1926); *Perkins v. State*, 135 So. 357 (Miss. 1931).

61. *Perkins v. State*, 135 So. 357 (Miss. 1931).

62. See, e.g., Cortner, *Scottsboro Case in Mississippi*, 147–54 (describing *Brown* defendants' decision to accept jail sentences rather than undergo a second trial); *Patton v. State*, 40 So.2d 592 (Miss. 1949) (second conviction following reversal of initial conviction by US Supreme Court); see also Klarman, *Jim Crow to Civil Rights*, 130–34.

63. *Carter v. Texas*, 177 U.S. 442 (1900), *reversing* 46 S.W. 236 (Tex. Crim. App. 1898); *Norris v. Alabama*, 294 U.S. 587 (1935), *reversing* 156 So. 556 (Ala. 1934); see also, e.g., *Pierre v. Louisiana*, 306 U.S. 365, *reversing* 180 So. 630 (La. 1938); see generally Klarman, *Jim Crow to Civil Rights*, 123–35.

64. *Patton v. State*, 29 So.2d 96 (Miss. 1947); *reversed*, 332 U.S. 463, 469 (Black); *on appeal following remand*, 40 So.2d 592, 594 (Miss. 1949) (Alexander); *appeal dismissed*, 338 U.S. 855 (1949); *Patton v. State*, 43 So.2d 216 (Miss. 1949).

65. See, e.g., *Coleman v. State*, 164 So.2d 704 (Ala. 1964) (holding that defendant had presented insufficient evidence of systematic discrimination, and criticizing *Norris*), *reversed*, 377 U.S. 129 (1964); *on remand*, 195 So.2d 800 (Ala. 1967) (holding that fact that 10-to-20 percent of grand and petit jury members were black in a county whose population was 80 percent black was not sufficient to show discrimination); *reversed*, 389 U.S. 22 (1967).

66. *McGee v. State*, 26 So.2d 680 (Miss. 1946); *McGee v. State*, 33 So.2d 843 (Miss. 1948); *McGee v. State*, 40 So.2d 169, 171 (Miss. 1949), *certiorari denied*, 338 U.S. 805 (1949); Joseph Crespino, *In Search of Another Country: Mississippi and the Conservative Counterrrevolution* (2007), 47–49; Craig Zahm, "Trial by Ordeal: The Willie McGee Case," 65 *Journal of Mississippi History* 215 (2003); Leandra Zarnow, "Braving Jim Crow to Save Willie McGee: Bella Abzug, the Legal Left, and Civil Rights Innovation, 1948–1951," 33 *Law & Soc. Inquiry* 1003 (2008). The McGee case continues to attract interest and attention today. See Alex Heard, *The Eyes of Willie McGee: A Tragedy of Race, Sex and Secrets in the Jim Crow South* (2010).

67. Mary Ellen Maatman, "Lawyering in the Lion's Mouth: The Story of S. D. Redmond and Pruitt v. State," 83 *Mississippi Law Journal* 459, 465–74, 498–504 (2014); *Pruitt v. State*, 139 So. 861 (Miss. 1932); *Carraway v. State*, 137 So. 325 (Miss. 1931); *Carraway v. State*, 141 So. 342 (Miss. 1932); *Carraway v. State*, 148 So. 340, 346 (Miss. 1933) (Griffith dissent); McMillen, *Dark Journey*, 206–212. In 1935, Governor Conner, perhaps influenced by the *Pruitt* and *Carraway* cases, held a "Court of Mercy" in which he commuted the sentences of about two dozen prisoners who he felt had been unjustly convicted. McMillen, *Dark Journey*, 216–17. District Attorney Colmer, like Stennis, went on to higher office, representing the Gulf Coast area in the US House of Representatives (1933–1972).

68. Irvin C. Mollison, "Negro Lawyers in Mississippi," 15 *Journal of Negro History* 38, 40–55 (1930); J. Clay Smith Jr., *Emancipation: The Making of the Black Lawyer, 1844–1944* (1993), 289–96.

69. McMillen, *Dark Journey*, 63, 167–69, 298; Mollison, "Negro Lawyers," 65–67.

70. *Ex parte Redmond*, 125 So. 833 (Miss. 1930); *Missouri ex rel. Gaines v. Canada*, 305 U.S. 337 (1938); Maatman, "Lawyering in the Lion's Mouth"; Smith, *Making of the Black Lawyer*, 298–99; Smith, "The Black Bar Association and Civil Rights," 15 *Creighton Law Review* 651, 657–59 (1982); Charles Hamilton Houston, "The Need for Negro Lawyers," 4 *Journal of Negro Education* 49, 52 (1935); Charles H. Wilson Sr., *God! Make Me a Man: A Biographical Sketch of Dr. Sidney Dillion Redmond* (1950), 5.

71. Virginia Drachman, *Sisters in Law: Women Lawyers in Modern American History* (1998), 2–35; Karen Berger Morello, *The Invisible Bar: The Woman Lawyer in America, 1638 to the Present* (1986); *Bradwell v. Illinois*, 83 U.S. 130 (1873); see also, e.g., *Robinson's Case*, 131

Mass. 376 (1881); *In re Hall*, 50 Conn. 131 (1882); *In re Ricker*, 29 A. 559 (N.H. 1890); *In re Petition of Leach*, 34 N.E. 641 (Ind. 1893).

72. Kris Gilliland, Bette Bradley, and Ellie Campbell, "'Dared to Enter A "Man's World"': Mississippi Women Lawyers, 1914–1964," 85 *Mississippi Law Journal* 1479, 1493–94 (2017); 1898 Miss. Laws, ch. 78; Martha. Swain, Elizabeth Anne Payne, and Marjorie Julian Spruill, eds., *Mississippi Women: Their Histories, Their Lives* (2003), 1:43–45, 49 (Somerville), 61–66 (Kearney).

73. See James C. Cobb and Michael V. Namorato, eds., *The New Deal and the South* (1984), 5–8 (arguing that the New Deal era was the crucial transitional period); Roger Biles, *The South and the New Deal* (1994), 154 (arguing that the New Deal era was "largely preparatory" for the transition during and after the war).

74. National Emergency Council, *Report to the President on the Economic Conditions of the South* (1938); Cobb, *Selling of the South*, 1–2; see also Cobb and Namorato, *New Deal and the South*, 13–18 (conceding that World War II may have been a more important transitional event for Mississippi than the New Deal, but also arguing that the state's transition to its modern era had begun in the 1920s). As to statistics of demographic and economic change in Mississippi during and after the Depression and World War II, see Chapter 6 and Figure 6.1.

75. Busbee, *Mississippi*, 225–30; Susan Estabrook Kennedy, *The Banking Crisis of 1933* (1973), 6–18; Benjamin J. Klebaner, *American Commercial Banking: A History* (1990), 131–38; Roger D. Tate Jr., "Easing the Burden: The Era of Depression and New Deal in Mississippi" (PhD dissertation, University of Tennessee, 1978), 3–10, 36–40; Daniel, *Standing at the Crossroads*, 13–20, 111–12.

76. 1914 Miss. Laws, ch. 124; Busbee, *Mississippi*, 225–30. By 1932, per-capita income in Mississippi had fallen by more than half since 1929; nearly half of all manufacturing jobs had disappeared, and the state treasury was nearly empty. Daniel, *Standing at the Crossroads*, 131–32.

77. 1932 Miss. Laws, ch. 251; *Dunn v. Love*, 155 So. 331, 333 (Miss. 1934). See Busbee, *Mississippi*, 230–35; Klebaner, *American Commercial Banking*, 138–47; Kennedy, *Banking Crisis*, 64–66, 97–107, 131–47; Biles, *South and the New Deal*, 21–22.

78. Chester M. Morgan, "At the Crossroads: World War II, Delta Agriculture, and Modernization in Mississippi," 57 *Journal of Mississippi History* 353, 355 (1995); Biles, *South and the New Deal*, 2–3.

79. 290 U.S. 398, 426, 435 (1933); William L. Prosser, "The Minnesota Mortgage Moratorium," 7 *Southern California Law Review* 353 (1934).

80. 1934 Miss. Laws, ch. 247. The 1931 legislature had also tried to give debtors relief by extending the annual date for tax foreclosure sales from April to September and providing that farms must be sold in separate forty-acre parcels rather than as a whole in order to satisfy taxes. 1931 Miss. Laws, ch. 25.

81. See, e.g., *Lingo Lumber Co. v. Hayes*, 64 S.W.2d 834 (Tex. Civ. App., Dallas, 1933) (upholding Texas moratorium law); *Langever v. Miller*, 76 S.W.2d 1025 (Tex. 1934) (striking down law); *Des Moines Joint Stock Land Bank v. Nordholm*, 253 N.W. 701 (Iowa 1934) (upholding Iowa moratorium law by 5–4 vote).

82. See, e.g., *Waterville Realty Corp. v. City of Eastport*, 8 A.2d 898 (Me. 1939); *Hanauer v. Republic Building Co.*, 225 N.W. 136 (Wis. 1934); *Brown v. Ferdon*, 54 P.2d 712 (Cal. 1936).

83. 161 So. 623 (Miss. 1934), 130 (Anderson dissent).

84. 1936 Miss. Laws, ch. 287; 1938 Miss. Laws, ch. 346; *Jefferson Standard Life Insurance Co. v. Noble*, 188 So. 289 (Miss. 1939).

85. Compare, e.g., *First Trust Co. of Lincoln v. Smith*, 277 N,W, 762 (Neb. 1938) and *First Trust Joint Stock Land Bank v. Arp*, 283 N.W. 441 (Iowa 1939) (overturning extensions) with *Onsrud v. Kenyon*, 300 N.W. 359 (Wis. 1941) and *East New York Savings Bank v. Hahn*, 59 N.E.2d 625 (N.Y. 1944) (upholding extensions).

86. See, e.g., editors of the *Economist, The New Deal: An Analysis and Appraisal* (1937), 44; Edward A. Filene, "What Business Men Think: See the New Deal Through," 139 *Nation* 707 (December 9, 1934), reprinted in Howard Zinn, ed., *New Deal Thought* (1966), 64, 68.

87. 1931 Miss. Laws, ch. 1; 1932 Miss. Laws, ch. 350; see Biles, *South and the New Deal*, 18–19; George B. Tindall, A *History of the South, Vol. X: The Emergence of the New South, 1913–1945* (1967), 356–57.

88. 48 U.S. Stats. 31 (1933); *United States v. Butler*, 297 U.S. 1 (1936); Daniel, *Standing at the Crossroads*, 117–24. After the *Butler* decision, the act was revised to meet the *Butler* court's criticisms and was reenacted in 1938. 52 U.S. Stats. 31 (1938).

89. 48 U.S. Stats. 195 (1933); see Note, "State Legislation in Support of the NIRA," 34 *Columbia Law Review* 1077 (1934); S. G. Tipton, Note, "State Acts in Aid of the NIRA," 29 *Illinois Law Review* 777 (1935).

90. 295 U.S. 495 (1935). Milk-industry codes were an exception: they were upheld by the US Supreme Court and many state courts because they involved public-health concerns and, thus, were a justifiable use of states' police powers. *Nebbia v. New York*, 291 U.S. 502 (1934); see also, e.g., *Franklin v. State ex rel. Alabama State Milk Control Board*, 169 So. 295 (Ala. 1936); *Miami Home Milk Producers Association v. Milk Control Board*, 169 So. 541 (Fla. 1936). State courts had mixed reactions to codes for other industries. See, e.g., *Joseph Triner Corp. v. McNeil*, 2 N.E.2d 929 (Ill. 1936), *affirmed*, 299 U.S. 183 (1936) (upholding state NIRA law); *State ex rel. Fulton v. Ives*, 167 So. 394, 402 (Fla. 1936) (denouncing state NIRA law as "a species of socialistic leveling").

91. The 1940 legislature authorized formation of a committee to recommend a code of business practices for vegetable growers and shippers, but it carefully provided that any such code would be promulgated and enforced by state authorities. 1940 Miss. Laws, ch. 312.

92. 49 U.S. Stat. 620 (1935); David M. Kennedy, *Freedom from Fear: The American People in Depression and War, 1929–1945* (1999), 266–78.

93. 1935 Miss. Laws (Spec. Sess.), ch. 18.

94. 1935 Miss. Laws (Spec. Sess.), ch. 18; 1936 Miss. Laws, ch. 175.

95. 1935 Miss. Laws (Spec. Sess.), chs. 51, 63; 1936 Miss. Laws, chs. 185, 187–88.

96. *Steward Machine Co. v. Davis*, 301 U.S. 548 (1937) (challenge to taxation under Social Security Act); *Carmichael v. Southern Coal & Coke Co.*, 301 U.S. 495 (1937) (challenge to Alabama's unemployment compensation act passed in response to Social Security Act). Both cases originated in the Alabama federal courts.

97. *Beeland Wholesale Co. v. Kaufman*, 174 So. 516 (Ala. 1937); *Tatum v. Wheeless*, 178 So. 95, 100 (Miss. 1938).

98. Section 183 provided that a municipality could not purchase corporate stock, appropriate funds, or "loan its credit in aid of [a] corporation." Section 258 provided that "the credit of the state shall not be pledged or loaned in aid of any person, association or corporation."

99. Miss. Const. (1890), § 183, § 258; Cobb, *Selling of the South*, 6–10. Tennessee municipalities made similar efforts in the early twentieth century despite a similar prohibition in the Tennessee constitution. *Id.*, 6–7.

100. *Carothers v. Town of Booneville*, 153 So. 670 (Miss. 1934); Cobb, *Selling of the South*, 13–14. The *Albritton* court distinguished *Carothers* on the ground that the ordinance at issue

in *Carothers* did not give the town the right to control the property developed for the benefit of industry but BAWI did. *Albritton*, 178 So. at 809.

101. Cobb, *Selling of the South*, 20–21; *Albritton*, 178 So. at 805.

102. Cobb, *Selling of the South*, 22–31; Jere Nash and Andy Taggart, *Mississippi Politics: The Struggle for Power, 1976–2006* (2006), 291–92.

103. Cobb, *Selling of the South*, 33–40; 1944 Miss. Laws, ch. 241. Courts in other states whose BAWI laws were challenged upheld the laws, although some divided as had Mississippi's court. See, e.g., *City of Fernandina v. State*, 197 So. 454 (Fla. 1940).

104. W. J. Cash, *The Mind of the South* (1941; 1971 ed.), 427 (stating that BAWI "gives away the wealth of the South on a scale hitherto unprecedented in a region which has always too eagerly given away its wealth"); Cobb, *Selling of the South*, 23–38. But some of these critics also concede that Mississippi may have obtained a competitive advantage by being the first to implement a BAWI program. *See* Cobb, *Selling of the South*, 27–30; Anthony J. Badger, "How Did the New Deal Change the South?" in Cobb, ed., *New Deal/New South: An Anthony J. Badger Reader* (2007), 39–40.

105. Cobb, *Selling of the South*, 1–2; Skates, "World War II as a Watershed."

Chapter Six

1. Skates, *Mississippi Supreme Court*, 60–61; Anders Walker, "The Violent Bear It Away: Emmett Till and the Modernization of Law Enforcement in Mississippi," 46 *San Diego Law Review* 459, 464–65 (2009); Orley B. Caudill, "Oral History with the Honorable J. P. Coleman," 11 *Journal of Southern Legal History* 117, 117–19 (2003); Leslie H. Southwick, "Four for the Fifth: The First Mississippi Judges on the Fifth Circuit," 34 *Mississippi College Law Review* 252, 252–54 (2015).

2. See *Belton v. Gebhart*, 87 A.2d 862 (Del. Ch. 1952), *affirmed*, 91 A.2d 137 (Del. 1952); Klarman, *Jim Crow to Civil Rights*, 146–52, 253–58; Mark V. Tushnet, *The NAACP's Legal Strategy Against Segregated Education, 1925–1950* (1987), 127–31.

3. Skates, "World War II as a Watershed"; Daniel, *Standing At the Crossroads*, 135–49; Crespino, *Conservative Counterrevolution*, 11–12, 21–26; Erle Johnston, *Mississippi's Defiant Years, 1953–1973: An Interpretive Documentary with Personal Experiences* (1990), 3–15; Klarman, *Jim Crow to Civil Rights*, 173–93; James T. Patterson, *Grand Expectations: The United States, 1945–1974* (1996), 16–17, 344–49, 446–47.

4. Johnston, *Defiant Years*, 31.

5. Crespino, *Conservative Counterrevolution*, 21–28, 143–45; Johnston, *Defiant Years*, 48–49; 1956 Miss. Laws, ch 365; 1958 Miss. Laws, ch. 472.

6. Johnston, *Defiant Years*, 55–59, 80–81; 1958 Miss. Laws, ch. 472. In 1958, the US Supreme Court struck down an Alabama regulation similar to Mississippi's 1958 law as an infringement of NAACP members' constitutional rights of free speech and association. *NAACP v. Patterson*, 357 US. 449 (1958).

7. Coleman stated in later years that he was glad he turned down President John F. Kennedy's offer to appoint him Secretary of the Army, because he would have resigned rather than sent federal troops to the University of Mississippi to enforce court decisions requiring the university to admit James Meredith as its first black student in 1962. Jack Bass, *Unlikely Heroes* (1981), 190–91; Deborah J. Barrow and Thomas G. Walker, *A Court Divided: The Fifth Circuit Court of Appeals and the Politics of Judicial Reform* (1988), 133.

8. Johnston, *Defiant Years*, 366–74; see J. Anthony Lukas, *Common Ground: A Turbulent Decade in the Lives of Three American Families* (1985); *Milliken v. Bradley*, 418 U.S. 717 (1974).

9. *Singleton v. Jackson Municipal Separate School District*, 419 F.2d 1211 (5th Cir. 1969), *reversed*, 396 U.S. 290 (1970), *on remand*, 425 F.2d 1211, 1216 (Coleman, dissenting).

10. *Baker v. Carr*, 369 U.S. 186 (1962); *Reynolds v. Sims*, 377 U.S. 533 (1964); *Connor v. Johnson*, 256 F. Supp. 962 (S.D. Miss. 1966) (striking down the 1890 Constitution's apportionment provisions and inviting the legislature to make a redistricting plan before the court acted); *Connor v. Johnson*, 265 F. Supp. 492 (S.D. Miss. 1967) (rejecting the legislature's proposed plan due to excessive population variation between districts and establishing court plan).

11. *Connor v. Johnson*, 330 F. Supp. 506 (1971) (presenting initial court plan); *stay granted*, 402 U.S. 690 (1971) (staying the Coleman plan because it contained multi-member districts); *on remand*, 330 F. Supp. 521 (1971) (panel replied that it did not have sufficient information to divide some multi-member counties into equally populated single-member districts); *vacated*, 404 U.S. 549 (1972) (repeating that the plan must be limited to single-member districts); *on remand, Connor v. Waller*, 396 F. Supp. 1308 (S.D. Miss. 1975) (approving a new plan devised by the 1975 legislature); *reversed*, 421 U.S. 656 (1975) (striking down the plan because the US Department of Justice had not approved it as required by the 1965 Voting Rights Act).

12. Miss. Const. (1890), §§ 241, 243–44, 251; Kirwan, *Revolt of the Rednecks*, 67–72; McNeilly, "History of Measures," 135–38; *Connor v. Coleman*, 425 U.S. 675 (1976) (instructing Coleman's panel to devise a new plan); *Connor v. Finch*, 419 F. Supp. 1072, 1112 (S.D. Miss. 1976) (acceding to Supreme Court but complaining about the court's lack of respect for the county-line tradition); *Connor v. Finch*, 431 U.S. 407 (1977) (reversing Coleman panel's 1976 plan); *Connor v. Coleman*, 440 U.S. 612 (1979) (ordering panel to formulate interim plan while state awaited federal approval of a 1978 plan formulated by the legislature; Marshall dissent and criticism of Coleman panel); *Mississippi v. United States*, 490 F. Supp. 569 (D.D.C. 1979) (approving legislature's 1978 plan pursuant to Voting Rights Act); *affirmed without opinion*, 444 U.S. 1050 (1979).

13. Skates, "World War II as a Watershed," 136; Cobb, *New Deal/New South*, 43–47; Busbee, *Mississippi*, 268–72; Klarman, *Jim Crow to Civil Rights*, 173–93. The figures in the chart are compiled from Donald B. Dodd and Wynelle S. Dodd, *Historical Statistics of the South 1790–1970* (1973), 34–37, 70; *Statistical Abstract of the United States* (1942), 54; *id.* (1992), 32, 395, 404, 458, 644, 652; *id.* (1972), 326, 331; *id.* (1982), 144, 444, 458; *id.* (2002), 27, 393, 426; *id.* (2012), 24, 36, 153, 407, 463, 536.

14. 1912 Miss. Laws, ch. 5 (providing $5,000 in supplemental funds to counties); *State Board of Education v. Pridgen*, 63 So. 416 (Miss. 1913) (striking down the 1912 law on the ground that it violated the school-aid distribution formula set forth at § 206 of the 1890 Constitution); Miss. Const. § 286 (1919) (§ 206 amended by initiative to allow equalization); *Miller v. State ex rel. Russell*, 94 So. 706 (Miss. 1922) (upholding amendment process); William F. Winter, "Development of Educational Policy in Mississippi," 58 *Mississippi Law Journal* 223, 225 (1988).

15. *Pearson v. Murray*, 182 A. 590 (Md. 1936); see also, e.g., *State ex rel. Gaines v. Canada*, 305 U.S. 337 (1938) (applying equal-means-equal doctrine to graduate programs at the University of Missouri); *Sipuel v. Board of Regents of University of Oklahoma*, 332 U.S. 631 (1948) (law school); *Sweatt v. Painter*, 339 U.S. 629 (1950) (Texas state law school). Several state courts followed the Supreme Court in applying the doctrine during this period. See, e.g., *State ex rel. Bluford v. Canada*, 153 S.W.2d 12 (Mo. 1941) (journalism school); *State ex rel.*

Michael v. Witham, 165 S.2d 2d 378 (Tenn. 1942) (colleges); *see generally* Tushnet, *NAACP's Legal Strategy Against Segregated Education*, 78–81, 127–31.

16. At least one prominent state judge, Delaware chancellor Collins Seitz, openly advocated that step prior to *Brown. See Parker v. University of Delaware*, 76 A.2d 225 (Del. Ch. 1950) (requiring immediate provision of truly equal college facilities or immediate desegregation); *Belton v. Gebhart*, 87 A.2d 862, 865 (Del. Ch. 1952); see also Richard Kluger, *Simple Justice: The History of Brown v. Board of Education and Black America's Struggle for Equality* (2004).

17. Johnston, *Defiant Years*, 3–6; 1952 Miss. Laws, chs. 271, 277–78, 281; 1953 Miss. Laws (Ex. Sess.), chs. 12, 20.

18. 347 U.S. 483 (1954); Charles C. Bolton, "Mississippi's School Equalization Program, 1945–1954: 'A Last Gasp to Try to Maintain a Segregated Educational System,'" 66 *Journal of Southern History*, 781, 784–85 (2000); Johnston, *Defiant Years*, 6.

19. 1956 Miss. Laws, ch. 466, Sen. C. Res. 125.

20. *See Constantin v. Anson County*, 93 S.E.2d 163 (N.C. 1956); *Harrison v. Day*, 106 S.E.2d 636 (Va. 1959). South Carolina and Georgia went one step further than Mississippi by directly eliminating the right to a public education from their constitutions, but those measures eventually proved unpopular. Brian J. Daugherity and Charles C. Bolton, eds., *With All Deliberate Speed: Implementing Brown v. Board of Education* (2008), 44–56, 94–106, 128–30.

21. 1952 Miss. House Concurrent Res. 33; 1954 Miss. (Ex. Sess.) Sen Concurrent Res. 13, House Concurrent Res. 2; Johnston, *Defiant Years*, 6–7, 22–24; see also discussion in *United States v. Mississippi*, 229 F. Supp. 925 (S.D. Miss. 1964). The 1890 Constitution had required voters to give a "reasonable interpretation" of the state constitution to officials. Miss. Const. (1890), § 244 (amended 1954).

22. Charles Eagles, *The Price of Defiance: James Meredith and the Integration of Ole Miss* (2009), 88–98; Johnston, *Defiant Years*, 53; Robert E. Luckett Jr., *Joe T. Patterson and the White South's Dilemma: Evolving Resistance to Black Advancement* (2015), 70; Yasuhiro Katagiri, *The Mississippi State Sovereignty Commission: Civil Rights and States' Rights* (2001), 41–42; Klarman, *Jim Crow to Civil Rights*, 259–60; Nash and Taggart, *Mississippi Politics*, 19–20. For a trenchant analysis of Coleman as an exemplar of practical-segregation advocates, see Walker, "The Violent Bear It Away," 467–71, 503.

23. Crespino, *Conservative Counterrevolution*, 29–32; Katagiri, *Sovereignty Commission*, 55–61; Johnston, *Defiant Years*, 53–54; Klarman, *Jim Crow to Civil Rights*, 412–13; Branch, *Parting the Waters*, 344. Mississippi's supreme court, which had little involvement in civil rights cases, held there was sufficient evidence to support Kennard's burglary conviction and rejected his claim that the local jury-selection process discriminated against blacks. *State v. Kennard*, 128 So.2d 572 (Miss. 1961); see also *Kennard v. State*, 148 So.2d 660 (Miss. 1963) (denying petition for a new trial based on newly discovered evidence)

24. See Barrow and Walker, *A Court Divided*, 18–26, 39–40; Note, "Judicial Performance in the Fifth Circuit," 73 *Yale Law Journal* 90, 91–103 (1963) (analyzing in detail the strategy of delay followed by Mississippi judges hostile to civil rights reform).

25. Bass, *Unlikely Heroes*, 84–88.

26. *Boman v. Birmingham Transit Co.*, 292 F.2d 531, 4, 16, 29 (5th Cir. 1961) (dissent); *United States v. Wood*, 295 F.2d 772 (5th Cir. 1961) (dissent).

27. Tuttle and Brown spent their early years in Hawaii and Nebraska, respectively, and migrated to the South as young men in search of professional opportunity. Wisdom and another Tuttle ally, Alabama's Richard Rives, were members of old, patrician families that

accepted the benefits of the Jim Crow system but tended to view it with paternalistic detachment. Bass, *Unlikely Heroes*, 32–38 (Tuttle), 46–51 (Wisdom), 69–74 (Rives), 101–106 (Brown).

28. *United States v. Harrison County*, 265 F. Supp. 76 (S.D. Miss. 1967), *reversed*, 399 F.2d 485 (5th Cir. 1968); *Harrison County v. Guice*, 140 So.2d 838 (Miss. 1962); Johnston, *Defiant Years*, 105–111.

29. J. Michael Butler, "The Mississippi State Sovereignty Commission and Beach Integration, 1959–1963: A Cotton-Patch Gestapo?" 68 *Journal of Southern History* 107 (2002); Johnston, *Defiant Years*, 129, 171–78; Branch, *Parting the Waters*, 814–18, 831–32.

30. See, e.g., *State v. Goldfinch*, 132 So.2d 860 (La. 1961), *reversed*, 373 U.S. 267 (1963); *City of Greenville v. Peterson*, 122 S.E.2d 826 (S.C. 1961), *reversed*, 373 U,S. 244 (1963); see also *Shuttlesworth v. City of Birmingham*, 373 U.S. 374 (1963). Defendant store owners sometimes argued that they were purely private businesses and that calling the police to maintain order did not constitute state-sponsored discrimination that was subject to the federal Fourteenth Amendment, but the Supreme Court rejected this argument. *Peterson v. City of Greenville*, 373 U.S. 244 (1963). Some state court complied readily with the Supreme Court's directives, see, e.g., *City of Rock Hill v. Hamm*, 128 S.E.2d 907 (S.C. 1962), *vacated on other grounds*, 379 U.S. 306 (1964); others put up resistance through narrow interpretation of the directives. See *Banks v. State*, 170 So.2d 417 (Ala. App. 1964).

31. Branch, *Parting the Waters*, 470–75, 482–85; Klarman, *Jim Crow to Civil Rights*, 373–74.

32. *Bailey v. Patterson*, 199 F. Supp. 595 (S.D. Miss. 1961), *vacated*, 369 U.S. 31 (1962), *on remand*, 206 F. Supp. 67 (S.D. Miss. 1962); *reversed*, 323 F.2d 201 (5th Cir. 1963).

33. *United States v. City of Jackson*, 206 F. Supp. 45 (S.D. Miss. 1962), *reversed*, 318 F.2d 1, 5–6 (5th Cir. 1963). Judge Clayton, more temperamentally inclined to Coleman's view, was less obdurate in his civil rights rulings than Mize and Cox. Neil R. McMillen, "Black Enfranchisement in Mississippi: Federal Enforcement and Black Protest in the 1960s," 43 *Journal of Southern History* 351, 358 (1977).

34. Eagles, *Price of Defiance*, 221–55.

35. *Meredith v. Fair*, 199 F. Supp. 754 (S.D. Miss. 1961), *affirmed*, 298 F.2d 696 (5th Cir. 1961); Eagles, *Price of Defiance*, 254–57.

36. *Meredith v. Fair*, 202 F. Supp. 224 (S.D. Miss. 1962), *reversed*, 305 F.2d 343 (5th Cir. 1963), Eagles, *Price of Defiance*, 257–60.

37. *Meredith*, 305 F.2d at 344, 358 (Wisdom), 362 (DeVane dissent); Eagles, *Price of Defiance*, 260–68.

38. Eagles, *Price of Defiance*, 277–370; David G. Sansing, *Making Haste Slowly: The Troubled History of Higher Education in Mississippi* (1990), 117–45; Branch, *Parting the Waters*, 647–53, 657–72; Johnston, *Defiant Years*, 146–67. Shortly before Meredith's enrollment, the legislature officially commended Barnett for his "courageous stand" against "political aggression . . . designed to disrupt and destroy Southern institutions, traditions, and ways of living," an effort at "subjugation of the sovereignty of our state to the demands of a minority group not qualified by training or experience." 1962 Miss. Laws (1st Ex. Sess.), ch. 9.

39. David J. Garrow, *Bearing the Cross: Martin Luther King, Jr. and the Southern Christian Leadership Conference* (1986), 236–51, 291–300; 78 U.S. Stat. 241 (1964); 79 U.S. Stat. 435 (1965).

40. *Singleton v. Jackson Municipal Separate School District*, 348 F.2d 729, 729 (5th Cir. 1965).

41. Johnston, *Defiant Years*, 308–312; 1964 Miss. Laws (Ex. Sess.), ch. 31. The private-school subsidy law was struck down in *Coffey v. State Education Finance Commission*, 296 F.

Supp. 1383 (S.D. Miss. 1969), and the US Supreme Court later eliminated some of the attraction of private schools by holding that federal anti-discrimination laws applied to them. *Runyon v. McCrary*, 427 U.S. 160 (1976).

42. *Green*, 391 U.S. 430 (1968); *Anthony v. Marshall County Board of Education*, 409 F.2d 1287 (5th Cir. 1968). For an evaluation of Keady's jurisprudence as to racial and other matters, see James L. Robertson, "Judge William C. Keady and the Bill of Rights," 68 *Mississippi Law Journal* 3 (1988).

43. *Swann*, 401 U.S. 1 (1971); Daugherity and Bolton, *With All Deliberate Speed*, x-xii; Raymond Wolters, *Race and Education, 1954–2007* (2009), 130–35.

44. 418 U.S. 747 (1974); see Lukas, *Common Ground*; Kevin M. Kruse, *White Flight, Atlanta and the Making of Modern Conservatism* (2007); Mark T. Mulder, *Shades of White Flight: Evangelical Congregations and Urban Departure* (2015).

45. *Alexander v. Holmes County Board of Education*, 417 F.2d 852 (5th Cir. 1969), *reversed*, 396 U.S. 19 (1969); *Singleton*, 419 F.2d 211 (5th Cir. 1969) (requiring integration of schools by fall 1970 in light of the Supreme Court's decision in *Alexander*); *reversed*, 396 U.S. 290 (1970); *on remand*, 425 F.2d 1211 (5th Cir. 1970); Bass, *Unlikely Heroes*, 312–15.

46. Clark had served Mississippi as a special assistant attorney general during the late 1950s and early 1960s. He had ably defended in court the state's and Judge Mize's efforts to delay and evade desegregation, but he had also counseled state officials that in the end they must yield, winning the respect of both his clients and Fifth Circuit judges as a result. Bass, *Unlikely Heroes*, 176–77; Barrow and Walker, *A Court Divided*, 140.

47. *Singleton*, 425 F.2d at 1216 (Coleman dissent), 1221 (Clark dissent); see also Craig S. Piper, "Breakthrough: The Desegregation of the Starkville Public Schools," 66 *Journal of Mississippi History* 265 (2004).

48. Crespino, *Conservative Counterrevolution*, 127–32; see Chapter 4.

49. 79 U.S. Stat. 437 (1965), §§ 4–5.

50. 369 U.S. 186 (1962); see also *Reynolds v. Sims*, 377 U.S. 533 (1964); Stephen Ansolabehere, *The End of Inequality: One Person, One Vote and the Transformation of American Politics* (2008); Leroy Hardy, Alan Heslop, and Stuart Anderson, eds., *Reapportionment Politics: The History of Redistricting in the Fifty States* (1981).

51. *United States v. Wood*, 295 F.2d 772 (5th Cir. 1961), 785 (Wisdom), 787 (Cameron dissent); see United States Commission on Civil Rights, *Voting In Mississippi* (1965).

52. Miss. Const. (1890) § 241A (amended 1960); 1962 Miss. Laws, chs. 570–75.

53. Cameron had recently replaced Wisdom on the three-judge panel in question, enabling him to join with Cox to form an anti-reform majority. The substitution took place soon after Cameron had accused Tuttle of using his power as chief judge of the Fifth Circuit to exclude Mississippi judges from panels that heard desegregation and voting-rights cases, and Tuttle had agreed to modify court assignment procedures. See *Armstrong v. Board of Education of City of Birmingham*, 323 F.2d 333, 352 (5th Cir. 1963) (Cameron dissent); Barrow and Walker, *A Court Divided*, 40–41, 56–58. Wisdom later defended Tuttle's policy: "[A]ssigning two Mississippi district judges and Ben Cameron to a civil rights case," he said, "would be the equivalent of deciding it for the defense." *Id.*, 60.

54. Nash and Taggart, *Mississippi Politics*, 100–102; *United States v. Mississippi*, 229 F. Supp. 925 (S.D. Miss. 1964), *reversed*, 380 U.S. 128 (1965), *on remand*, 256 F. Supp. 344 (S.D. Miss. 1966). See also Kathryn Healy Hester, "Mississippi and the Voting Rights Act: 1965–1982," 52 *Mississippi Law Journal* 803 (1982). For an example of Cox's uses of delaying tactics in voting-rights cases, see *United States v. Lynd*, 301 F.2d 818 (5th Cir. 1962) (reversing Cox's denial of a temporary injunction requiring local officials to register black voters).

55. Johnston, *Defiant Years*, 324–25; Hester, "Mississippi and the Voting Rights Act," 803, 808 n. 43; Nash and Taggart, *Mississippi Politics*, 104–108; 1965 Miss. Laws (Ex. Sess.), ch. 36; Miss. Const. (1890) §§ 241A, 244 (amended 1965). The 1965 Voting Rights Act rendered the literacy requirement unenforceable. *United States v. Mississippi*, 256 F. Supp. at 347.

56. Business interests on the Gulf Coast, which had grown rapidly since the 1930s and was seriously underrepresented in the legislature, filed a challenge to the 1890 reapportionment plan even before *Baker* was decided, and in 1962, Hinds County Judge W. T. Horton ruled in their favor. After an abortive effort to comply with Horton's order, an effort that both he and Mississippi voters rejected, the legislature was able to put together a plan that passed muster under the order, but the plan was revisited soon after the 1965 act went into effect. 1963 Miss. Laws (1st Ex. Sess.), ch. 34; Nash and Taggart, *Mississippi Politics*, 103–106.

57. Nash and Taggart, *Mississippi Politics*, 103–106, quoting Thomas Vocino, John H. Morris and D. Steve Gill, "The Population Apportionment Principle: Its Development and Application to Mississippi's State and Local Legislative Bodies," 47 *Mississippi Law Journal* 943, 952–68 (1976).

58. *Connor v. Johnson*, 256 F. Supp. 962 (S.D. Miss. 1966); 1967 Miss. Laws (Ex. Sess.), ch. 41; *Connor v. Johnson*, 265 F. Supp. 492 (S.D. Miss. 1967).

59. *Connor v. Johnson*, 330 F. Supp. 506 (S.D. Miss. 1971) *reversed*, 402 U.S. 690 (1971); *Connor v. Johnson*, 330 F. Supp. 521 (S.D. Miss. 1971), *vacated and remanded*, 404 U.S. 549 (1972); *Connor v. Waller*, 396 F. Supp. 1308 (S.D. Miss. 1975), *reversed*, 421 U.S. 656 (1975); *Connor v. Finch*, 419 F. Supp. 1072 (S.D. Miss. 1976), 419 F. Supp. 1089 (S.D. Miss. 1976), 422 F. Supp. 1014 (S.D. Miss. 1976), *reversed*, 431 U.S. 407 (1977); *Connor v. Coleman*, 425 U.S. 675 (1976); *Connor v. Coleman*, 440 U.S. 612 (1979); see also *Mississippi v. United States*, 490 F. Supp. 569 (D.D.C. 1979) (approving legislature's 1978 apportionment plan pursuant to 1965 act), *affirmed without opinion*, 444 U.S. 1050 (1979).

60. *Evers v. State Board of Election Commissioners*, 327 F. Supp. 640, 641 (S.D. Miss. 1971); *South Carolina v. Katzenbach*, 383 U.S. 301 (1966). Federal courts had to draw district lines for other offices as well. See, e.g., *Fairley v. Patterson*, 282 F. Supp. 165 (S.D. Miss. 1967); *Bunton v. Patterson*, 281 F. Supp. 918 (S.D. Miss. 1967); *Whitley v. Johnson*, 296 F. Supp. 754 (S.D. Miss. 1967), all *affirmed* in *Allen v. State Board of Elections*, 393 U.S 544 (1969) (challenges to apportionment of county-supervisor districts).

61. Cobb, *New Deal/New South*, 56, 110, 172–79; Ted Ownby, ed., *The Civil Rights Movement in Mississippi* (2013), 237–48. In 1968, Charles Evers, brother of Mississippi civil rights leader Medgar Evers, became the Democratic nominee in a congressional election by gaining a plurality in a multi-candidate primary. After Evers was narrowly defeated in the general election, the legislature enacted an open-primary law to ensure that future black candidates could not obtain nominations with a plurality. Party primaries were eliminated; there would be one general primary for all candidates, and if no candidate received a majority, the top two candidates would advance to the general election. Opponents of the law obtained an injunction against its enforcement in 1971, and eventually the injunction was made permanent. The legislature's effort also prompted Congress to amend the Voting Rights Act to prohibit primary systems that had racially discriminatory effects. Crespino, *Conservative Counterrevolution*, 223–27; Frank R. Parker, *Black Votes Count: Political Empowerment in Mississippi after 1965* (1990), 60–63, 184–85; *Evers v. State Board of Election Commissioners*, 327 F. Supp. 640 (S.D. Miss. 1971).

62. Another way in which the civil rights movement has shaped Mississippi's legal system is the emergence of black lawyers as a significant part of the state's bar and the appearance of black judges in the system. When the modern civil rights struggle began in

earnest in the early 1960s, there were few black lawyers in Mississippi and only a handful, including R. Jess Brown, Jack Young, and Carsie Hall, dared to assist the NAACP and other groups in pursuing Mississippi desegregation cases. They were joined in the mid- and late 1960s by others, including Marian Wright Edelman, Reuben Anderson, and Fred L. Banks Jr. In 1985, Anderson became the first black Mississippian to serve on the Supreme Court (1985–90); Banks (1991–2001), James Graves (2001–11), and Leslie King (2011–) have also served on the court. The first black trial judges were appointed and elected to the late 1980s, and several black judges have served on the Court of Appeals since its creation in 1994. Judge Graves has also served on the federal Fifth Circuit (2011–), and Carlton Reeves (2010–) and Debra Brown (2013–) have served as federal district judges. Jack Greenberg, *Crusaders in the Courts: How a Dedicated Band of Lawyers Fought for the Civil Rights Revolution* (1994), 38; Willie L. Rose, "Historical Notes on Black Lawyers in Mississippi," 33 *Mississippi Lawyer* 5:14 (Mar.-Apr. 1987); Dale Krane and Stephen D. Shaffer, *Mississippi Government and Politics: Modernizers Versus Traditionalists* (1992).

63. Nash and Taggart, *Mississippi Politics*, 177–82; Ownby, *Civil Rights Movement in Mississippi*, 237–48; Scott E. Buchanan and Branwell DuBose Kapeluck, *Second Verse, Same as the First: The 2012 Presidential Election in the South* (2013), 83–99; E. C. Foster, "A Time of Challenge: Afro-Mississippi Political Developments Since 1965," 68 *Journal of Negro History* 185 (1983); Charles S. Bullock III and Mark J. Rozell, eds., *The New Politics of the Old South: An Introduction to Southern Politics* (5th ed. 2014), 89–111. In 1983, the Supreme Court directed the federal redistricting panel, now headed by Judge Clark, to reconsider its plan in light of Congress's recent decision to renew the 1965 act. By now, Clark had abandoned or at least suppressed his resentment of the act's requirements; his opinion matter-of-factly recognized that he and his colleagues had to fashion the best plan they could consistent with the act's requirements. *Jordan v. Winter*, 541 F. Supp. 1135 (N.D. Miss. 1982), *vacated*, 461 U.S. 921 (1983), *on remand*, 604 F. Supp. 807 (N.D. Miss. 1984), *affirmed without opinion*, 469 U.S. 1002 (1984).

64. Nash and Taggart, *Mississippi Politics*, 237–45; *Mauldin v. Branch*, 866 So.2d 429, 436 (Miss. 2003); see also *Smith v. Clark*, 189 F. Supp.2d 548 (S.D. Miss. 2002), *affirmed*, 538 U.S. 254 (2003) (enjoining state court's attempt to control redistricting). As to the state's post-2000 reapportionment, see *id.*; as to the post-2010 reapportionment, see *Smith v. Hosemann*, 852 F. Supp.2d 757 (S.D. Miss. 2011).

65. The literature touching on this subject is vast. Important sources include Daniel T. Rodgers, *The Age of Fracture* (2011); Pietro S. Nivola and David W. Brady, eds., *Red and Blue Nation? Characteristics and Causes of America's Polarized Politics* (2006); and Robert D. Putnam, *Bowling Alone: The Collapse and Revival of American Community* (2000), 173–80, 283–85. A source particularly relevant in the legal-history context is Naomi Cahn and June Carbone, *Red Families v. Blue Families: Legal Polarization and the Creation of Culture* (2010).

66. Rodgers, *Age of Fracture*, 3–5, 220–22.

67. *See* Sydney Ahlstrom, *A Religious History of the American People* (1972), 828–33, 842–65; John Higham, *Strangers in the Land: Patterns of American Nativism, 1860–1925* (1963), 54–59; Robert S. Michaelsen, *Piety in the Public Schools: Trends and Issues in the Relationship Between Religion and the Public Schools in the United States* (1970), 69–74, 87–89; Donald E. Boles, *Bible, Religion and the Public Schools* (1965), 26–28.

68. *Coffey v. State Education Finance Commission*, 296 F. Supp. 1383 (S.D. Miss. 1969); Crespino, *Conservative Counterrevolution*, 229–40, 255–59; 1964 Miss. Laws (Ex. Sess.), ch. 31. In 1970, a new point of conflict arose over private-school tax exemptions when the Internal

Revenue Service announced it would deny exemptions to schools that excluded black pupils but indicated that schools that formally disavowed segregation would not be closely scrutinized to determine if they were actually desegregated. The following year, a federal court held that Southern private schools' role in resistance to integration created a "badge of doubt" as to their good faith and that more than nominal compliance would be required in order to obtain a tax exemption. In 1978, the IRS strengthened its review policies, eliciting a series of court challenges. The US Supreme Court eventually upheld the IRS's authority to implement strict rules, but after Ronald Reagan was elected president in 1980 the rules were once again loosened *Green v. Connally*, 330 F. Supp. 1150 (D.D.C. 1971), *affirmed*, 404 U.S. 997 (1971); *Bob Jones University v. United States*, 461 U.S. 574 (1983); Note, "The Supreme Court, 1982 Term: Tax-Exempt Status of Discriminatory Private Schools," 97 *Harvard Law Review* 261 (1983).

69. Nash and Taggart, *Mississippi Politics*, 133–40; 1982 Miss. Laws, ch. 17.

70. See John F. Witte, *The Market Approach to Education: An Analysis of America's First Voucher Program* (2000), 34–35, 43–46; 1989 Wis. Laws, ch. 336, § 228; 1995 Ohio Laws, ch. 117.

71. *Davis v. Grover*, 480 N.W.2d 460 (Wis. 1992); *Jackson v. Benson*, 578 N.W.2d 602 (Wis. 1998); *Simmons-Harris v. Goff*, 711 N.E.2d 203 (Ohio, 1999), *affirmed sub nom. Zelman v. Simmons-Harris*, 536 U.S. 629 (2002); Julie F. Mead, "The Right to an Education or the Right to Shop for Schooling: Examining Voucher Programs in Relation to State Constitutional Guarantees," 42 *Fordham Urban Law Journal* 703, 707–713 (2015); National Conference of State Legislatures, "School Voucher Laws: State-by-State Comparison," www.ncsl.org/research/education/voucher-law-comparison.aspx. In the wake of *Zelman*, voucher opponents turned to state constitutional "Blaine clauses," products of a late nineteenth-century nativist movement that explicitly prohibit all state aid to sectarian schools, and that strategy has gained them some victories. See *Bush v. Holmes*, 919 So.2d 392 (Fla. 2006); *Cain v. Horne*, 202 P.3d 1178 (Ariz. 2009); *Taxpayers for Public Education v. Douglas County School District*, 351 P.3d 461 (Colo. 2015); Benjamin M. Superfine, *Equality in Education Law and Policy, 1954–2010* (2013), 147–50; Mead, "Examining Voucher Programs."

72. 2012 Miss. Laws, ch. 560 (dyslexic students); 2013 Miss. Laws, ch. 564 (students with speech and language impairments); 2015 Miss. Laws, ch 441 (special-needs students).

73. Michael Nelson and John Lyman Mason, *How the South Joined the Gambling Nation: The Politics of State Policy Innovation* (2007), 4–7; "A law to regulate Taverns and retailers of Liquors, and concerning Indians" (February 28, 1799); Ethridge, "Introduction to Sargent's Code," 180; Miss. Act of June 18, 1822; Hutchinson Code, 940; John L. Mason and Michael Nelson, *Governing Gambling: A Century Foundation Report* (2001), 8–10.

74. Nash and Taggart, *Mississippi Politics*, 215–25; Mason and Nelson, *Gambling Nation*, 7–16; 1989 Miss. Laws, ch. 481; 1990 Miss. Laws (Ex Sess.), ch. 45; 102 U.S. Stats. 2467 (1988).

75. Miss. Const. (1868), XIII:15; Miss. Const. (1890), § 98; Mason and Nelson, *Gambling Nation*, 15–25.

76. After the 1990 legislature failed to approve a lottery amendment, lottery supporters proposed enacting a constitutional amendment through the initiative and referendum process. They asked the Mississippi Supreme Court to overrule *Power v. Robertson*, 169 So. 769 (1922), in which the court had reversed an earlier decision upholding a constitutional amendment authorizing the initiative-and-referendum process. See Chapter 5. In 1991, the court, while recognizing that its predecessors had performed an "about-face" in *Power*, held that the decision had long been accepted as law in Mississippi and therefore should not be overturned. *State ex rel. Moore v. Molpus*, 578 So.2d 624, 630) (Miss. 1991). The 1992 legislature then approved a lottery amendment, which the voters approved by a vote of 481,848 to 427,335.

77. Mason and Nelson, *Gambling Nation*, 15–25; *Knight v. State ex. rel. Moore*, 574 So.2d 662 (Miss. 1990) (allowing bingo); *Casino Magic Corp. v. Ladner*, 666 So.2d 452 (Miss. 1995) (discussing casino licensing and regulation).

78. Jerome Start, "A State-By-State Examination of Nondiscrimination Laws and Policies," Center for American Progress Action Fund (2012), 3–4, 22–80.

79. *Baehr v. Lewin*, 852 P.2d 44 (Hawaii 1993); 1997 Hawaii Laws, ch. 383; William N. Eskridge Jr., "Backlash Politics: How Constitutional Litigation Has Advanced Marriage Equality in the United States," 93 *Boston University Law Review* 275 (2013); see also *Baker v. Nelson*, 191 N.W.2d 185 (Minn, 1971); *Jones v. Hallahan*, 501 S.W.2d 588 (Ky. 1973); *Singer v. Hara*, 522 P.2d 1187 (Wash. App. 1974) (early rejections of a constitutional right to gay marriage).

80. *Baker v. State*, 744 A.2d 864 (Vt. 1999); *Goodridge v. Department of Public Health*, 798 N.E.2d 941 (Mass. 2003).

81. See *Lewis v. Harris*, 908 A.2d 196 (N.J. 2006) (constitutional right to civil unions); *Kerrigan v. Commissioner of Public Health*, 957 A.2d 407 (Conn. 2008) (constitutional right to gay marriage); *In re Marriage Cases*, 183 P.3d 384 (Cal. 2008) (same); *Varnum v. Brien*, 763 N.W.2d 862 (Iowa 2009) (same). Court decisions holding that there was no constitutional right to gay marriage or civil unions included *Hernandez v. Robles*, 855 N.E.2d 1 (N.Y. 2006); *Conaway v. Deane*, 932 A.2d 571 (Md. 2007); *Andersen v. King County*, 138 P.2d 963 (Wash. 2006); *State v. Carswell*, 872 N.E.2d 547 (Ohio 2007), and *National Pride at Work v. Governor*, 748 N.W.2d 525 (Mich. 2008).

82. *Campaign for Southern Equality v. Bryant*, 64 F. Supp.3d 906, 914–15, 930–32 (Miss. 2014); 1997 Miss. Laws, ch. 301; Miss. Const. (1890), § 263A (amended 2004); see http:// en.wikipedia.org/wiki/ List_of_former_U.S_.state_constitutional_amendments_banning _same_sex_unions_by_type.

83. *Perry v. Schwarzenegger*, 704 F. Supp. 2d 921 (N.D. Cal. 2010), *affirmed*, 671 F.3d 1052 (9th Cir. 2012), *vacated*, 133 S. Ct. 2652 (2013).

84. For a list of decisions, see *Obergefell v. Hodges*, 135 S. Ct. 2584, 2607–12 (2015).

85. *Campaign for Southern Equality*, 64 F. Supp.3d at 912–13; *Obergefell*, 135 S. Ct. at 2590.

86. *Obergefell*, 135 U.S. at 2611–43 (Roberts, C.J. and Scalia, Thomas and Alito, JJ., dissenting); see also, e.g., *Goodridge*, 798 N,E.2d at 970–71 (Greaney, J., concurring), 974 (Spina, J., dissenting), 1002 n.34 (Cordy, J., dissenting).

87. Kathleen C. Berkeley, *The Women's Liberation Movement in America* (1999), 7–12; Joan Hoff, *Law, Gender and Injustice: A Legal History of U.S. Women* (1991), 108–118, 206–215.

88. Swain et al., *Mississippi Women*, 43–53, 148–55; 1921 Wis. Laws, ch. 529; National Woman's Party, "How Mississippi Laws Discriminate Against Women" (1922, pamphlet).

89. Berkeley, *Women's Liberation Movement*, 33–34; Kris Gilliland, Bette Bradley, and Ellie Campbell, "'Dared to Enter a "Man's World': Mississippi Women Lawyers, 1914–1944," 86 *Mississippi Law Journal* 1479, 1481 n. 5 (2017); *Pendergraft v. State*, 213 So.2d 560 (Miss. 1968); 1968 Miss. Laws, ch. 463.

90. Mary Caruthers Gholson of Holly Springs, who worked as an attorney for the US Department of Labor (DOL) after graduating from law school in 1939, played an important role in the inclusion of gender-discrimination provisions in the 1964 Civil Rights Act. She was active in the National Woman's Party and the National Organization of Women and prosecuted many gender-discrimination cases on behalf of the DOL. Gilliland et al., "Mississippi Women Lawyers," 1548–49.

91. Berkeley, *Women's Liberation Movement*, 85–90; Mary Frances Berry, *Why ERA Failed* (1986), 66–85; Kathryn Cullen-DuPont, ed., *American Women Activists' Writings: An Anthology, 1637-2002* (2002), 510 (Schlafly); Swain et al., *Mississippi Women*, 279–87. The

women's movement has also influenced Mississippi's legal system in that since 1970, the number of women law students, lawyers, and judges in Mississippi has increased dramatically. Mississippi has had women trial judges since at least 1953, when Zelma Price of Greenville became the first woman to join the trial bench. Lenore Prather became the first woman to serve on the Mississippi Supreme Court (1982–2001), and Mary Bickerstaff Payne became the first to serve on the state's Court of Appeals (1994–2001) after it was created in 1994. Gilliland et al., "Mississippi Women Lawyers," 1494–95, 1500, 1559–62. As of this writing, one of nine Supreme Court justices and three of ten Court of Appeals justices are women.

92. See Cahn and Carbone, *Red Families v. Blue Families*, 91–95; Kelefa Sanneh, "The Intensity Gap: Can a Pro-Life Platform Win Elections?," *New Yorker*, October 27, 2014.

93. See 1880 Miss. Code, § 2884: 1906 Miss. Code, §§ 1157, 1217; David Garrow, "Abortion Before and After Roe v. Wade: An Historical Perspective," 62 *Albany Law Review* 833, 846–48 (1999).

94. Garrow, "Abortion Before and After Roe v. Wade," 846–48; Maya Manian, "Lessons from Personhood's Defeat: Abortion Restrictions and Side Effects on Women's Health," 74 *Ohio State Law Journal* 75, 83–84 (2013).

95. 410 U.S. 113, 163–65 (1973); 1986 Miss. Laws, ch. 448; 1991 Miss. Laws, ch. 439; *Casey*, 505 U.S. 833, 877, 880–84 (1992). The 1990 legislature approved a bill providing a twenty-four-hour waiting period and requiring all abortion clinics to be specially licensed, but Governor Ray Mabus vetoed the bill, a decision that contributed to his defeat for re-election in 1991. Nash and Taggart, *Mississippi Politics*, 230–31.

96. 970 F.2d 12 (5th Cir. 1992). The Fifth Circuit later divided over whether the 1986 law's "judicial bypass" provisions, allowing minors to obtain court permission for an abortion in lieu of parental permission and prescribing hearing procedures, gave applicants an adequate opportunity to be heard. A majority of the judicial panel upheld the provisions. *Barnes v. Mississippi*, 992 F.2d 1335 (5th Cir. 1992).

97. *Pro-Choice Mississippi v. Fordice*, 716 So.2d 645 (Miss. 1998).

98. Cahn and Carbone, *Red Families v. Blue Families*, 91–95. In 2000, 36 percent of states were "low regulation" states that had enacted at most a single restrictive law and 24 percent were "high regulation" states with four or more restrictive laws; in 2016, the figures were 26 percent and 54 percent, respectively. See Rachel Benson Gold and Elizabeth Nash, "Troubling Trend: More States Hostile to Abortion Rights and Middle Ground Shrinks," 15 *Guttmacher Policy Review* 14 (2012) (2000 statistics); Heather D. Boonstra and Elizabeth Nash, "A Surge of State Abortion Restrictions Puts Providers—and the Women They Serve—in the Crosshairs," 17 *Guttmacher Policy Review* 9 (2014) (2013 statistics).

99. See Guttmacher Institute, "State Politics in Brief: An Overview of Abortion Laws as of September 1, 2015," available at www.guttmacher-org./statecenter/spibs/spib_ OAL.pdf.

100. Like the Fifth Circuit in *Barnes*, most courts have upheld such laws except those whose legislative history too openly indicated that their real purpose was to restrict abortion rather than promote health, and those that failed to provide medical-emergency exceptions. See, e.g., *Stuart v. Camnitz*, 774 F.3d 238 (4th Cir. 2014) (striking down requirement that mother be given opportunity to view sonogram); *Texas Medical Providers Performing Abortion Services v. Lakey*, 667 F.3d 570 (5th Cir. 2012) (upholding similar provision that was accompanied by recitation of ways in which it promoted health); Christine L. Raffaele, "Validity of State 'Informed Consent' Statutes," 119 *American Law Reports 5th* 315 (2004, updated 2017).

101. 2002 Miss. Laws, ch. 604. The US Supreme Court has approved a law banning funding, as have several state courts, all on condition that the laws create exceptions for

preserving the mother's life or health. But other courts have struck down such bans as violative of their state constitutions' equal-protection and right-to-privacy clauses and other clauses. See *Harris v. McRae*, 448 U.S. 297 (1980) and *Renee B. v. Florida Agency for Health Care Administration*, 790 So.2d 1036 (Fla. 2001) (upholding bans); *Doe v. Gomez*, 542 N.W.2d 17 (Minn. 1995) and *Women's Health Center of West Virginia, Inc. v. Panepinto*, 446 S.E.2d 659 (W.Va. 1993) (striking down bans as violative of state constitutional provisions). See also Tracey Bateman Farrell, "Validity of State Statutes and Regulations Limiting or Restricting Public Funding for Abortion South by Indigent Women," 118 *American Law Reports 5th* 463 (2007, updated 2017).

102. 2004 Miss. Laws, ch. 584; *Jackson Women's Health Organization v. Amy*, 330 F. Supp. 2d 820 (S.D. Miss. 2004).

103. *Jackson Women's Health Organization v. Currier*, 940 F. Supp.2d 416 (S.D. Miss. 2013), *affirmed*, 760 F.3d 448 (5th Cir. 2014). Similar TRAP laws in Wisconsin and Texas met similar fates, the latter at the hands of the U.S. Supreme Court. *Planned Parenthood of Wisconsin, Inc. v. Van Hollen*, 94 F. Supp. 3d 949 (W.D. Wis. 2015), *affirmed*, 806 F.3d 908 (7th Cir. 2015), *certiorari denied*, 134 S.Ct. 2841 (2015); *Whole Women's Health v. Cole*, 790 F.3d 563 (5th Cir. 2015), *reversed*, 136 S. Ct. 2292 (2016).

104. 2014 Miss. Laws, ch. 506; see, e.g., *Isaacson v. Horne*, 716 F.3d 1213 (9th Cir. 2013) (Arizona law); *Edwards v. Beck*, 786 F.3d 1113 (8th Cir. 2015) (Arkansas law).

105. 2007 Miss. Laws, ch. 441.

106. *See* Lawrence M. Friedman, *A History of American Law* (3rd ed. 2005), 356–64, 516–23; G. Edward White, *Tort Law in America: An Intellectual History* (2003), 164–73; Kenneth S. Abraham, *The Liability Century: Insurance and Tort Law from the Progressive Era to 9/11* (2008), 39–68, 114–21; John Fabian Witt, "The Long History of State Constitutions and American Tort Law," 6 *Rutgers Law Journal* 1159, 1171–95 (2005); John T. Nockleby and Shannon Curreri, "100 Years of Conflict: The Past and Future of Tort Retrenchment," 38 *Loyola of Los Angeles Law Review* 1021, 1026–30 (2005).

107. Nockleby, "Tort Retrenchment," 1029–30; David F. Maron and Samuel D. Gregory, "A Decade Examined: A Review of the Recovery Under Mississippi's Civil Justice Reforms," 34 *Mississippi College Law Review* 203, 203–206 (2015); Mark A. Behrens and Cary Silverman, "Building on the Foundation: Mississippi's Civil Justice Reform Success and a Path Forward," 34 *Mississippi College Law Review* 113, 113–14 (2015); Bryan A. Jones, Comment, "The End of Tort Reform? The Constitutional Battle Looms Over Mississippi," 80 *Mississippi Law Journal* 87, 95 (2011); Nash and Taggart, *Mississippi Politics*, 291–97.

108. 1993 Miss. Laws, ch. 302; Nash and Taggart, *Mississippi Politics*, 295–97; Philip L. McIntosh, "Tort Reform in Mississippi: An Appraisal of the New Law of Products Liability, Part I," 16 *Mississippi College Law Review* 393, 394–99 (1996).

109. 2002 Miss. Laws (3d Ex. Sess.), ch. 2 (punitive damages limits); 2004 Miss. Laws (1st Ex. Sess.), ch. 1 (non-economic damages cap); Nockleby, "Tort Retrenchment," 1029–30; Maron and Gregory, "A Decade Examined," 213–16; Behrens and Silverman, "Building on the Foundation," 117–24; Nash and Taggart, *Mississippi Politics*, 297–301. The 2002 and 2004 legislatures also made less-publicized changes in the state's tort law, most notably limiting the extent to which multiple defendants in tort cases could be held jointly and severally liable for all defendants' fault. The scope of joint and several liability is vitally important in cases where multiple defendants with widely varying resources (for example, a negligent supervisor with few personal assets and a corporation with millions or billions of dollars in assets) are partly responsible for an injury. 2002 Miss. Laws (3d Ex. Sess.), ch. 2.

110. *Learmonth v. Sears, Roebuck & Co.*, 631 F.3d 724 (5th Cir. 2011) (requesting advisory opinion as to cap's constitutionality); *Sears, Roebuck & Co. v. Learmonth*, 95 So.2d 633 (Miss. 2012) (declining to give opinion).

111. *Learmonth v. Sears, Roebuck & Co.*, 710 F.3d 249 (5th Cir. 2013). In *Clemons v. United States*, 2013 WL 3943494, *14 (S.D. Miss. 2013), Judge Reeves confirmed that the cap was constitutional but noted that it could lead to discriminatory and unfair results in some cases. One Mississippi trial judge has held the cap unconstitutional, but other state trial judges have disagreed. See Maron and Gregory, "A Decade Examined," 216–17.

112. See Theodore Eisenberg and Geoffrey P. Miller, "Reversal, Dissent and Variability in State Supreme Courts: The Centrality of Jurisdictional Source," 89 *Boston University Law Review* 1451, 1483–84 (2009); Ranney, *Shaping of American Law*, 209–210.

113. 1993 Miss. Laws, ch. 518. The information in Figure 6.3 is compiled from the *Mississippi Reports* for 1940 and 1960 and from the *Southern Reporter* for 1980, 2000, and 2010. The compilation is in the author's possession.

114. Eisenberg and Miller, "Variability in State Supreme Courts," 1483–84. This study indicates that in 2003, Mississippi's supreme court had the highest rate of dissent of any in the nation. *Id.* See also Leslie Southwick, "Mississippi Supreme Court Elections: A Historical Perspective 1916–1996," 18 *Mississippi College Law Journal* 115 (1998).

115. See McDonald, *States Rights and the Union*, 76–79; Shirley S. Abrahamson, "Criminal Law and State Constitutions: The Emergence of State Constitutional Law," 63 *Texas Law Review* 1141 (1985).

116. Abrahamson, "Emergence of State Constitutional Law," 1147–48; William J. Brennan Jr., "State Constitutions and the Protection of Individual Rights," 90 *Harvard Law Review* 489 (1977).

117. See Kenneth P. Miller, "Defining Rights in the States: Judicial Activism and Popular Response," 76 *Albany Law Review* 2061, 2070–71, 2080–83 (2013); Gerald F. Uelmen, "Crocodiles in the Bathtub: Maintaining the Independence of State Supreme Courts in an Era of Judicial Politicization," 72 *Notre Dame Law Review* 1133, 1133–34, 1139 (1997); Stephen B. Bright and Patrick J. Keenan, "Judges and the Politics of Death: Deciding Between the Bill of Rights and the Next Election in Capital Cases," 75 *Boston University Law Review* 759, 763–65 (1995).

118. See *Penick v. State*, 440 So.2d 547, 551 (Miss. 1983) (stating: "While of great persuasion, we will not concede that simply because the United States Supreme Court may interpret a U.S. Constitutional provision that we must give the same interpretation to essentially the same words in a provision of our state Constitution"); *Sanders v. State*, 429 So.2d 245 (Miss. 1983) (favoring congruent interpretation); *McCrory v. State*, 342 So.2d 897 (Miss. 1977) (same).

119. *Stringer v. State*, 491 So.2d 837 (Miss. 1986); *White v. State*, 842 So.2d 565 (Miss. 2003). The court has also interpreted Mississippi's bill of rights to give indigent defendants a broader right to legal counsel than the federal bill of rights, and it has rejected an argument that it should march in lockstep with federal courts on that issue. *Killingsworth v. State*, 490 So.2d 849 (Miss. 1986), refusing to adopt the narrower interpretation of the right to counsel announced in *Anders v. California*, 386 U.S. 738 (1967).

120. See Sharkey's opinion in *Brien v. Williamson*, 8 Miss. at 16 (accepting US Supreme Court's decision that an 1833 Mississippi constitutional amendment restricting the slave trade was not enforceable because of a lack of implementing legislation). See also *Grand Gulf Railroad & Banking Co. v. State*, 18 Miss. at 434 and *Montgomery v. Galbraith*, 19 Miss. at 574 (accepting US Supreme Court decision striking down a banking law that the Mississippi court had upheld); see generally Chapters 3–4.

121. See Chapters 2 and 5.

TABLE OF MISSISSIPPI CASES

Brown v. State, 167 So. 82 (Miss. 1936).

Bryant v. Barnes, 106 So. 113 (Miss. 1925).

Buchanan v. Smith, 43 Miss. 90 (1870).

Bunton v. Patterson, 281 F. Supp. 918 (S.D. Miss. 1967), *affirmed*, 393 U.S 544 (1969).

Butler v. State, 135 So. 357 (Miss. 1931).

Byrd v. State, 123 So. 867 (Miss. 1929).

Campaign for Southern Equality v. Bryant, 64 F. Supp.3d 906 (Miss. 2014).

Carothers v. Town of Booneville, 153 So. 670 (Miss. 1934).

Carraway v. State, 137 So. 325 (Miss. 1931).

Carraway v. State, 141 So. 342 (Miss. 1932).

Carraway v. State, 148 So. 340 (Miss. 1933).

Casino Magic Corp. v. Ladner, 666 So.2d 452 (Miss. 1995).

Cassell v. Backrack, 42 Miss. 56 (1868).

Clemons v. United States, 2013 WL 3943494 (S.D. Miss. 2013).

Coffey v. State Education Finance Commission, 296 F. Supp. 1383 (S.D. Miss. 1969).

Collins v. Sherman, 31 Miss. 679 (1856).

Connor v. Coleman, 425 U.S. 675 (1976).

Connor v. Coleman, 440 U.S. 612 (1979).

Connor v. Finch, 419 F. Supp. 1072 (S.D. Miss. 1976), *reversed*, 431 U.S. 407 (1977).

Connor v. Finch, 422 F. Supp. 1014 (S.D. Miss. 1976), *reversed*, 431 U.S. 407 (1977).

Connor v. Johnson, 256 F. Supp. 962 (S.D. Miss. 1966).

Connor v. Johnson, 265 F. Supp. 492 (S.D. Miss. 1967).

Connor v. Johnson, 330 F. Supp. 506 (1971), *reversed*, 402 U.S. 690 (1971).

Connor v. Johnson, 330 F. Supp. 521 (1971), *vacated*, 404 U.S. 549 (1972).

McInnis v. Thames, 32 So. 286 (Miss. 1902).

McIntyre v. Ingraham, 35 Miss. 525 (1858).

Meredith v. Fair, 199 F. Supp. 754 (S.D. Miss. 1961), *affirmed*, 298 F.2d 696 (5th Cir. 1961).

Meredith v. Fair, 202 F. Supp. 224 (S.D. Miss. 1962), *reversed*, 305 F.2d 343 (5th Cir. 1963).

Miller v. State ex rel. Russell, 94 So. 706 (Miss. 1922).

Mississippi v. United States, 490 F. Supp. 569 (D.D.C. 1979), *affirmed*, 444 U.S. 1050 (1979).

Mitchell v. Wells, 37 Miss. 235 (1859).

Montgomery v. Galbraith, 19 Miss. 555 (1848).

Murrell v. Jones, 40 Miss. 465 (1866).

Netterville v. Barber, 52 Miss. 168 (1876).

Nevitt v. Bank of Port Gibson, 14 Miss. 513 (1846).

Oliver v. State, 39 Miss. 526 (1860).

Patton v. State, 29 So.2d 96 (Miss. 1947), *reversed*, 332 U.S. 463.

Patton v. State, 40 So.2d 592 (Miss. 1949), *appeal dismissed*, 338 U.S. 855 (1949).

Patton v. State, 43 So.2d 216 (Miss. 1949).

Payne v. Baldwin, 11 Miss. 661 (1844), *reversed*, 47 U.S. 301 (1848).

Pendergraft v. State, 213 So.2d 560 (Miss. 1968).

Penick v. State, 440 So.2d 547 (Miss. 1983).

Perkins v. State, 135 So. 357 (Miss. 1931).

Peter v. State, 12 Miss. 31 (1844).

Pickens v. Eskridge, 42 Miss. 114 (1868).

Planters Bank v. Sharp, 12 Miss. 17 (1844), *reversed*, 47 U.S. 301 (1848).

Power v. Robertson, 93 So. 769 (Miss. 1922).

Pruitt v. State, 139 So. 861 (Miss. 1932).

State v. Jones, 1 Miss. 83 (1821).

State v. Kennard, 128 So.2d 572 (Miss. 1961).

State v. McGinty, 41 Miss. 435 (1867).

State Board of Education v. Pridgen, 63 So. 416 (Miss. 1913).

Story v. State, 97 So. 806 (Miss. 1923).

Stringer v. State, 491 So.2d 837 (Miss. 1986).

Sykes v. State, 42 So. 875 (Miss. 1907).

Tatum v. Wheeless, 178 So. 95 (Miss. 1938).

Thomas v. Taylor, 42 Miss. 651 (1869).

Thompson v. Box, 112 So. 597 (Miss. 1927).

Thompson v. Young, 30 Miss. 17 (1855).

Trotter v. McCall, 26 Miss. 410 (1853).

Trustees of Walton School v. Board of Supervisors of Covington County, 75 So. 833 (Miss. 1917).

United States v. City of Jackson, 206 F. Supp. 45 (S.D. Miss. 1962), *reversed*, 318 F.2d 1 (5th Cir. 1963).

United States v. Harrison County, 265 F. Supp. 76 (S.D. Miss. 1967), *reversed*, 399 F.2d 485 (5th Cir. 1968).

United States v. Lynd, 301 F.2d 818 (5th Cir. 1962).

United States v. Mississippi, 229 F. Supp. 925 (S.D. Miss. 1964), *reversed*, 380 U.S. 128 (1965).

United States v. Mississippi, 256 F. Supp. 344 (S.D. Miss. 1966).

United States v. Wood, 295 F.2d 772 (5th Cir. 1961).

Van Buren v. State, 24 Miss. 512 (1852).

Waldauer v. Vicksburg Ry. & Light Co., 40 So. 751 (Miss. 1906).

Warren v. Brown, 25 Miss. 66 (1852).

SELECTED BIBLIOGRAPHY

Abernethy, Thomas P. *A History of the South, Vol. IV: The New Nation, 1789–1819*. Baton Rouge: Louisiana State University Press, 1961.

Abraham, Kenneth S. *The Liability Century: Insurance and Tort Law from the Progressive Era to 9/11*. Cambridge: Harvard University Press, 2008.

Abrahamson, Shirley S. "Criminal Law and State Constitutions: The Emergence of State Constitutional Law." 63 *Texas Law Review* 1141 (1985).

Ahlstrom, Sydney. *A Religious History of the American People*. New Haven, CT: Yale University Press, 1972.

Ames, Herman V., ed. *State Documents on Federal Relations: The States and the United States*. Philadelphia: University of Pennsylvania Department of History, 1900.

Ansolabehere, Stephen. *The End of Inequality: One Person, One Vote and the Transformation of American Politics*. New York: Norton, 2008.

Arnold, Morris S. *Unequal Laws unto a Savage Race: European Legal Tradition in Arkansas, 1686–1836*. Fayetteville: University of Arkansas Press, 1985.

Aucoin, Brent J. *Thomas Goode Jones: Race, Politics and Justice in the New South*. Tuscaloosa: University of Alabama Press, 2016.

Ayers, Edward L. *The Promise of the New South: Life after Reconstruction*. New York: Oxford University Press, 1992.

———. *Vengeance and Justice: Crime and Punishment in the Nineteenth Century American South*. New York: Oxford University Press, 1984.

Baggett, James A. *The Scalawags: Southern Dissenters in the Civil War and Reconstruction*. Baton Rouge: Louisiana State University Press, 2003.

Baldwin, Joseph G. *The Flush Times of Alabama and Mississippi*. New York: D. Appleton, 1853.

Balesi, Charles J. *The Time of the French in the Heart of North America, 1673–1818*. Chicago: Alliance Francaise Chicago, 1991.

Barrow, Deborah J., and Thomas G. Walker. *A Court Divided: The Fifth Circuit Court of Appeals and the Politics of Judicial Reform*. New Haven, CT: Yale University Press, 1988.

Basch, Norma. *In the Eyes of the Law: Women, Property and Marriage in Nineteenth-Century New York*. Ithaca, NY: Cornell University Press, 1982.

Bass, Jack. *Unlikely Heroes*. New York: Simon and Schuster, 1981.

Beckert, Sven. *Empire of Cotton: A Global History*. New York: Alfred A. Knopf, 2014.

Behrens, Mark A., and Cary Silverman. "Building on the Foundation: Mississippi's Civil Justice Reform Success and a Path Forward." 34 *Mississippi College Law Review* 113 (2015).

Benedict, Michael Les. "Laissez-Faire and Liberty: A Re-Evaluation of the Meaning and Origins of Laissez-Faire Constitutionalism." 3 *Law & History Review* 293 (1985).

Berlin, Ira. *Slaves without Masters: The Free Negro in the Antebellum South.* New York: Pantheon, 1975.

Biles, Roger. *The South and the New Deal.* Lexington: University Press of Kentucky, 1994.

Blackstone, William. *Commentaries on the Law of England.* Oxford: Clarendon Press, 1765.

Blume, William Wirt. "Legislation on the American Frontier." 60 *Michigan Law Review* 317 (1962).

Boles, Donald E. *Bible, Religion and the Public Schools.* Ames: Iowa State University Press, 1965.

Bolton, Charles C. "Mississippi's School Equalization Program, 1945–1954: 'A Last Gasp to Try to Maintain a Segregated Educational System.'" 66 *Journal of Southern History* 781 (2000).

Bond, Bradley G. *Political Culture in the Nineteenth-Century South: Mississippi, 1830–1900.* Baton Rouge: Louisiana State University Press, 1995.

Branch, Taylor. *Parting the Waters: America in the King Years.* New York: Simon and Schuster, 1988.

Brennan, William J., Jr. "State Constitutions and the Protection of Individual Rights." 90 *Harvard Law Review* 489 (1977).

Bridgeforth, Lucie Robertson. "Mississippi's Response to Nullification, 1833." 45 *Journal of Mississippi History* 1 (1983).

Bright, Stephen B., and Patrick J. Keenan. "Judges and the Politics of Death: Deciding Between the Bill of Rights and the Next Election in Capital Cases." 75 *Boston University Law Review* 759 (1995).

Brown, Elizabeth Gaspar. Note, "Husband and Wife—Memorandum on the Mississippi Woman's Law of 1839." 42 *Michigan Law Review* 1110 (1944).

Buchanan, Scott E., and Branwell DuBose Kapeluck. *Second Verse, Same as the First: The 2012 Presidential Election in the South.* Fayetteville: University of Arkansas Press, 2013.

Bullock, Charles S. III, and Mark J. Rozell, eds. *The New Politics of the Old South: An Introduction to Southern Politics.* 5th ed. Lanham, MD: Rowman and Littlefield, 2014.

Busbee, Wesley F., Jr. *Mississippi: A History.* Wheeling, IL: Harlan Davidson, 2005.

Butler, J. Michael. "The Mississippi State Sovereignty Commission and Beach Integration, 1959–1963: A Cotton-Patch Gestapo?" 68 *Journal of Southern History* 107 (2002).

Cadman, John W. *The Corporation in New Jersey: Business and Politics, 1791–1875.* Cambridge: Harvard University Press, 1949.

Cahn, Naomi, and June Carbone. *Red Families v. Blue Families: Legal Polarization and the Creation of Culture.* New York: Oxford University Press, 2010.

Calhoon, S. S. "The Causes and Events that Led to the Calling of the Constitutional Convention of 1890." 6 *Publications of the Mississippi Historical Society* 105 (1902).

Campbell, Josiah A. P. "Planters and Union Bank Bonds." 4 *Publications of the Mississippi Historical Society* 493 (1901).

Carter, Clarence E., ed. *Territorial Papers of the United States.* Washington, DC: US Government Printing Office, 1937.

Caruso, John A. *The Mississippi Valley Frontier: The Age of French Exploration and Settlement.* Indianapolis: Bobbs-Merrill, 1964.

Cash, W. J. *The Mind of the South*. London: Thames and Hudson, 1971.

Caudill, Orley B. "Oral History with the Honorable J.P. Coleman." 11 *Journal of Southern Legal History* 117 (2003).

Censer, Jane Turner. "'Smiling Through Her Tears': Ante-Bellum Southern Women and Divorce." 25 *American Journal of Legal History* 24 (1981).

Chused, Richard H. "Married Women's Property Law: 1800–1850." 71 *Georgetown Law Journal* 1359 (1983).

Claiborne, J. F. H. *Mississippi as a Province, Territory and State*. Jackson: Power and Barksdale, 1880.

Clark, Eric C. "Legislative Adoption of BAWI, 1936." 52 *Journal of Mississippi History* 283 (1990).

———. "Legislative Apportionment in the 1890 Constitutional Convention." 42 *Journal of Mississippi History* 298 (1980).

———. "Regulation of Corporations in the Mississippi Constitutional Convention of 1890." 48 *Journal of Mississippi History* 31 (1986).

Cobb, James C., ed. *New Deal/New South: An Anthony J. Badger Reader*. Fayetteville: University of Arkansas Press, 2007.

———. *Redefining Southern Culture: Mind and Identity in the Modern South*. Athens: University of Georgia Press, 1999.

Cobb, James C. *The Selling of the South: The Southern Crusade for Industrial Development, 1936–1990*. 2nd ed. Urbana: University of Illinois Press, 1993.

Cobb, James C., and Michael Namorato, eds. *The New Deal and the South: Essays*. Jackson: University Press of Mississippi, 1984.

Cohen, Felix S. *Cohen's Handbook of Federal Indian Law*. Nell Jessup Newton, ed. Charlottesville, VA: Michie/Bobbs-Merrill, 1982.

Cohen, William. "Negro Involuntary Servitude in the South, 1865–1940: A Preliminary Analysis." 42 *Journal of Southern History* 31 (1976).

Coleman, Peter J. *Debtors and Creditors in America: Insolvency, Imprisonment for Debt, and Bankruptcy, 1607–1900*. Madison: State Historical Society of Wisconsin, 1974.

Commons, John R., ed. *History of Labor in the United States, 1896–1932*. New York: Macmillan, 1935.

Cooley, Thomas B. *A Treatise on the Constitutional Limitations Which Rest Upon the Legislative Power of the States of the American Union*. Boston: Little, Brown, 1868.

Cortner, Richard C. *A "Scottsboro" Case in Mississippi: The Supreme Court and Brown v. Mississippi*. Jackson: University Press of Mississippi, 1986.

Crane, J. Michael. "Controlling the Night: Perceptions of the Slave Patrol System in Mississippi." 61 *Journal of Mississippi History* 119 (1999).

Crespino, Joseph. *In Search of Another Country: Mississippi and the Conservative Counterrevolution*. Princeton, NJ: Princeton University Press, 2007.

Cresswell, Stephen. "Enforcing the Enforcement Acts: The Department of Justice in Northern Mississippi, 1870–1900." 53 *Journal of Southern History* 421 (1987).

———. *Multiparty Politics in Mississippi, 1877–1902*. Jackson: University Press of Mississippi, 1995.

———. *Rednecks, Redeemers and Race: Mississippi after Reconstruction, 1877–1917*. Jackson: University Press of Mississippi, 2006.

Cutler, James Elbert. *Lynch-Law: An Investigation into the History of Lynching in the United States*. New York: Longmans, Green, 1905.

Daniel, Pete. *Shadow of Slavery: Peonage in the South, 1901–1969*. Urbana: University of Illinois Press, 1972.

Daniel, Pete. *Standing at the Crossroads: The South Since 1900*. New York: Hill and Wang, 1986.

Dargo, George. *Jefferson's Louisiana: Politics and the Clash of Legal Traditions*. Cambridge: Harvard University Press, 1975.

Daugherity, Brian J., and Charles C. Bolton, eds. *With All Deliberate Speed: Implementing Brown v. Board of Education*. Fayetteville: University of Arkansas Press, 2008.

Davis, Reuben. *Recollections of Mississippi and Mississippians*. Hattiesburg: University and College Press of Mississippi, 1972.

Dillon, John F. *Law of Municipal Corporations*. New York: J. Cockroft, 1873.

Dodd, Donald B., and Wynelle S. Dodd. *Historical Statistics of the South, 1790–1970*. Tuscaloosa: University of Alabama Press, 1973.

Drachman, Virginia. *Sisters in Law: Women Lawyers in Modern American History*. Cambridge: Harvard University Press, 1998.

Drake, Winborne Magruder. "The Framing of Mississippi's First Constitution." 29 *Journal of Mississippi History* 301 (1967).

Du Bois, W. E. B. *Black Reconstruction*. Philadelphia: A. Saifer, 1935.

Eagles, Charles. *The Price of Defiance: James Meredith and the Integration of Ole Miss*. Chapel Hill: University of North Carolina Press, 2009.

Eblen, Jack E. *The First and Second United States Empires: Governors and Territorial Government, 1784–1912*. Pittsburgh: University of Pittsburgh Press, 1968.

Editors of the *Economist*. *The New Deal: An Analysis and Appraisal*. New York: Alfred A. Knopf, 1937.

Eisenberg, Theodore, and Geoffrey P. Miller. "Reversal, Dissent and Variability in State Supreme Courts: The Centrality of Jurisdictional Source." 89 *Boston University Law Review* 1451 (2009).

Eskridge, William N., Jr. "Backlash Politics: How Constitutional Litigation Has Advanced Marriage Equality in the United States." 93 *Boston University Law Review* 275 (2013).

Ethridge, George H. *Mississippi Constitutions*. Jackson, MS: Tucker Printing House, 1938.

Ethridge, William N., Jr. "An Introduction to Sargent's Code of the Mississippi Territory (1799–1800)." 11 *American Journal of Legal History* 148 (1967).

Fairman, Charles E. *History of the Supreme Court of the United States, Vol. 6: Reconstruction and Reunion, 1864–1888*. New York: Macmillan, 1971.

The Federalist. New York: Modern Library, 1937.

Finkelman, Paul. *An Imperfect Union: Slavery, Federalism and Comity*. Chapel Hill: University of North Carolina Press, 1980.

Fishback, Price V., and Shawn E. Kanter. "The Adoption of Workers' Compensation in the United States, 1900–1930." 41 *Journal of Law and Economics* 305 (1998).

Fisher, William W. "Ideology and Imagery in the Law of Slavery," 68 *Chicago-Kent Law Review Review* 1051 (1993).

Fiss, Owen M. *History of the Supreme Court of the United States, Vol. 8: Troubled Beginnings of the Modern State, 1888–1910*. New York: Macmillan, 1993.

Flanigan, Daniel J. "Criminal Procedure in Slave Trials in the Antebellum South." 40 *Journal of Southern History* 537 (1974).

Foner, Eric S. *Free Soil, Free Labor, Free Men: The Ideology of the Republican Party before the Civil War*. New York: Oxford University Press, 1971.

———. *Reconstruction: America's Unfinished Revolution, 1863–1877.* New York: Harper & Row, 1988.

Foster, E. C. "A Time of Challenge: Afro-Mississippi Political Developments Since 1965." 68 *Journal of Negro History* 185 (1983).

Franklin, John Hope. *The Militant South, 1800–1861.* Cambridge: Harvard University Press, 1956.

Fredrickson, George M. *The Black Image in the White Mind: The Debate on Afro-American Character and Destiny, 1817–1914.* New York: Harper & Row, 1971.

Friedman, Lawrence E. *A History of American Law.* 3rd ed. New York: Simon and Schuster, 2005.

Garner, James W. *Reconstruction in Mississippi.* New York: Macmillan, 1901.

Garrison, Tim A. *The Legal Ideology of Removal: The Southern Judiciary and the Sovereignty of Native American Nations.* Athens: University of Georgia Press, 2002.

Garrow, David J. "Abortion Before and After Roe v. Wade: An Historical Perspective." 62 *Albany Law Review* 833 (1999).

———. *Bearing the Cross: Martin Luther King, Jr., and the Southern Christian Leadership Conference.* New York: William Morrow, 1986.

Gates, Paul W. *History of Public Land Law Development.* Washington, DC: US Government Printing Office, 1968.

Gilliland, Kris, Bette Bradley, and Ellie Campbell. "'Dared to Enter a "Man's World': Mississippi Women Lawyers, 1914–1944," 86 *Mississippi Law Journal* 1479 (2017).

Glaeser, Edward L., and Claudia Goldin, eds. *Corruption and Reform: Lessons from America's Economic History.* Chicago: University of Chicago Press, 2006.

Goodman, Paul. "The Emergence of the Homestead Exemption in the United States: Accommodation and Resistance to the Market Revolution, 1840–1880." 80 *Journal of American History* 470 (Sept. 1993).

Goodrich, Carter. *Government Promotion of American Canals and Railroads, 1800-1890.* New York: Columbia University Press, 1960.

Grandy, Christopher. *New Jersey and the Fiscal Origins of Modern American Corporation Law.* New York: Garland, 1993.

Grantham, Dewey. *Southern Progressivism: The Reconciliation of Progress and Tradition.* Knoxville: University of Tennessee Press, 1983.

Greenberg, Jack. *Crusaders in the Courts: How a Dedicated Band of Lawyers Fought for the Civil Rights Revolution.* New York: Basic Books, 1994.

Grimke, Frederick. *Considerations on the Nature and Tendency of Free Institutions.* Cincinnati: H. W. Derby & Co., 1848.

Guice, John D. W. "The Cement of Society: Law in the Mississippi Territory." 1 *Gulf Coast Historical Review* 76 (1986).

Hall, Kermit L. *The Magic Mirror: Law in American History.* New York: Oxford University Press, 1989.

Hamilton, Charles G. *Progressive Mississippi.* Aberdeen, MS: Hamilton, 1948.

Hamilton, William Baskerville. *Anglo-American Law on the Frontier: Thomas Rodney and his Territorial Cases.* Durham, NC: Duke University Press, 1953.

Hardy, Leroy, Alan Heslop, and Stuart Anderson, eds. *Reapportionment Politics: The History of Redistricting in the Fifty States.* Beverly Hills: Sage Publications, 1981.

Harris, William C. "The Creed of the Carpetbaggers: The Case of Mississippi." 40 *Journal of Southern History* 199 (1974).

———. *The Day of the Carpetbagger: Republican Reconstruction in Mississippi*. Baton Rouge: Louisiana State University Press, 1979.

———. "Formulation of the First Mississippi Plan: The Black Code of 1865." 29 *Journal of Mississippi History* 181 (1967).

———. *Presidential Reconstruction in Mississippi*. Baton Rouge: Louisiana State University Press, 1967.

Heard, Alex. *The Eyes of Willie McGee: A Tragedy of Race, Sex and Secrets in the Jim Crow South*. New York: Harper, 2010.

Hermann, Janet Sharp. *Pursuit of A Dream*. Jackson: University Press of Mississippi, 1999.

Hester, Kathryn Healy. "Mississippi and the Voting Rights Act: 1965–1982." 52 *Mississippi Law Journal* 803 (1982).

Hicks, Frederick. *Men and Books Famous in the Law*. Rochester, NY: Lawyers Co-Op, 1921.

Hicks, Paul D. *Joseph Henry Lumpkin: Georgia's First Chief Justice*. Athens: University of Georgia Press, 2002.

Higham, John. *Strangers in the Land: Patterns of American Nativism, 1860–1925*. New York: Athenaeum, 1963.

Hill, Karlos K. "Black Vigilantism: The Rise and Decline of African American Lynch Mob Activity in the Mississippi and Arkansas Deltas, 1883–1923." 95 *Journal of African-American History* 26 (2010).

Hoff, Joan. *Law, Gender and Injustice: A Legal History of U.S. Women*. New York: New York University Press, 1991.

Hoffman, Ronald, and Peter J. Albert, eds. *The Transforming Hand of Revolution: Reconsidering the American Revolution as a Social Movement*. Charlottesville: University Press of Virginia, 1996.

Horton, John T. *James Kent: A Study in Conservatism*. New York: D. Appleton-Century, 1939.

Huebner, Timothy S. *The Southern Judicial Tradition: State Judges and Sectional Distinctiveness, 1790–1890*. New York: Oxford University Press, 1999.

Huffman, Alan. *Mississippi in Africa: The Saga of the Slaves of Prospect Hill Plantation and Their Legacy in Liberia Today*. New York: Gotham Books, 2010.

Hume, Richard L. "Carpetbaggers in the Reconstruction South: A Group Portrait of Outside Whites in the 'Black and Tan' Constitutional Conventions." 64 *Journal of American History* 313 (1977).

Hurst, J. Willard. *The Growth of American Law: The Law Makers*. Boston: Little, Brown, 1950.

Hutchinson, A., and V. Howard. *Code of Mississippi, Being an Analytical Compilation of the Public and General Statutes of the Territory and State, with Tabular References to the Local and Private Acts, from 1798–1848*. Jackson, MS: Price and Fall, 1848.

Jacobs, Clyde. *Law Writers and the Courts: The Influence of Thomas M. Cooley, Christopher G. Tiedeman, and John F. Dillon upon American Constitutional Law*. New York: Da Capo Press, 1973.

Johnston, Erle. *Mississippi's Defiant Years, 1953–1973: An Interpretive Documentary with Personal Experiences*. Forest, MS: Lake Harbor Pub., 1990.

Jones, Alan R. *The Constitutional Conservatism of Thomas McIntyre Cooley: A Study in the History of Ideas*. New York: Garland, 1987.

Jones, Bryan A. Comment, "The End of Tort Reform? The Constitutional Battle Looms Over Mississippi." 80 *Mississippi Law Journal* 87 (2011).

Journal of the Convention of the State of Mississippi (1850). Jackson, MS: T. Palmer, 1851.

Journal of the Convention of the Western Part of the Mississippi Territory (1817), reprinted in 29 *Journal of Mississippi History* 443 (1967).

Journal of the Proceedings and Debates in the Constitutional Convention of the State of Mississippi, August, 1865. Jackson, MS: E. M. Yerger, 1865.

Journal of the Proceedings in the Constitutional Convention of the State of Mississippi (1868). Jackson, MS: E. Stafford, 1871.

Journal of the Proceedings of the Constitutional Convention, of the State of Mississippi, Begun at the City of Jackson on August 12, 1890. Jackson, MS: E. L. Martin, 1890.

Journal of the Constitutional Convention of the State of South Carolina (1895). Columbia, SC: C. A. Calvo, 1895.

Kaczorowski, Robert. *The Politics of Judicial Interpretation: The Federal Courts, Department of Justice and Civil Rights, 1866–1876.* New York: Fordham University Press, 1985.

Kahrl, Andrew W. "The Power to Destroy: Discriminatory Property Assessments and the Struggle for Tax Justice in Mississippi." 82 *Journal of Southern History* 579 (2016).

Katagiri, Yasuhiro. *The Mississippi State Sovereignty Commission: Civil Rights and States' Rights.* Jackson: University Press of Mississippi, 2001.

Keller, William F. *The Nation's Advocate: Henry Marie Brackenridge and Young America.* Pittsburgh: University of Pittsburgh Press, 1956.

Kennedy, David M. *Freedom from Fear: The American People in Depression and War, 1929–1945.* New York: Oxford University Press, 1999.

Kennedy, Susan Estabrook. *The Banking Crisis of 1933.* Lexington: University Press of Kentucky, 1973.

Kent, James. *Commentaries on American Law.* New York: O. Halsted, 1826.

Kerr, Norwood Allen. "The Mississippi Colonization Society (1831–1860)." 43 *Journal of Mississippi History* 1 (1981).

Keynes, Edward. *Liberty, Property, and Privacy: Toward a Jurisprudence of Substantive Due Process.* University Park: Pennsylvania State University Press, 1996.

Kight, Lawrence E. "'The State Is On Trial': Governor Edmund F. Noel and the Defense of Mississippi's Legal Institutions against Mob Violence." 60 *Journal of Mississippi History* 191 (1998).

Kilbourne, Richard H., Jr. *A History of the Louisiana Civil Code: The Formative Years, 1803–1839.* Baton Rouge: Paul M. Hebert Law Center, Louisiana State University, 1987.

Kirwan, Albert D. *Revolt of the Rednecks: Mississippi Politics, 1876–1925.* Lexington: University of Kentucky Press, 1951.

Klarman, Michael J. *From Jim Crow to Civil Rights: The Supreme Court and the Struggle for Racial Equality.* New York: Oxford University Press, 2004.

Klebaner, Benjamin J. *American Commercial Banking: A History.* Boston: Twayne Publishers, 1990.

Klein, Herbert J., and Jacob Klein. *The Atlantic Slave Trade.* New York: Cambridge University Press, 1999.

Kluger, Richard. *Simple Justice: The History of Brown v. Board of Education and Black America's Struggle for Equality.* New York: Knopf, 2004.

Kruse, Kevin M. *White Flight, Atlanta and the Making of Modern Conservatism.* Princeton, NJ: Princeton University Press, 2007.

Kuehnl, George J. *The Wisconsin Business Corporation.* Madison: University of Wisconsin Press, 1959.

Kutler, Stanley I. "Ex Parte McCardle, Judicial Incompetency? The Supreme Court and Reconstruction Reconsidered." 72 *American Historical Review* 835 (1967).

Lang, Meredith. *Defender of the Faith: The High Court of Mississippi, 1817–1875.* Jackson: University Press of Mississippi, 1977.

Lebsock, Suzanne D. "Radical Reconstruction and the Property Rights of Southern Women." 43 *Journal of Southern History* 195 (1977).

Lemann, Nicholas. *Redemption: The Last Battle of the Civil War.* New York: Farrar, Straus and Giroux, 2006.

Lester, Connie. "Balancing Agriculture with Industry: Capital, Labor and the Public Good in Mississippi's Home-Grown New Deal." 70 *Journal of Mississippi History* 225 (2008).

Levy, Leonard W., ed. *The Virginia Report of 1799–1800: Touching the Alien and Sedition Laws.* New York: Da Capo Press, 1970.

Lewis, Anna. *Chief Pushmataha, American Patriot: The Story of the Choctaws' Struggle for Survival.* New York: Exposition Press, 1959.

Lewis, Herbert James. *Clearing the Thickets: A History of Antebellum Alabama.* New Orleans: Quid Pro Books, 2013.

Libby, David J. *Slavery in Frontier Mississippi, 1720–1835.* Jackson: University Press of Mississippi, 2004.

Library of America. *Abraham Lincoln: Speeches and Writings, 1859–1865.* New York: Library of America, 1989.

Link, Arthur S., and Richard L. McCormick. *Progressivism.* Arlington Heights, IL: Harlan Davidson, 1983.

Litwack, Leon F. *Been in the Storm So Long: The Aftermath of Slavery.* New York: Knopf, 1979.

Luckett, Robert E., Jr. *Joe T. Patterson and the White South's Dilemma.* Jackson: University Press of Mississippi, 2015.

Lukas, J. Anthony. *Common Ground: A Turbulent Decade in the Lives of Three American Families.* New York: Knopf, 1985.

Maier, Pauline. *American Scripture: Making the Declaration of Independence.* New York: Knopf, 1998.

Maatman, Mary Ellen. "Lawyering in the Lion's Mouth: The Story of S. D. Redmond and Pruitt v. State." 83 *Mississippi Law Journal* 459 (2014).

Manian, Maya. "Lessons from Personhood's Defeat: Abortion Restrictions and Side Effects on Women's Health." 74 *Ohio State Law Journal* 75 (2013).

Maron, David F., and Samuel D. Gregory. "A Decade Examined: A Review of the Recovery Under Mississippi's Civil Justice Reforms." 34 *Mississippi College Law Review* 203 (2015).

Mason, John L., and Michael Nelson. *Governing Gambling: A Century Foundation Report.* New York: Century Foundation Press, 2001.

Mayes, Edward. *Lucius Q. C. Lamar: His Life, Times, and Speeches, 1825–1893.* Nashville, TN: Publishing House of the Methodist Episcopal Church, South, 1896.

McDonald, Forrest. *States' Rights and the Union: Imperium in Imperio, 1776–1876.* Lawrence: University Press of Kansas, 2000.

McIntosh, Philip L. "Tort Reform in Mississippi: An Appraisal of the New Law of Products Liability, Part I." 16 *Mississippi College Law Review* 393 (1996).

McKibben, Davidson B. "Negro Slave Insurrections in Mississippi, 1800–1865." 34 *Journal of Negro History* 73 (1949).

McLemore, Richard A., ed. *A History of Mississippi.* Hattiesburg: University and College Press of Mississippi, 1973.

McMillen, Neil R. "Black Enfranchisement in Mississippi: Federal Enforcement and Black Protest in the 1960s." 43 *Journal of Southern History* 351 (1977).

———. *Dark Journey: Black Mississippians in the Age of Jim Crow.* Urbana: University of Illinois Press, 1989.

McMillen, Sally G. *Southern Women: Black and White in the Old South*. 2nd ed. Wheeling, IL: Harlan Davidson, 2002.

McNeilly, J. S. "History of Measures Submitted to the Committee on Elective Franchise, Apportionment, and Elections in the Constitutional Convention of 1890." 6 *Proceedings of the Mississippi Historical Society* 129 (1902).

Mead, Julie F. "The Right to an Education or the Right to Shop for Schooling: Examining Voucher Programs in Relation to State Constitutional Guarantees." 42 *Fordham Urban Law Journal* 703 (2015).

Merriam, Charles E., and Louise Overacker. *Primary Elections*. Chicago: University of Chicago Press, 1928.

Meyers, Marvin. *The Jacksonian Persuasion: Politics and Belief*. Stanford: Stanford University Press, 1957.

Michaelsen, Robert S. *Piety in the Public Schools: Trends and Issues in the Relationship Between Religion and the Public Schools in the United States*. New York: Macmillan, 1970.

Miles, Edwin A. "The Mississippi Slave Insurrection Scare of 1835." 42 *Journal of Negro History* 48 (1957).

Milkis, Sidney M. *Theodore Roosevelt, the Progressive Party, and the Transformation of American Democracy*. Lawrence: University Press of Kansas, 2009.

Miller, Edward A. *Gullah Statesman: Robert Smalls from Slavery to Congress, 1838–1915*. Columbia: University of South Carolina Press, 1995.

Miller, Kenneth P. "Defining Rights in the States: Judicial Activism and Popular Response." 76 *Albany Law Review* 2061 (2013).

Mills, Michael P. "Slave Law in Mississippi from 1817–1861: Constitutions, Codes and Cases." 71 *Mississippi Law Journal* 153 (2001).

Mollison, Irvin C. "Negro Lawyers in Mississippi." 15 *Journal of Negro History* 38 (1930).

Moncrief, Sandra. "The Mississippi Married Women's Property Act of 1839." 47 *Journal of Mississippi History* 110 (1985).

Moore, John Hebron. *The Emergence of the Cotton Kingdom in the Old Southwest: Mississippi, 1770–1860*. Baton Rouge: Louisiana State University Press, 1988.

Moreau-Lislet, Louis, and Henry Carleton. *Law of Las Siete Partidas, Which are Still in Force in the State of Louisiana*. New Orleans: James M'Karaher, 1820.

Morgan, Chester M. "At the Crossroads: World War II, Delta Agriculture, and Modernization in Mississippi." 57 *Journal of Mississippi History* 353 (1995).

Morris, Christopher. *Becoming Southern: The Evolution of a Way of Life, Warren County and Vicksburg, Mississippi, 1770–1860*. New York: Oxford University Press, 1999.

Morris, Thomas D. *Free Men All: The Personal Liberty Laws of the North, 1780–1861*. Baltimore: Johns Hopkins University Press, 1974.

———. *Southern Slavery and the Law, 1619–1860*. Chapel Hill: University of North Carolina Press, 1996.

Mulder, Mark T. *Shades of White Flight: Evangelical Congregations and Urban Departure*. New Brunswick, NJ: Rutgers University Press, 2015.

Mushkat, Jerome, and Joseph G. Rayback. *Martin Van Buren: Law, Politics, and the Shaping of Republican Ideology*. DeKalb, IL: Northern Illinois University Press, 1997.

Nash, A. E. Keir. "Negro Rights, Unionism, and Greatness on the South Carolina Court of Appeals: The Extraordinary Chief Justice John Belton O'Neall." 21 *South Carolina Law Review* 141 (1969).

———. "Reason of Slavery: Understanding the Judicial Role in the Peculiar Institution." 32 *Vanderbilt Law Review* 1 (1979).

Nash, Jere, and Andy Taggart. *Mississippi Politics: The Struggle for Power, 1976–2006.* Jackson: University Press of Mississippi, 2006.

National Emergency Council. *Report to the President on the Economic Conditions of the South.* Washington, DC: US Government Printing Office, 1938.

Nelson, Caleb. "A Re-Evaluation of Scholarly Explanations for the Rise of the Elective Judiciary in Antebellum America." 37 *American Journal of Legal History* 190 (1993).

Nelson, Michael, and John Lyman Mason. *How the South Joined the Gambling Nation: The Politics of State Policy Innovation.* Baton Rouge: Louisiana State University Press, 2007.

Nieman, Donald G. "The Freedmen's Bureau and the Mississippi Black Code." 40 *Journal of Mississippi History* 91 (1978).

Nivola, Pietro S., and David W. Brady, eds. *Red and Blue Nation? Characteristics and Causes of America's Polarized Politics.* Washington, DC: Brookings Institute Press, 2006.

Nockleby, John T., and Shannon Curreri. "100 Years of Conflict: The Past and Future of Tort Retrenchment." 38 *Loyola of Los Angeles Law Review* 1021 (2005).

Note. "Judicial Performance in the Fifth Circuit." 73 *Yale Law Journal* 90 (1963).

Note. "State Legislation in Support of the NIRA." 34 *Columbia Law Review* 1077 (1934).

Note. "The Supreme Court, 1982 Term: Tax-Exempt Status of Discriminatory Private Schools." 97 *Harvard Law Review* 261 (1983).

Nye, Russel B. *Midwestern Progressive Politics: A Historical Study of Its Origins and Development, 1870–1958.* East Lansing: Michigan State University Press, 1959.

Oberholtzer, Ellis P. *The Referendum in America.* New York: Charles Scribner's Sons, 1912.

Osborn, George C. *James Kimble Vardaman: Southern Commoner.* Jackson, MS: Hederman Brothers, 1981.

Ownby, Ted, ed. *The Civil Rights Movement in Mississippi.* Jackson: University Press of Mississippi, 2013.

Parker, Frank R. *Black Votes Count: Political Empowerment in Mississippi after 1965.* Chapel Hill: University of North Carolina Press, 1990.

Patterson, James T. *Grand Expectations: The United States, 1945–1974.* New York: Oxford University Press, 1996.

Paul, Randolph E. *Taxation in the United States.* Boston: Little, Brown, 1954.

Perman, Michael. *Struggle for Mastery: Disfranchisement in the South, 1888–1908.* Chapel Hill: University of North Carolina Press, 2001.

Pfeifer, Michael J. *The Roots of Rough Justice: Origins of American Lynching.* Urbana: University of Illinois Press, 2011.

———. *Rough Justice: Lynching and American Society, 1874–1947.* Urbana: University of Illinois Press, 2004.

Phelps, Edith M., ed. *Selected Articles on the Recall: Including the Recall of Judges and Judicial Decisions.* 2nd ed. New York: H. W. Wilson, 1915.

Piper, Craig S. "Breakthrough: The Desegregation of the Starkville Public Schools." 66 *Journal of Mississippi History* 265 (2004).

Poindexter, George. *The Revised Code of the Laws of Mississippi, In Which Are Comprised All Such Acts of the General Assembly of a Public Nature, As Were In Force at the End of the Year 1823.* Natchez: F. Baker, 1824.

Polk, Noel, ed. *Natchez Before 1830.* Jackson: University Press of Mississippi, 1989.

Poore, Benjamin Perley. *The Federal and State Constitutions, Colonial Charters and Other Organic Laws of the United States.* Washington, DC: US Government Printing Office, 1877.

Pound, Roscoe. *The Spirit of the Common Law.* Boston: Marshall Jones, 1921.

Prentiss, George L. *Memoir of S. S. Prentiss.* New York: C. Scribner, 1856.

Prest, Wilfrid R. *William Blackstone: Law and Letters in the Eighteenth Century.* New York: Oxford University Press, 2008.

Prosser, William L. "The Minnesota Mortgage Moratorium." 7 *Southern California Law Review* 353 (1934).

Prucha, Francis P. *American Indian Policy in the Formative Years.* Lincoln: University of Nebraska Press, 1962.

Pruitt, Paul M. *Taming Alabama: Lawyers and Reformers, 1804–1929.* Tuscaloosa: University of Alabama Press, 2010.

Putnam, Robert D. *Bowling Alone: The Collapse and Revival of American Community.* New York: Simon and Schuster, 2000.

Rabinowitz, Howard N., ed. *Southern Black Leaders of the Reconstruction Era.* Urbana: University of Illinois Press, 1982.

Ranney, Joseph A. *In the Wake of Slavery: Civil War, Civil Rights and the Reconstruction of Southern Law.* Westport, CT: Praeger, 2006.

———. "'This New and Beautiful Organism': The Evolution of American Federalism in Three State Supreme Courts." 87 *Marquette Law Review* 253 (2003).

———. *Wisconsin and the Shaping of American Law.* Madison: University of Wisconsin Press, 2017.

Reeves, Carolyn Keller, ed. *The Choctaw Before Removal.* Jackson: University Press of Mississippi, 1985.

Report of the Debates and Proceedings of the Convention for the Revision of the Constitution of the State of Indiana (1851). Indianapolis: A. H. Brown, 1851.

Report of the Debates and Proceedings of the Convention for the Revision of the Constitution of the State of New York, 1846. Albany, NY: Evening Atlas, 1846.

Remini, Robert V. *The Life of Andrew Jackson.* New York: Harper & Row, 1988.

Roark, James L. *Masters without Slaves: Southern Planters in the Civil War and Reconstruction.* New York: Norton, 1977.

Robertson, James L. "Judge William C. Keady and the Bill of Rights." 68 *Mississippi Law Journal* 3 (1988).

Rodgers, Daniel T. *The Age of Fracture.* Cambridge: Harvard University Press, 2011.

Rosen, George. *A History of Public Health.* Baltimore: Johns Hopkins University Press, 1977.

Ross, Steven J. "Freed Soil, Freed Labor, Freed Men: John Eaton and the Davis Bend Experiment." 44 *Journal of Southern History* 351 (1978).

Rothman, Joshua D. "The Hazards of the Flush Times: Gambling, Mob Violence and the Anxieties of America's Market Revolution." 95 *Journal of American History* 651 (2008).

Rowland, Dunbar. *Courts, Judges and Lawyers of Mississippi, 1798–1935.* Jackson, MS: State Department of Archives and History, 1935.

———. "Mississippi's First Constitution and Its Makers." 6 *Publications of the Mississippi Historical Society* 79 (1902).

Rushdy, Ashraf H. A. *American Lynching.* New Haven, CT: Yale University Press, 2012.

Salmon, Marylynn. *Women and the Law of Property in Early America.* Chapel Hill: University of North Carolina Press, 1986.

Sansing, David G. "The Failure of Johnsonian Reconstruction in Mississippi, 1865–1866." 34 *Journal of Mississippi History* 373 (1972).

———. *Making Haste Slowly: The Troubled History of Higher Education in Mississippi.* Jackson: University Press of Mississippi, 1990.

Schlesinger, Arthur M., Jr. *The Age of Jackson.* Boston: Little, Brown, 1950.

Schmidt, Benno C., Jr. "Principle and Prejudice: The Supreme Court and Race in the Progressive Era, Part 2: The Peonage Cases." 82 *Columbia Law Review* 646 (1982).

Scott, Anne Firor. *The Southern Lady: From Pedestal to Politics, 1830–1930.* Charlottesville: University Press of Virginia, 1995.

Sedgwick, Theodore, Jr. *A Collection of the Political Writings of William Leggett.* New York: Taylor & Dodd, 1840.

Segal, Ronald. *The Black Diaspora: Five Centuries of the Black Experience Outside Africa.* New York: Farrar, Straus and Giroux, 1995.

Severns, Roger L. *Prairie Justice: A History of Illinois Courts Under French, English and American Law.* Carbondale: Southern Illinois University Press, 2015.

Shambaugh, Benjamin F., ed. *Fragments of the Debates of the Iowa Constitutional Conventions of 1844 and 1846.* Iowa City: State Historical Society of Iowa, 1900.

Skates, John Ray. *A History of the Mississippi Supreme Court, 1817–1848.* Jackson: Mississippi Bar Foundation, 1973.

———. "World War II as a Watershed in Mississippi History." 37 *Journal of Mississippi History* 131 (1975).

Smith, Alice E. *James Duane Doty: Frontier Promoter.* Madison: State Historical Society of Wisconsin, 1954.

Smith, Franklin A. *Judicial Review of Legislation in New York, 1906–1938.* New York: Columbia University Press, 1952.

Smith, J. Clay, Jr. *Emancipation: The Making of the Black Lawyer, 1844–1944.* Philadelphia: University of Pennsylvania Press, 1993.

Smith, Mark M. "Remembering Mary, Shaping Revolt: Reconsidering the Stono Rebellion." 67 *Journal of Southern History* 513 (2001).

Southwick, Leslie H. "Four for the Fifth: The First Mississippi Judges on the Fifth Circuit." 34 *Mississippi College Law Review* 252 (2015).

———. "Mississippi Supreme Court Elections: A Historical Perspective, 1916–1996." 18 *Mississippi College Law Journal* 115 (1998).

Stephenson, Gilbert T. *Race Relations in American Law.* New York: D. Appleton, 1910.

Stone, Alfred H. "Mississippi's Constitution and Statutes in Reference to Freedmen, and Their Alleged Relation to the Reconstruction Acts and War Amendments." 4 *Proceedings of the Mississippi Historical Society* 143 (1901).

Stover, John F. "Colonel Henry S. McComb, Mississippi Railroad Adventurer." 17 *Journal of Mississippi History* 177 (1955).

Stroud, George M. *A Sketch of the Laws Relating to Slavery in the Several States of the United States of America.* Philadelphia: Henry Longstreth, 1856.

Summers, Mark W. *The Ordeal of the Reunion: A New History of Reconstruction.* Chapel Hill: University of North Carolina Press, 2014.

———. *Railroads, Reconstruction and the Gospel of Prosperity: Aid Under the Radical Republicans, 1865–1877.* Princeton, NJ: Princeton University Press, 1984.

Superfine, Benjamin M. *Equality in Education Law and Policy, 1954–2010.* New York: Cambridge University Press, 2013.

Swain, Martha, Elizabeth Anne Payne, and Marjorie Julian Spruill, eds. *Mississippi Women: Their Histories, Their Lives, Vol. I.* Athens: University of Georgia Press, 2003.

Sydnor, Charles S. *A History of the South, Vol. V: The Development of Southern Sectionalism 1819–1848.* Baton Rouge: Louisiana State University Press, 1948.

———. *Slavery in Mississippi.* New York: D. Appleton-Century Co., 1933.

Tate, Roger D., Jr. "Easing the Burden: The Era of Depression and New Deal in Mississippi." PhD dissertation, University of Tennessee, 1978.

Timberlake, Elise. "Did the Reconstruction Regime Give Mississippi Her Public Schools." 12 *Proceedings of the Mississippi Historical Society* 72 (1912).

Tindall, George B. *A History of the South, Vol. X: The Emergence of the New South, 1913–1945.* Baton Rouge: Louisiana State University Press, 1967.

———. "The Question of Race in the South Carolina Convention of 1895." 37 *Journal of Negro History* 227 (1952).

Tipton, S. G. Note, "State Acts in Aid of the NIRA." 29 *Illinois Law Review* 777 (1935).

Toulmin, Harry. *The Statutes of the Mississippi Territory, Revised and Digested by the Authority of the General Assembly.* Natchez, MS: Samuel Terrell, 1807.

Trelease, Allen W. *White Terror: The Ku Klux Klan Conspiracy and Southern Reconstruction.* Westport, CT: Greenwood Press, 1971.

Tucker, St. George. *Blackstone's Commentaries: With Notes of Reference to the Constitution and Laws of the Federal Government of the United States and the Commonwealth of Virginia.* 1996 ed. Union, NJ: Lawbook Exchange, 1996.

Turner, Edward. *Statutes of the Mississippi Territory* (1816). Natchez, MS: Peter Isler, 1816.

Tushnet, Mark. "The American Law of Slavery, 1810–1860: A Study in the Persistence of Legal Autonomy." 10 *Law and Society Review* 119 (1975).

———. *The NAACP's Legal Strategy Against Segregated Education, 1925–1950.* Chapel Hill: University of North Carolina Press, 1987.

Tyrrell, Ian R. *Sobering Up: From Temperance to Prohibition in Antebellum America, 1800–1860.* Urbana: University of Illinois Press, 1979.

Uelmen, Gerald F. "Crocodiles in the Bathtub: Maintaining the Independence of State Supreme Courts in an Era of Judicial Politicization." 72 *Notre Dame Law Review* 1133 (1997).

Vocino, Thomas, John H. Morris, John H., and D. Steve Gill. "The Population Apportionment Principle: Its Development and Application to Mississippi's State and Local Legislative Bodies." 47 *Mississippi Law Journal* 943 (1976).

Volk, Kyle G. *Moral Minorities and the Making of American Democracy.* New York: Oxford University Press, 2014.

Waldrep, Christopher. *Roots of Disorder: Race and Criminal Justice in the American South, 1817–80.* Urbana: University of Illinois Press, 1998.

Walker, Anders. "The Violent Bear It Away: Emmett Till and the Modernization of Law Enforcement in Mississippi." 46 *San Diego Law Review* 459 (2009).

Warner, Hoyt L. *Progressivism in Ohio, 1897–1917.* Columbus: Ohio State University Press, 1964.

Wax, Darold D. "'The Great Risque We Run': The Aftermath of Slave Rebellion at Stono, South Carolina, 1739–1745." 67 *Journal of Negro History* 136 (1982).

Wesser, Robert F. *Charles Evans Hughes: Politics and Reform in New York, 1905–1910.* Ithaca, NY: Cornell University Press, 1967.

Wilson, Charles H., Sr. *God! Make Me a Man: A Biographical Sketch of Dr. Sidney Dillion Redmond.* Boston: Meador Publishing Co., 1950.

Woodford, Frank B. *Mr. Jefferson's Disciple: A Life of Justice Woodward.* East Lansing: Michigan State University Press, 1953.

Wyatt-Brown, Bertram. *The Shaping of Southern Culture: Honor, Grace and War, 1790s–1860s.* Chapel Hill: University of North Carolina Press, 2001.

White, G. Edward. "The Chancellor's Ghost." 74 *Chicago-Kent Law Review* 229 (1998).

———. *Tort Law in America: An Intellectual History.* New York: Oxford University Press, 2003.

White, G. Edward, and Gerald Gunther. *The Marshall Court and Cultural Change, 1815–1835.* New York: Macmillan, 1988.

Whites, Lee Ann. *The Civil War as a Crisis in Gender: Augusta, Georgia, 1860–1890.* Athens: University of Georgia Press, 1995.

Wilson, Theodore B. *The Black Codes of the South.* Tuscaloosa: University of Alabama Press, 1965.

Winter, William F. "Development of Educational Policy in Mississippi." 58 *Mississippi Law Journal* 223 (1988).

Witt, John Fabian. "The Long History of State Constitutions and American Tort Law." 6 *Rutgers Law Journal* 1159 (2005).

Witte, John F. *The Market Approach to Education: An Analysis of America's First Voucher Program.* Princeton, NJ: Princeton University Press, 2000.

Wolters, Raymond. *Race and Education, 1954–2007.* Columbia: University of Missouri Press, 2009.

Woodman, Harold. *King Cotton and His Retainers: Financing and Marketing the Cotton Crop of the South, 1800–1915.* Lexington: University of Kentucky Press, 1968.

Woodward, C. Vann. *A History of the South, Vol. IX: Origins of the New South, 1877–1913.* Baton Rouge: Louisiana State University Press, 1951.

———. *The Strange Career of Jim Crow.* New York: Oxford University Press, 1966.

Wunder, John. "American Law and Order Comes to Mississippi Territory: The Making of Sargent's Code, 1798–1800." 38 *Journal of Mississippi History* 131 (1976).

Zahm, Craig. "Trial by Ordeal: The Willie McGee Case." 65 *Journal of Mississippi History* 215 (2003).

Zarnow, Leandra. "Braving Jim Crow to Save Willie McGee: Bella Abzug, the Legal Left, and Civil Rights Innovation, 1948–1951." 33 *Law & Soc. Inquiry* 1003 (2008).

Zinn, Howard, ed. *New Deal Thought.* Indianapolis: Bobbs-Merrill, 1966.

INDEX

CPSIA information can be obtained
at www.ICGtesting.com
Printed in the USA
BVHW032020280319
544020BV00001B/1/P

9 781496 822574